JUDGMENT
BEFORE
NUREMBERG

JUDGMENT BEFORE NUREMBERG

THE HOLOCAUST IN THE UKRAINE
AND THE FIRST NAZI WAR CRIMES TRIAL

GREG DAWSON

PEGASUS BOOKS

NEW YORK

JUDGMENT BEFORE NUREMBERG

Pegasus Books LLC
80 Broad Street, 5th Floor
New York, NY 10004

First Pegasus Books edition March 2012

Interior design by Maria Fernandez

Library of Congress Cataloging-in-Publication Data is available.

ISBN: 978-1-60598-290-8

10 9 8 7 6 5 4 3 2 1

Printed in the United States of America
Distributed by W. W. Norton & Company

For my mother

JUDGMENT
BEFORE
NUREMBERG

FOREWORD

This is not a book I ever expected to write. I ended up writing it because no one else has, and because a book like mine is overdue—by several decades. It's a byproduct of *Hiding in the Spotlight*, my account of my Ukrainian mother's escape from the Holocaust, published in 2009, but it's not exactly a sequel.

In the course of making public appearances for *Hiding in the* Spotlight, now close to 150, I was startled to find that most people in these interested audiences knew virtually nothing about the Holocaust in Ukraine—as little as I had before doing research for my mother's memoir.

Like me, they were not aware that what we think of as the Holocaust—the mass extermination of Jews by the Nazis—did not begin in Germany or Poland, but in Ukraine after Hitler invaded the Soviet Union in June 1941. Nor did they know that at least 750,000

Jews—mostly Ukrainian—were murdered by gunfire before the gas chambers at Auschwitz-Birkenau began operation, the majority even before the tenets of the Final Solution had been formally laid down by Hitler and Himmler.

While I had encountered a few people here and there during my travels who knew about those events, I have yet to find a single person out of the many hundreds I have addressed, from university professors to families of survivors, who could answer this question correctly: When and where was the first trial of Nazis for their crimes during the war?

Nuremberg, Germany, in 1945 is a good guess. But it is wrong. The correct answer is Kharkov, Ukraine, December 1943.

I happened on this startling fact at the Holocaust museum in Kharkov in 2006 while doing research for *Hiding in the Spotlight*. I mentioned it in the epilogue of that book and did not expect to return to it—until my book-tour experience revealed a gaping black hole in public knowledge of the Holocaust that cried out to be filled.

I said a book "like mine" is overdue because although there are many books about the Holocaust in Ukraine on library shelves, few even touch on the Kharkov trial. Nearly all were written by historians and scholars and, sadly, it seems that nearly all of them have been read only by other historians and scholars, not general readers, resulting in this rather disturbing gap in popular understanding of the Holocaust.

I am neither historian nor scholar. I am a newspaper reporter of more than four decades, accustomed to writing stories that assume the reader may not know anything about my subject, be it a basketball game, oil spill, or city zoning law. I am used to writing for the intellectually curious but under-informed, something that could be a byword when it comes to Ukrainian Holocaust scholarship.

Ukraine is the final frontier of Holocaust scholarship and literature. Since the dissolution of the Soviet Union in 1991, a mother lode of secret and suppressed material about the Holocaust in Ukraine has been made available to academics and journalists, and the flow continues nearly two decades later. In early 2011 the archives of the Ukrainian KGB agreed to open its wartime files to the Yad Vashem Holocaust Memorial after more than fifty years of secrecy. All this promises to keep historians busy for decades doing the grueling work of real scholarship.

Judgment Before Nuremberg is the tip of the tip of the iceberg, a very personal journey through one small corner of history. If casual readers learn as much reading the book as I did writing it, I will have accomplished one of my goals—and the credit will belong to the master historians: Raul Hilberg, Christopher Browning, Richard Rhodes, Deborah Lipstadt, Yitzhak Arad, Alexander

Prusin, and many others, without whose work this book could not have been written.

And if *Judgment Before Nuremberg* moves readers to seek out those sources of my own illumination and inspiration, and to discover the full breadth of their majestic work, I will have accomplished both my goals.

PROLOGUE

Even under many layers of warmth including a bulky new coat—a final-hour gift from my mother—my blood ran cold on a December night in Ukraine as I boarded a shuttle bus at Borispol International Airport in Kiev. It was the second time that night that the shuttle had made the trip from the terminal to an Aerosvit Airlines commuter jet on the tarmac for the flight east to Kharkov near the Russian border, the final leg of my journey which had begun 15 hours earlier in Orlando, Fla.

On the first attempt, the plane had reached Kharkov but could not land due to icy runways, and returned to Borispol. The shuttle took us back to Terminal A, the departure point for regional flights. It was late Friday night and the terminal was teeming with passengers on the way to Odessa, Lviv, Donetsk, and other weekend destinations. Maybe the plane would try again in a few hours. Maybe not.

For those accustomed to spacious, mall-like American airports, "terminal" belies the reality of Terminal A at Borispol, which is closer to a bus station in size and amenities. There was a kiosk offering hot drinks, hard liquor, and snacks, but no TV screens tuned to CNN, no gift shops to browse or newsstands selling English-language newspapers. There was little for me to do but people-watch, and for a long while I was diverted by the antics of a pixyish girl about eight years old who raced and pirouetted across the waiting room, mugging for an invisible camera.

By the time we left Kiev several hours later, I understood the significance—the meaning for me—of this little Ukrainian dervish.

This was my second trip to Ukraine. I had come in 2006 to do research for *Hiding in the Spotlight*, a book about my mother, Zhanna Arshanskaya Dawson. She and her younger sister, Frina, are the only known survivors of a Nazi death march in January 1942 that led 16,000 Jews, including Frina and Zhanna's parents and paternal grandparents, to Drobitsky Yar (Russian for "ravine"), a killing field outside Kharkov. It was thought that no one could have possibly escaped the march, so when a memorial was erected with the names of victims etched on walls, the sisters' names appeared next to those of their parents and grandparents.

Brushing my fingertips across the Cyrillic letters spelling out my mother's name was a jolting brush with my own mortality—a reminder that the Nazis meant for half my genes to have been interred in that deep ravine with her bones. SS chief Heinrich Himmler made that clear in describing the steps necessary to ensure the extermination of the Jewish race.

"We have come to the question: how is it with the women and children?" he told an assembly of SS officers. "I have resolved on a completely clear solution. I do not consider myself justified in eradicating the men and allowing the avengers in the shape of the children to grow up for our sons and grandsons. The difficult decision had to be taken to cause this *Volk* to disappear from the Earth."

Why had I decided to return, to *reappear* in Ukraine? Not to taunt Himmler's ghost with my presence and thereby avenge the murder of my grandparents and great-grandparents. There is no commensurate vengeance for these crimes. I had come back to do what I could to end the coverup of this crime, the darkness surrounding Drobitsky Yar and Ukraine's Jews. It's been said that history is written by the winners, but in the history of the Holocaust it's as though the chapter on Ukraine had been written by Himmler himself. For all practical purposes, the pages are blank.

While Hitler did not succeed in making "this Volk disappear from the Earth," he destroyed most of European Jewry in trying—and he began here, in Ukraine, in the summer of 1941. Upwards of a million Ukrainian Jews—give or take 100,000 "kikes" as Himmler, who often used the slur, might have blithely put it—were shot and dumped like garbage in mass graves in their native soil before the first Jews died in the gas chambers at Auschwitz-Birkenau in May of 1942.

In their later retreat from Ukraine, the defeated Nazis attempted to destroy the evidence of their mass murder by digging up and burning the corpses, but there were too many corpses and not enough time. Witnesses told of the earth at the killing fields moving, heaving like a distended belly from the gases emitted by thousands of decomposing bodies, blood seeping up to the surface. The gassings—and ovens—at Auschwitz were antiseptic in comparison.

The slaughter by gunfire in Ukraine should have become Hitler's original sin and Babi Yar—where 34,000 Jews were murdered in two days—the darkest icon of the Shoah. But when the war ended, Stalin abetted Himmler's coverup by throwing an Iron Curtain around the crime scene, off limits to writers, journalists, and historians. The only deaths in the great war to defend the Motherland would be "Russian" deaths. And so, by default, the liberation of Auschwitz and other camps became the defining images of the Holocaust. Hitler's crime in Ukraine began to fade slowly from public view and consciousness till it became what it is today—barely a footnote in popular understanding of the Holocaust.

By the 1970's when "Never forget" had become a familiar mantra of Holocaust remembrance, the Holocaust in Ukraine had already been forgotten, if it had even been remembered to begin with. It was as an ironic fulfillment of Himmler's macabre coverup—as if the Nazis had actually succeeded in unearthing and burning the evidence of their monstrous crime.

On a Thursday night in February 2008, I was slicing vegetables for dinner in the kitchen of our Orlando home and half listening to the NBC Nightly News when anchorman Brian Williams said something that made me look up.

"Tonight some extraordinary reporting by our friend and colleague Ann Curry. It's a story of a kind of invisible part of the Holocaust where more than a million Jews simply disappeared," Williams said, using the same portentous inflection reserved for discovery of a lost tribe in New Guinea or ice crystals on the moon. Curry did not skip a beat.

"In fact, this is *stunning* new information about an unknown part of the Holocaust," she reported. "We are learning in detail now about what happened to 1.3 million Jews who simply disappeared in Ukraine between 1941 and 1944."

It was a surreal moment that made me want to check the calendar. Was it really 2008? Was NBC News—67 years after the fact—really reporting the Holocaust in Ukraine as "news"? So it seemed. It's hard to find a better working definition of "news" than "stunning new information." The pretext—or "hook," in journalese—for Curry's story was Father Patrick Desbois, a French Catholic priest who had undertaken the noble mission of finding undiscovered killing fields in Ukraine and interviewing witnesses to the shootings. He told his story in *Holocaust by Bullets*, published in 2008.

Father Desbois had not, as the NBC report breathlessly suggested, solved a great historical mystery—a vanishing act by a million Ukrainian Jews. Rather, he had corroborated and shed welcome new light on the voluminously documented Nazi Holocaust in Ukraine. And although the professional journalists at NBC should have checked the record before presenting "new information" that was not, Curry's report undoubtedly *was* news to virtually everyone watching. That would have included me too, had I not spent the previous eight years researching and writing *Hiding in the Spotlight*.

Curry's report was stark illustration of how completely the Nazi crimes in Ukraine have been erased from our collective memory and body of common knowledge about the Holocaust. NBC was not the first or last to rediscover the story. In recent years there has been a spate of reports, most focusing on the *Einsatzgruppen*, mobile killing squads which followed the German army across Ukraine, murdering Jews. Like Curry's story, these reports, many an hour long, come packaged as "news," like "Hitler's Hidden Holocaust," which aired on The National Geographic cable channel in September 2010.

The historical amnesia, the deep black hole, is not confined to the general reading public or TV audience—it can be found among those who have made study of the Holocaust their lifework. A focal point of this book is the first trial—and conviction and execution—of Nazis for their wartime crimes. It was held in Kharkov in December 1943, well before the end of the war and the celebrated postwar trials in Nuremberg, Germany. I have encountered Holocaust scholars in the U.S. who know nothing about this trial, though it's no historical secret. The trial and executions—witnessed by tens of thousands of Kharkov residents—were reported in *The New York Times, The Christian Science Monitor, Time,* and *Life Magazine,* which even included photos.

Time and inattention have since relegated these facts to a netherworld of library archives and academic symposia. The seminal event of the Holocaust—the rape of Ukraine—has become obscure knowledge held by a tiny priesthood of professional historians and amateur aficionados. I had come to my mother's homeland a second time to gather material for a book that I hoped would help elevate Ukraine from the footnotes to the forefront of Holocaust history where it rightfully belongs.

I was not prepared for the sense of being surrounded by spirits in the corporeal form of the Ukrainians all around me. Touching my mother's name on the wall of the dead four years earlier at Drobitsky Yar—my own epitaph, in a way—sent an existential shiver up my spine, and it cloaked all I surveyed in an air of unreality, as if I were visiting a parallel universe populated not by the living but by symbols and apparitions.

After two hours in the waiting area of Terminal A, we were informed that landing conditions had improved in Kharkov and we were herded back onto the shuttle bus. The adult travelers stood silent or murmuring in the rolling ice box. A few feet away from me, the same exuberant young girl who had lit up the dreary terminal with her theatrics now jumped up onto a seat, grabbed the overhead straps, and was showing off—twisting, turning, swaying, pretending to fall— her smiling eyes alive with mischief and pure joy.

"Mama!" she cried. "Papa!"

Her seated parents cast mock scowls and waved for her to get down, but the show went on. At that moment, I thought that she was the happiest child I had ever seen. This was a peculiar reaction. After all, I had seen a lifetime of happy children on playgrounds. What was it about *this* child that filled me with such joy and also, oddly, deep melancholy?

In this beaming, blithe spirit I saw my mother as I imagine her at eight, a carefree wanderer in her beloved seaside hometown of Berdyansk in southern Ukraine when life was good, before the storm.

And so it was everywhere I went in Ukraine—spirits and flashbacks and omens. On the flight to Kharkov, the flight attendant serving us was "Marina," the fictitious name used by my mother's sister, Frina, during the war. On the side of a bus in Kharkov was a poster for a young entertainer named Zhanna, my mother's name, who became a pianist and was performing around Ukraine by the time she was ten. I visited the school in Kharkov my mother attended when she was thirteen and spoke to a class of students the same age. Looking out at the sea of fresh faces, I saw . . . survivors.

I returned to Kharkov State Music Conservatory where my mother and Frina studied as children, starting at ages eight and six. A student symphony was rehearsing Prokofiev's Third Piano Concerto, an electrifying piece full of darkness and light that only a Russian could have written. My mother recalls sitting cross-legged on the stage of the elegant concert hall as virtuosos performed only feet away, knowing at that moment, so very young, that she wanted to become a great artist too. I climbed the stairs to the balcony and took a seat at one end.

After a while, my gaze drifted from the stage to the opposite end of the balcony and a most incongruous sight. Seated in the second row up from the rail was a babushka in a bulky gray coat, a headscarf tied under her chin in

classic fashion. Babushkas, or "grandmothers," many of
them war widows, are a common sight on street corners in
Ukraine where they sell dried fruit, nuts, and seeds. Not in
balconies of concert halls. The babushka seemed to be listening intently. From time to time she would bend forward,
as if reaching into a bag.

I wondered—as Hemingway did of the frozen leopard
found on Mount Kilimanjaro—what she was seeking
at this altitude, in this empty balcony. Not warmth, I
decided. If it was warmth she sought late on a December
afternoon, surely there were other options—stores, cafes,
subways—which did not entail climbing several flights of
stairs. I wanted to know what had brought her there, but
I would not ask and interrupt her reverie. I could only
imagine.

At a distance, the babushka appeared to be a few years
older than my mother, who was born in 1927. Perhaps
she had fond memories of coming to the hall as a girl to
hear a brother or sister perform—or perhaps a boyfriend
or husband lost in the war. Perhaps she herself had been
a student at the conservatory and had seen her dreams
shattered, as my mother had, on June 22, 1941, when the
Nazis invaded. I could only imagine. The babushka was
still in the second row of the balcony, staring at the stage,
when I left.

Later, downstairs, I saw her drifting silently, ghostlike,
through the hallways crowded with students, much as

Ukraine still moves silently, unseen, through the hallways of Holocaust history.

I had come to liberate the ghosts of Ukraine, and to face my own.

CHAPTER ONE

Wout did I know about the Holocaust, and when did
I know it?

As a baby boomer growing up in the Midwest in the
fifties and sixties attending public schools, I knew as much
as the guy at the next desk—nothing. There was no mention of the Holocaust in our textbooks, nor do I remember
any teacher telling us about it. This may seem incredible to
anyone, say, thirty years old who was in middle school in
1993 when *Schindler's List* debuted and the U.S. Holocaust
Museum opened in Washington, D.C. That student may
even have met one of the many Holocaust survivors who
regularly visit schools to share their stories.

But in the context of 1961 when I was in sixth grade—
the level that Holocaust education commonly begins
today—the invisibility of the Holocaust was hardly surprising. In fact, any mention of it by Mr. Mize, my teacher

at Rogers Elementary in Bloomington, Indiana, would have been startling—wildly out of sync with mainstream America where "Holocaust" would not be a household word for another decade.

Nineteen sixty-one was still early dawn of Holocaust awareness in America, even though sixteen years had passed since GIs entered the gates of Auschwitz and other Nazi death camps—newsreel moments imprinted indelibly on the American mind. The *New York Times* did not use "holocaust" to describe the murder of Jews until May 1959 in a story about dedication of the Yad Vashem memorial in Jerusalem. The first graduate seminar on the Holocaust in the U.S. was at Emory College in 1959–60. *Night*, Elie Wiesel's transformative memoir, was published in the U.S. in 1960 but sold only a few copies that first year. American TV had extensive coverage of the trial of Adolf Eichmann in Israel in 1961, and *Judgment at Nuremberg*, starring Spencer Tracy, was released that year and won two Academy Awards.

I believe I speak for my immediate twelve-year-old peers at the time in admitting that I did not watch the Eichmann trial or go to see *Judgment at Nuremberg*. My favorite movie that year was *The Absent-Minded Professor* in which Fred MacMurray invented an anti-gravity goop called Flubber that made his old jalopy fly and let the vertically challenged slam-dunk a basketball. I saw it twice. Above all, I remember 1961 as the year Mickey Mantle and

Roger Maris chased Babe Ruth's record of sixty home runs in a season. Holocaust awareness was still a long way down the road and around the bend for my friends and me.

You might think it would have been different for me since my mother was a Holocaust survivor—the only one on the block!—but she did not share that part of her life with me and my younger brother, Bill, deciding it was "too cruel" to burden young children with such information. My information was sketchy. All I knew was that my mother had been caught up in the war and had somehow made it to America. Had we gone to synagogue and been surrounded by Jews with their own survivor stories, it would have been impossible for my mother to keep her secret. But ours was a secular home, my mother a non-observant Jew, my father a lapsed Roman Catholic from Virginia. Sunday the rabbi stayed home, and so did the Dawsons.

On the other hand, my mother made no secret of the fact that she was Russian. She was fiercely proud of her heritage, and made it known often in the kitchen by fixing borscht and other traditional meals, and she spoke Russian to me from birth. I was bilingual until age seven when I became aware of the childhood pitfalls of being "different" and begged her to stop speaking Russian to me around my friends. Unfortunately, she caved to my demand, and we now agree it was a bad decision in the long run. Fluent Russian would have satisfied my college language requirement the easy way and broadened career choices later. What was coming naturally to me in childhood, when the mind is at its ripest to absorb new languages, is nearly impossible for the ossifying adult mind short of a total immersion program. But my aversion to Russian was understandable at the time. It was the 1950s, the height of McCarthyism and the Red Scare. With people checking under their beds for Communists each night, it was not the best time for a kid in the Indiana heartland to be caught speaking the language of America's mortal enemy.

I tell the story of how I became monolingual because it helps explain, in part, why America—Main Street and Washington—was slow to make the Holocaust a focus of our national conversation and education. "Better dead than Red!" went the McCarthyite cry. Only a decade after liberation of the death camps, America was more obsessed with the Red than the dead. In paranoia over the perceived threat from our recent ally, the *actual* horrific crimes of our recent enemy were, if not exactly forgotten, placed on a distant back burner of benign neglect.

Hardball geopolitics clearly was at play. The U.S. government was anxious about offending West Germany, its new ally against the evil empire in Moscow. Intense lobbying by West German government and church officials led to reduced sentences and early freedom for many officers of the *Einsatzgruppen,* the mobile killing squads responsible for murdering over a million Ukrainian Jews. At Nuremberg in 1948, the tribunal sentenced 14 *Einsatzgruppen* functionaries and field commanders to death, two to life sentences, and five to prison terms of 10 to 20 years.

Under the Nuremberg Charter, sentence reduction was the "sole prerogative" of the American Military Governor for Germany, John McCloy, former Assistant Secretary of War, who replaced General Lucius Clay in 1950. Clay had affirmed the death sentences and stoutly rebuffed all appeals, but McCloy, eager to nurture U.S.-German solidarity for the Cold War, succumbed to the deluge of demands for clemency and established an Advisory Group to review all the sentences. Subsequently, four of the convicted killers were hanged at Landsberg Prison near Munich in 1951. By 1958 all the rest, including nine men originally sentenced to death, had been set free.

Such sweeping absolution for perpetrators of the crime induces a sort of philosophical vertigo. It is difficult to put any name on this head-spinning nullification of justice other than "Holocaust denial"—perpetrated, incredibly, by representatives of the same country that went to war to stop the criminal in chief. Is it any wonder, then, that it was possible—in fact more than likely—to grow up in the American heartland in the 1950s and '60s and know nothing of the Holocaust?

That's the way my mother wanted it, of course—my innocence preserved—and the world cooperated by providing me with no information. Yes, I knew who Hitler was—who didn't?—but only from capsule descriptions in grade-school texts and as the slightly ridiculous figure in grainy newsreel footage—a ranting, fist-pumping, bug-eyed lunatic who didn't know when to stop. I also knew that Hitler killed many Jews, but more as collateral damage, it seemed, than by design.

In the absence of more and better information, my unfortunate impression of Hitler as cartoonish was reinforced by *Hogan's Heroes*, a TV sitcom which hilariously satirized Nazis. Colonel Klink, the buffoonish commander of the prisoner-of-war camp, was played by Werner Klemperer, who3 only a few years earlier had given a fine dramatic performance as a remorseless defendant in *Judgment at Nuremberg*. John Banner played Sergeant Schultz, the genial, strudel-fed, risk-averse guard who repeatedly claimed, "I know nothing—*nothing*." Just like me!

It was about the time *Hogan's Heroes* came on the air in 1965 that I became fully aware that I was Jewish. Like the Holocaust, it may seem incredible that I would not have this crucial data. How could this be? Well, not only did we not go to church or synagogue, religion was not discussed at the dinner table. It was not *verboten*, just irrelevant—not as interesting to me as sports, politics, food, and the doings at the Indiana University School of Music where my mother, a pianist, and my father, a violist, were on the faculty. I also don't recall religion being discussed *outside* the home— being asked by virtual strangers which church I attended, which today often comes right after "hello." In those days people's religion (or lack of it) was their own business. So, I had no particular reason to consider my religious or ethnic identity. I thought of myself as half Russian, half Virginian, and 100% Hoosier.

I say that as a teenager I became "fully aware" of being Jewish because I had been dimly aware of it for many years. Except for religion, ours was culturally a very Jewish home, filled with Jewish food, Jewish humor. Most of my parents' friends, colleagues on the music faculty, were Jewish. It was a matter of putting two and two and two together—but who was counting? I don't remember precisely when and how I learned that I was officially Jewish—there was no dramatic come-to-Jesus talk with my mother—but I considered it a diversity upgrade. No offense to my father's English-Scotch ancestry, but Russian Jewish, with a dollop of Mongolian, added zest and exotic flair missing from the monochrome (yawn) Dawson line.

The revelation did not kindle a religious awakening for me or prompt questions that might have led to discovering my mother's great untold story. Most children, at some point, would wonder why their mother had never spoken of her own parents. Why were there no photos? Why no stories from her childhood? I never thought to ask my mother about her parents—my phantom grandparents— perhaps because my paternal grandparents had never been part of our lives either. My father's dad died when he was

thirteen; his mother when I was very young. The absence
of grandparents seemed normal.

My father, David, knew my mother's story *before* he
met her, from his brother, Larry, an Army lieutenant who
discovered her and Frina in the displaced-persons camp he
ran near Munich after the war. Beguiled by their musical
gifts and fiery personalities, he pulled strings to bring them
to America. Going through my mother's papers for *Hiding
in the Spotlight*, I found letters from Larry to my father, and
a Western Union telegram alerting him to the girls' arrival
in New York in May 1946. I also found the copy of an
affidavit, "Janna Dawson's story as told to David Dawson,"
submitted to a reparations board which awarded each sister
$800, an amount so slight and nonsensical that it illustrates
the notion of incalculable loss. I'm confident that my father
would have confided my mother's story had I asked, but I
never did while living under their roof. I was twenty-five—
working in Florida, a new husband and father—when he
died in Bloomington at the age of sixty-two of cigarette-
induced emphysema, without our ever speaking of the
subject.

I might never have learned my mother's story if not
for Irwin Segelstein. It was Segelstein, head programmer
for NBC in the 1970s, who had the idea for a miniseries
about the Holocaust, which seemed a farfetched, costly
gamble. From the early 1950s, when a camp survivor
appeared on the hugely popular reality series *This Is Your*

Life, prime time was peppered with teleplays and episodes of series such as *The Twilight Zone* which used Holocaust themes as background and allegory, but never explained what happened outright. Nine and a half hours of straight, unfiltered Holocaust four nights in a row was quite another thing. However, in those pre-cable days the three networks had a monopoly on viewers and money to burn, so NBC rolled the dice—and won, drawing an estimated 120 million viewers.

Holocaust followed the intersecting destinies of two fictional families, one German Jewish, the other German gentile with Nazi sympathies, against the backdrop of the unfolding cataclysm. As the first major pop-culture treatment of the Holocaust—it was the miniseries genre that put the *pop* in pop culture—*Holocaust* was not just a big TV event but a significant social and cultural milestone, like the *Roots* miniseries the year before.

At the time, April 1978, I was back in Bloomington working as a feature writer at *The Herald-Telephone,* eternally in search of fodder. Reading the massive hype surrounding the upcoming miniseries, I knew there was a story in there for me—somewhere. Perhaps my mother had some anecdotes from her wartime experience that I could spin into a piece. I phoned her in Milwaukee, where she had moved after my father's death to join the music faculty at the University of Wisconsin-Milwaukee. Oblivious to television and pop culture, she was predictably unaware of the miniseries. I described it and asked if she could recount her own experience, hoping for enough relevant scraps to build a feature.

What followed was the most astonishing hour of my life as my mother told me, for the first time, her miraculous story of escape and survival. Not the most proficient typist, my fingers flew erratically across the keyboard, my crooked neck aching from holding the receiver to my shoulder, my mind struggling to wrap itself around the idea that it was my mother at the center of this harrowing fairy tale, improbable even by Holocaust standards. My story began with Dmitri Arshansky, my maternal grandfather, bartering for his daughter's life.

A gold watch, the turn of a soldier's head, and she was gone. Zhanna Arshanskaya, fourteen years old, the coat off her father's back to resist the Russian winter, bolted from the sad column of marching Jews and disappeared into the landscape.

Something my mother said in the interview supplied the headline for the front-page story: "My father didn't think anything could be so savage."

My story ran the week *Holocaust* aired. Writing in *Time* magazine, critic Frank Rich called the miniseries "an uncommonly valuable achievement . . . likely to awaken more consciences to the horrors of the Holocaust than any single work since Anne Frank's diary nearly three decades ago."

He was correct. *Holocaust* proved to be a powerful catalyst in America for adding the Holocaust to secondary school textbooks, and in West Germany—where it drew enormous ratings—the miniseries triggered the first national conversation about the Holocaust since the end of the war, forcing Germans to confront pent-up demons and repressed guilt.

The impact was less profound for me and, as far as I could tell, my mother. There was no change in our relationship, which consisted of weekly phone calls and occasional trips to her home in Atlanta, where she moved in 1981. From time to time in ensuing years, as a columnist and later a TV critic, I would call and do a brief interview for a piece I was writing. In 1980, I spoke to her about *Playing for Time*, a CBS movie based on the true story of a prisoner who played in a band at Auschwitz—a story similar to her own. Just like two years earlier when she had told me her story for the first time, her recounting was vivid, colorful, and detailed, but not emotional—for either of us. Not once had she paused, unable to go on. Nor had I.

Perhaps this steely ability to maintain focus, to block out all intervening thoughts and feelings, simply was the discipline of an artist trained to keep going no matter what—as Dmitri Arshansky had trained his daughter, having six-year-old Zhanna practice in a darkened room so she would learn to play without looking at the piano keys. Or perhaps her eerie equanimity when we spoke of the past was something else altogether, akin to my own.

Not until after *Hiding in the Spotlight* was published in 2009 did I become aware of an entire genre of literature which had sprung up over the previous two decades or so—memoirs by people like me, children of Holocaust survivors. They even had a collective name, Second Generation Survivors. It turned out there were Second Generation clubs and associations *everywhere*, yet somehow they had escaped my notice.

Not long after my book came out, I attended a reading at the Holocaust Center in Maitland, a suburb of Orlando, by Alan Berger, a Holocaust scholar at Florida Atlantic University in Boca Raton. We traded books. I gave him *Hiding in the Spotlight,* he signed a copy of *Second Generation Voices: Reflections by Children of Holocaust Survivors & Perpetrators,* a collection of essays he edited with his wife, Naomi. It was my first exposure to this discrete universe of memory and suffering, and it left me feeling very much the outsider.

For me the most haunting essay was "The Lifelong Reporting Trip" by Julie Salamon, the author of several Holocaust-themed books including a novel, *White Lies,* and a memoir, *The Net of Dreams: A Family's Search for a Rightful Place.* Like me, Salamon was a journalist and Second Generation Survivor who grew up in the placid Midwest—southern Ohio, on the river—but both her parents were survivors.

"My parents raised me to be optimistic, to believe in goodness, the future, the possibility of beauty and love," she wrote in her *Reflections* essay. "Yet, they didn't hide their background from us, so we were also well aware of evil, no hope for the future, the reality of ugliness and hate." She recalled her "public declaration" as a child of survivors in 1979 in a review of Helen Epstein's book *Children of the Holocaust* that she volunteered to write for the *Wall Street Journal,* where she was covering the commodities market.

In the review, she wrote of being obsessed with concentration camps when she was young. "I read *Exodus* by Leon Uris for the first time when I was seven, lingering over his renditions of what happened to people in concentration camps. My dreams were filled with visions of mangled and bloodied Jewish bodies. I substituted fictional victims with my mother and father and would cry out in the night for Mommy and Daddy. I never told my parents why I cried so often at night. I'm not sure why."

All the essays in the collection echoed Salamon's. They left me profoundly grateful for the gift of my Mickey-Mantle-Flubber childhood. Unlike my mother's decision to stop speaking Russian to me, withholding her story was a good decision in the short and, especially, the long run. As a child, I had a recurrent nightmare of falling down the long, dark set of stairs in our first home in Bloomington. I can also recall a sharp sense of foreboding while waiting for my parents to return home at night after a party or concert, though they had been gone only a few hours, and always returned. On the whole, however, mine was an untroubled, blue-sky childhood. As a teenager and young adult, when many "Second Gens" began to experience delayed trauma from corrosive childhood memories, my subconscious was blessedly *tabula rasa*.

This, I believe, is why hearing my mother's story for the first time at age thirty did not faze or unsettle me. By then I was a husband and father with fully developed emotional armor. I was able to listen to my mother's story with nearly the same detachment as that of a stranger—then put it in a mental drawer and move on. Over the next fifteen years my wife, Candy, and journalism mentor, Bob Hammel, continually urged me to open the drawer and make the story into a book.

I continually resisted—on the grounds that I did not have the time; that my mother would not sit for more interviews (even though she had opened up, there was so much she still would not speak of); that I was a columnist, not a book writer, and I feared my own mother becoming the victim of a literary lab experiment gone horribly wrong—the Survivor Bride of Frankenstein. Whatever my grounds for resisting, conscious or buried, it would take a middle-school class assignment years later to unlock my mother's emotions and compel me to open the drawer once again.

CHAPTER TWO

I n 1994 our daughter, Aimee, was in eighth grade at Glenridge Middle School in Winter Park, near Orlando. She was fortunate to have a man named Ron Hartle as her history teacher, a passionate dynamo known for multimedia presentations that brought any subject to life. One day Aimee came home with an assignment from Mr. Hartle. Each student was to ask a grandparent, or other older relative, what their life had been like at the same age.

Aimee, thirteen, decided to ask "Zee," as she affectionately called my mother, about her teenage experiences. "Good luck with that!" we thought. Aimee knew little about her Russian grandmother's early life beyond the fact that she'd come to America after the war, and even less about the Holocaust. She had no idea "Zee" had been caught up in the Holocaust at age fourteen and was not eager to discuss that part of her life. So Aimee forged ahead.

"Dear Grandma (Zee): Hi, how are you doing? I hope everything is going well for you right now. I am writing this letter for a school history project we are doing. The project is to find out as much as possible about our grandparents, and what was going on when they were about 13 years old. I know some about your life then, but I would love to hear more. Some specific things I would like to know are what life was like overall in about 1940. What was your home life like? Also, what are some major world events that you remember from around that time? I look forward to hearing from you, and hope to see you soon. Love, Aimee Dawson."

We were surprised when, two weeks later, Aimee received from "Zee" a handwritten letter covering four pages of her 8-by-10 personalized stationery with the sketch of a grand piano in the upper right-hand corner. We were astonished when we read the letter.

Not only had my mother directly answered Aimee's questions about her life and "major world events," she had done so in wrenchingly personal terms—reaching emotional depths untouched in her interviews with me.

"Dearest Aimee. To start with you should know that I have loved my country truly passionately from very early childhood. Some easier times and mostly hard times did not take away this feeling of mine. My parents were the most devoted kind to my sister Frina and myself. There was no limit of their concern for us."

She described her idyllic early life in Berdyansk and later Kharkov where she and Frina studied piano at the conservatory, and how it all vanished in a flash when the Nazis arrived in 1941—when she was about Aimee's age.

"They hung anyone they wanted on the trees where people had to walk," she wrote. "They tore into our apartment first to press and hold my mother to the wall, and the second time they took my father's violin. It was with my father almost every day of his life. That horrified me and I can never tell anyone what hatred I had for them."

She recounted the march of 16,000 Jews from Kharkov to a killing field outside the city, and how the Nazis mocked the walking dead and took souvenir photos to send home to Germany.

"I found out how little death mattered to me if you weren't ridiculed, laughed at, or had your picture taken in your most humiliated moment of life. The realization came to me early in five years of war that humiliation is much worse than death. I never felt that I was a big enough person to endure humiliation and I don't think that has changed. Our honor is life itself to us, and dignity.

"Well, at this point of my story, I will have to make it very sketchy because it's too long, it's much too hard on me and also because one day I hope to make it known to this world of ours."

It was the first time I had heard those words from my mother—"I hope to make it known to this world of ours."

For fifteen years, since she first told me the story, she had resolutely resisted the idea. The letter from Aimee had changed everything. It's as if she flipped a light switch and suddenly my mother could see the importance of telling her story for Aimee's generation and others to follow. She grew more and more willing to share her story, agreeing two years later to an interview for Steven Spielberg's Shoah Project. After the phenomenal success of *Schindler's List* in 1993, Spielberg sent camera crews around the world to record the testimonies of as many survivors as he could find, knowing they would soon be gone.

My writing mentor, Bob Hammel, and Candy had never given up their campaign for a book, and now events were on their side. Aimee's letter, the Shoah Project taping, and my mother's stated desire to "make this known to the world" had given their effort real momentum. There was another event, wholly unexpected, which drove home for me the imperative of preserving the story.

After her sophomore year in high school, Aimee and a dozen classmates followed a venerable tradition—the chaperoned "If it's Tuesday this must be Belgium" summer tour of Europe, five countries in ten days by bus and train. Strange languages, stranger food, midnight pillow fights, picturebook scenery—all of it reflected in Aimee's scrapbook. Or so we thought. In fact, she had omitted one stop.

In Aimee's scrapbook and her postcards and calls home, there was no trace of the group's trip to Dachau.

The blank page, the silence, was out of character for Aimee, a garrulous, opinionated student-government leader. We learned of the Dachau tour from one of the chaperones, a teacher who knew Aimee well. Of all the students, she said, only Aimee was visibly shaken by what she saw at Dachau, and said nothing afterward. This was two years after she received my mother's letter, which did not include this detail: after the war, before leaving their displaced persons in Germany for America, my mother and sister played a long concert for two thousand survivors of Dachau.

While it's possible to engage in too much armchair psychology, it is difficult to account for Aimee's reaction to Dachau except as trauma—her subconscious connecting what she saw at Dachau to her grandmother's ordeal. Aimee's distress was deeper than anything I had ever felt. It almost seems as if the trauma of my mother's experience, which she spared me, had been transmitted to Aimee, who unmistakably inherited my mother's slender frame and fiery Russian temperament. Did she also inherit the winds of my mother's war?

Berger identifies common characteristics among Second Gens such as sensitivity to multicultural issues and concern for social justice. "Many of the second generation witnesses seek a post-Auschwitz mending of the world. For instance, numerous children of survivors enter the helping professions, for example, marriage and family therapists, mental health counselors, social workers, attorneys, and

teachers. Furthermore, many of the Jewish second generation speak with a moral voice, on issues ranging from social
justice to peace in the Middle East to counseling children
of Vietnamese boat people."[1]

This portrait of a Second Gen sounds less like me
than it does Aimee, who is technically the Third Gen.
Perhaps it had nothing to do with her grandmother
being a Holocaust survivor who despises prejudice, but as
student body president in high school Aimee appointed
rainbow cabinets and volunteered with the National
Conference for Community and Justice which combats
discrimination and hate. Her first job after college was
youth program director for the NCCJ in Washington,
D.C. Now she volunteers at urban high schools in Indianapolis, teaching reading and presentation skills. And the
bond with her grandmother, "Zee," grew, and continues
to grow, stronger each year.

As the new millennium neared, I was chafing under
the punishing iron yoke of the top editor at *The Orlando
Sentinel*, where I had been a columnist since 1986, and
began looking around. In early 2000, I was offered a job as
consumer columnist at *The Indianapolis Star*, just an hour
from Bloomington where Aimee was attending Indiana
University. I loved the idea of moving back to basketball
country and working for an editor, Tim Franklin, who
believed in using the First Amendment. The job itself
would be less time-consuming than my TV-critic and

columnist gigs in Orlando, which I always brought home with me.

But despite the bonus of Aimee becoming eligible for in-state tuition and seeing her more often (not necessarily in that order), it was not a slam-dunk decision for us. We had moved several times and hated it. We had sworn Orlando would be our last stop. Moreover, I was taking a $13,000 pay cut to escape Captain Queeg in the editor's office—though Candy would make that much more in Indianapolis for the same reading-specialist job she had in Orange County.

"Okay," Candy said one day, "let's do it—on one condition."

"That I do all the packing?"

"That you use the extra time to write the book."

"Deal," I said.

CHAPTER THREE

In the autumn of 2000, I left behind the gold and crimson foliage of central Indiana and traveled to Atlanta for an interview with my mother that I hoped would lead to a book about her Holocaust experience. I had written to her sister, Frina, about the project and asked when I could visit her in Buffalo, NY, to get the story through her eyes. I was still waiting to hear back.

The interviews were conducted at the dining table in my mother's condominium in northeast Atlanta using a Radio Shack cassette recorder with a plastic microphone stand. Having spent much of her life as a concert pianist, my mother was no stranger to microphones and performing on cue—to rehearsal and repetition until it was perfect. She was used to commanding the stage. At seventy-three, her memory and focus remained extraordinary. Only once in ten hours of questions and answers over two days did she succumb to emotion and stop momentarily to gather herself—when she spoke of her mother, "my greatest hero," crisscrossing Nazi-occupied Kharkov on foot in a futile search for a Russian Orthodox priest to baptize her daughters, to de-Jewdify them.

Back home in Indiana, I found an executive secretary in a bank who transcribed tape recordings on the side and was pleased to receive such a large order, though she warned me she knew little about the Holocaust. A few weeks later she returned a fine transcript with a personal note. "I loved listening to your mother tell her story. It is truly amazing. She sounds like a truly incredible person."

These unsolicited comments by a stranger were the first objective confirmation of my purely subjective view that an amazing story had fallen in my lap—or perhaps, more to the point, I had fallen in the *story's* lap at Bloomington Hospital in December 1949. Leafing through the transcript, I had the same thought I had that day in 1978 in *The Herald-Times* newsroom, typing in disbelief as my mother related her story to me for the first time over the phone: "This is incredible copy."

In fact, it was so incredible, so rich, I panicked. It was like finding a bag on your doorstep with a million dollars in unmarked bills. *Now* what? I didn't want to do anything impulsive—I needed a plan. I put the transcript in a drawer for safekeeping and deep thought. Meanwhile, I returned to Atlanta for a followup interview, which produced another transcript for the drawer. About that time I received a note from Frina that left me perplexed. Politely, without explanation, she declined my request to be interviewed for the book.

The doorstep bounty was still in the drawer, untouched, when in 2003 we did the unthinkable—for the sixth time—uprooted. This time it was back to Orlando where, ironically, Tim Franklin had succeeded the *Sentinel* editor who caused me to flee to Indiana to work for Franklin at *The Star*. The transcripts went from the drawer to a moving box marked "den." In Orlando we bought a house with an upstairs room with a view conducive to writing an overdue book. On my first official day as an "author," the silence from upstairs was so deafening that after a few hours Candy looked in to see if I had fallen asleep at the keyboard. She found me staring at a stubbornly blank screen.

As I struggled to give narrative form to the material, to transfer the music of my mother's words to the page, Candy repeated something she had said from the outset.

"You need to go to Ukraine."

"No, I don't," I repeated.

There was nothing to be gained by going to Ukraine, I argued. Nothing to see there that I couldn't see in pictures, no one left to talk to who knew my mother. I didn't speak the language. It would be a long, expensive trip for nothing. I had the whole story right here in my mother's words.

I was right—I had the story. And a year later, after writing in the mornings before work and on weekends, I had a manuscript. What I *didn't* have, it turned out, was a book. Pleased to be "finished" and eager for feedback, I gave the 35,000-word manuscript to a *Sentinel* colleague, Jean Patteson, a constant reader and wonderful writer. She read it over the weekend and flagged me down on Monday morning.

"This is the most amazing story I've ever read," Jean said.

My heart leapt. Then Jean dropped the hammer.

"But it's not a book. What you have is a great *outline* for a book."

The manuscript lacked emotion and sense of place, Jean said. The story felt distant, reportorial. The solution was obvious.

Candy was right. I had to go to Ukraine.

In September 2006, Candy and I traveled from Orlando to Kiev, the capital of Ukraine and unofficial line of demarcation between the west, where Ukrainian is the dominant language, and the east, where anything other than Russian raises bushy eyebrows. After two days in Kiev we hopped an eastbound train for Kharkov, where my mother had studied at the music conservatory. Later, we would travel south to her hometown of Berdyansk on the Sea of Azov where she had played her first public performance on the radio at age six.

To supplement my thirty words of Russian, which could be stitched together for basic greetings and questions, we were armed with a handwritten message of introduction, in Russian, from my mother, which we had printed on the back of cards to hand out to locals baffled by my pidgin Russian.

"Dear Countrymen!" she wrote, "I am turning to you because my son Greg and his wife Candy don't speak the language and need your help. He wrote a book about Ukraine and my family. My name is Zhanna Arshanskaya (married name Dawson). I was born in Berdyansk in 1927. Our family moved to Kharkov in 1935 and we were there when the Germans invaded. Everyone in my family was killed and it is only because of the help of the kind population in our wonderful country that my sister and I are still alive so the story of our life in Ukraine can be told. Greg's book is about the heroism of our people. He and Candy know a lot about Ukraine and fell in love with the country and decided to fly to you even though they don't know the language. Trust them 100%—they already love you the way their mother does. Thank you all for your generosity and colossal courage. Be happy and healthy. Zhanna Arshanskaya Dawson, who would love to be going to see you."

My mother *could* have been there. We invited her to come along, and she was in robust health, a daily walker with hand weights up and down the hills of her neighborhood in the Buckhead section of Atlanta. She declined, reminding us that she hated to travel. True. She had not left the country since arriving in 1946. It was hard enough getting my mother on a plane to Florida or Indiana, much less Ukraine. I ascribed her general aversion to travel to the fact she'd simply had her fill of it during the war. Yet, I wondered if turning down the opportunity to visit her homeland with us was rooted in something deeper than the hassle of going through security.

As stolid and unflinching as my mother had been through all our interviews, and despite her growing willingness to speak about her own experience, the fact was she had never read a book or seen a film about the Holocaust, even the less graphic and emotionally wrenching ones I recommended, such as *Schindler's List* and *Life is Beautiful*. I had the feeling she declined our invitation to Ukraine for the same unspoken reason.

As it turned out, her instincts probably served her well. The last time she had seen Kharkov, in December 1941, the city was in semi-ruins, occupied by Nazis. Returning to her former home and seeing the house down the street where she had been hidden for two weeks by a non-Jewish family would have been a mixed emotional moment, as would visiting the secondary school she attended and the music conservatory in the center of the city where she and her sister studied.

But around so many other corners lurked images freighted with nightmares for my mother, like the majestic statue of the Ukrainian poet Shevchenko which she saw festooned with Jewish corpses. The most terrible possibility is that she would have accompanied us to the memorial at Drobitsky Yar outside the city where her parents and grandparents were murdered—and where she and Frina were supposed to die, too—along with sixteen thousand other Jews.

I shudder to imagine my mother listening as the tour guide told how in summer there were strawberries and cranberries growing in the ravines, but when she looked at them all she could think of was blood. Worst of all would have been the subterranean "Mourning Hall" where on a wall engraved with the names of the dead she would have found the names of her grandparents, her parents, Dmitri and Sarah—and also her own and her sister's. I am certain that no flicker of triumph at having cheated fate would have mitigated the horror of that moment for my mother. She might, however, have found some solace at the Kharkov Holocaust Museum. And though I might have originally gone to Ukraine for *Hiding in the Spotlight*, it was at the museum that I found the inspiration for this book.

The museum is housed in three high-ceilinged rooms on the second story of a pre-war building on Petrovskogo Street in downtown Kharkov. When opened in 1996 without government support by a band of Jewish activists

45

led by Larisa Volovik, it became—and remains to this day—the only public Holocaust museum in Ukraine. That startling fact speaks volumes about denial of the Holocaust in the country where the mass extermination of Jews first began in 1941. That changed with the dissolution of the Soviet Union in 1991. It's no longer official policy to pretend the Holocaust happened to 6 million random people of no particular ethnic or religious identity. There has been a revival of Jewish life. In Kharkov I visited the synagogue and several thriving Jewish organizations that offer books and programs on the Holocaust. It's now taught in the schools. But there is still a long way to go.

I wish my mother had been with us the day we visited the museum in 2006. Volovik had put a story in the museum's monthly publication about our upcoming research trip to Ukraine. When we arrived, there were two surprise guests waiting for us whose presence refuted my facile assertion to Candy that there was no one left in Kharkov who knew my mother. These two gray-haired women—sisters—did. But they knew Zhanna only as Anna Morozova, the fictitious name she used during the war while trying to hide her Jewish identity

Through a translator, the sisters explained that they had been in an entertainment troupe with Anna (Zhanna) and Marina (Frina) that performed for Nazi troops occupying the city of Kremenchug in central Ukraine. One of them gave us a picture she had taken of the troupe. My mother is in the middle of the large group, the only one looking away from the camera, in hopes of not being noticed. Frina had stayed in her room and refused to be in the photo.

The museum offered a variety of artifacts—eyeglasses, pocket watches, lockets—documents, photos, and exhibits, including a scale model of the abandoned tractor factory outside Kharkov where the doomed Jews were held for two weeks without food and water in late December 1941 before being marched to Drobitsky Yar.

Another exhibit that caught my eye featured a series of black-and-white photos. There were images of a courtroom, close-ups of various individuals, and—most striking— photos of a public execution, four men hanging by their necks at the end of long ropes. A huge crowd, thousands, surrounded the rough gallows in what appeared to be a public square. The accompanying text said the four men were three Nazi officers and a Russian collaborator. They had been tried by Soviet authorities in a makeshift court-room in the Kharkov Opera House and been found guilty of heinous crimes against the people of Ukraine. I looked at the date under the photo of the hangings.

December 19, 1943.

I looked again—that couldn't be right. 1943? The war in Europe didn't end till May 1945. The war crime trials in Nuremberg began that November.

How was it possible, I wondered, that there was a Nazi war crime trial in Ukraine nearly two years before

Nuremberg and that there seemed to be no record of it except this exhibit?

But then, how was it possible that nearly a million Ukrainian Jews were murdered before the chimneys at Auschwitz began belching human ash, and almost no one seemed to know about that either?

Near the photo exhibit of the trial was a glass case with two faded red ticket stubs, good for admission to the Kharkov Opera House, December 13, 1943, for a trial now as forgotten as the million Jews who, in the words of NBC anchor Brian Williams sixty-five years later, "simply vanished" from Ukraine.

"Somebody," I thought, "needs to do a book about that someday."

CHAPTER FOUR

History has done Holocaust deniers a great favor by largely deleting Ukraine from our collective memory and common knowledge. What makes the omission as significant as it is tragic is not just the fact that more than a million Jews in Ukraine were murdered; it's the fact that these were the *first* of the 6 million. Ukraine is where the mass extermination of the Jews began, not Poland or Germany as nearly all Americans still believe.

The analogy is imperfect but will suffice: not placing Ukraine high up in Chapter 1 of the story of the Holocaust would be like teaching U.S. involvement in World War II by skipping Pearl Harbor and going straight to D-Day. The analogy is further imperfect because what Hitler did in Ukraine, and why, explains far more about the Holocaust than Pearl Harbor does about the war with Japan. Motive, weapons, plan—all the incontrovertible evidence of the greatest crime of the twentieth century is to be found at the start, in Ukraine. Allowing fate and circumstance to effectively quash the evidence—disconnecting the dots between motive and crime—helps deniers spread their fantasies in the court of public opinion.

I was not a student of the Holocaust—or much of anything, I'm sure my teachers would say—before writing *Hiding in the Spotlight.* I spent more time at the library doing research for the book than I did in all my years of high school and college combined. I was startled by what I found. I had gone in search of basic Holocaust history that would form the backdrop for my mother's story of escape and survival. I found the first hours of the Final Solution—Operation Barbarossa. On June 22, 1941, three million German troops and three thousand tanks invaded the Soviet Union. Following behind the *Wehrmacht* were mobile killing squads, *Einsatzgruppen,* whose specific mission was to find and kill Jews in large numbers, the start of the fulfillment of Hitler's malignant vision. By the end of the year, months before the gas chamber doors at Auschwitz would swing open, half a million Ukrainian Jews were already dead.

I was surprised by this information, but even more surprised—dumbfounded—that it was news to virtually everyone who heard it from me at events where I spoke about *Hiding in the Spotlight.* Between June 2009 when the book came out and January 2011, I made some 120 presentations at churches, synagogues, service clubs, retirement homes, private homes, middle schools, universities, museums, libraries, and bookstores in Florida, Georgia, Virginia, and Indiana. It would be generous to say that 10% of the listeners had a clue about the events in Ukraine in 1941.

At a middle school in Bloomington, Ind., my hometown, the percentage was half that, and would have been lower if I weren't such an easy grader. Before my wife and I visited the school to discuss the book and to show Candy's film about our trip to Ukraine in 2006, I had the teachers give a four-question pop quiz to the eighth-graders we would be addressing. No need for the kids to sign their papers, I told the teachers, I just want to see how much a group of typical middle schoolers knows about the Holocaust in 2010. These were not trick questions. They called for information that would be in chapter one of any history of the Holocaust in Ukraine—if only it were being taught.

1) In which country did the mass extermination of Jews begin? 2) What was the main method of killing in these exterminations? 3) What are *Einsatzgruppen*? 4) What is Babi Yar? The answers: 1) Ukraine (or Soviet Union or Russia); 2) Shooting; 3) Nazi killing squads; 4) A killing field in Ukraine where the Nazis murdered 34,000 Jews.

Two hundred twenty students took the quiz. Not one student aced it. Two students answered three questions correctly, five got two right, and seven students scored one—meaning 205 students were not able to answer a single question correctly. Only one student knew that the mass exterminations began in "Russia." The overwhelming majority said Germany. A dozen students identified Babi Yar as a Jewish holiday.

To put the dismal results in depressing perspective, this school is in a middle-class neighborhood in a university community with high rates of literacy and cultural awareness. The several classes of eighth-graders were brought to our presentation because they already were studying the Holocaust. Media students at the school have produced award-winning films of their visits to Auschwitz. If smart students with motivated teachers can't pass a quiz about basic Holocaust history, who could?

Not the tanned, well-spoken residents, many of them retirees, of an affluent community outside Orlando who came to my presentation on a balmy, sun-splashed morning. Two women told me their husbands would have been there, but they had tee times. Though equipped with much longer memories and experience, this group did only slightly better than the middle-schoolers in Bloomington, and I thought I noticed two or three furtively researching on their iPhones.

The most startling confirmation for me that Ukraine Holocaust blindness cuts across all ethnic, religious and generational lines came on a rainy Sunday night in March when I traveled to Minneola, forty-five miles south of Orlando in what used to be orange groves, to speak at a new synagogue that had just opened in a small strip shopping center. It was an older congregation, many of them retirees from New York and others points north. After my usual riff on the *Einsatzgruppen* and how the mass killings had begun in Ukraine, I asked for a show of hands from all those who had heard this before. Not one hand went up.

This information about Ukraine is so widely *un*known that once you come into possession of it, you feel as if you belong to a secret society and begin to notice its absence everywhere. I could not help noticing that it's virtually absent from the impressive Holocaust memorial in Miami Beach, an open-air exhibit with a plaza of Jerusalem stone, a meditation garden, a waterlily pond, and a magnificent sculpture—a giant hand and arm, tattooed with a number from Auschwitz, outstretched to the heavens. Nearby in "The Arbor of History" are fifty inscribed black granite slabs telling the history of the Jewish people and the Shoah in words and images.

It reads more like the history of Auschwitz and the Warsaw ghetto, both cited on many panels. Only two slabs contain any reference to Ukraine. (A third panel uses a photo of undressed women at a killing field in Ukraine, but it is not labeled as such.) One tells about the formation of the *Einsatzgruppen* but does not say where they operated. Panel #42 out of 50 has a photo of corpses in a ravine. "Many of these covered ravines were later discovered in the countryside of Poland and the Ukraine," the caption says. "In one such ravine in Babi Yar, outside of Kiev, the capital of the Ukraine, over 30,000 Jews were killed in 2 days shortly after the Germans arrived." (Every source I've seen gives a total closer to 34,000.)

The dates of the Babi Yar slaughter, Sept. 29–30, 1941, are not set in stone at the memorial. Nor is June 22, 1941, when the Nazis invaded the Soviet Union with the *Einsatzgruppen* in tow and ignited the mass exterminations which became the impetus for use of gas chambers and ovens at places like Treblinka, Sobibor, Belzec, and Auschwitz-Birkenau, which had not even been built at the time of the Babi Yar massacre. I am not suggesting that the creators of the Miami memorial intentionally marginalized the Holocaust in Ukraine. That would be antithetical to their greater purpose. My point is illustrative: the memorial was a product of its times—conceived in 1984 when there was little public awareness in the U.S. of wartime events in Ukraine, and opened in 1990 before the implosion of the Soviet Union, which assiduously maintained the fiction that the Holocaust was not a Jewish event. Still, considering the substantial scholarship available at the time—Raul Hilberg wrote at great length about the *Einsatzgruppen* in *The Destruction of the European Jews,* published in 1961—the scant mention of Ukraine at the Miami memorial is startling.

All the history on the panels at the Miami Beach memorial was written by Helen Fagin, a Polish survivor and scholar who served as chair of the committee in charge of developing educational material for the United States Holocaust Memorial Museum. In early 2011, I reached Fagin at her home in Sarasota, Fl., where she now lectures at the New College of Florida. After describing my project, I told Fagin I was puzzled by the fact that there was so little information on the memorial about events in Ukraine.

Fagin made no comment on the events themselves, these first mass exterminations of the Shoah, focusing instead on geography and national boundaries—Ukraine's history as a geopolitical football fought over by Poland, Romania, Czechoslovakia, and the Soviet Union, which she noted had "absorbed" it. As a mere republic of the Soviet Union, Fagin suggested, it did not merit or require special attention on the memorial. Well then, I said, how about the Nazi invasion of the Soviet Union? Was not June 22, 1941 as consequential a date as others on the memorial such as May 8, 1943, when the leader of the Warsaw ghetto, Mordechai Anielewicz, was killed? Or January 22, 1942, when Hitler's high command met at Wannsee to approve plans for the Final Solution, which had already consumed half a million Ukrainian Jews?

Getting no direct answer to that, either, I asked Fagin if she knew about the trial of three Nazi officers for war crimes in Kharkov in December 1943—the first such trial, long before the post-war trials at Nuremberg—and she confessed that she did not. She then proceeded to explain *why* the trial she had never heard of was of no special import.

"These soldiers were not on trial for what they did to the Jews or Ukrainian people—they were put on trial because they were political enemies of the Soviet Union," Fagin said.

This is a classic difference without a distinction. Yes, the *Einsatzgruppen* and the German army were "political enemies" of the Jews and other Ukrainians they murdered. But as Clausewitz said, war is the extension of politics by other means, and never was this more evident than it was in the planning for the invasion of the Soviet Union.

"By Hitler's definition, the war with the Soviet Union was different from the wars he had waged against Poland, France and the other countries in Europe," writes historian Yitzhak Arad in *The Holocaust in the Soviet Union*. "General Alfred Jodl was ordered by Hitler to prepare an appendix to the 'Special Orders to Directive No. 21' (Operation Barbarossa), saying, 'The forthcoming campaign is more than a mere armed conflict: it is a collision between two different ideologies.'"[1] The document gave SS chief Himmler authority to eliminate all elements of the Soviet "political system," including many Jews.

So, yes, Fagin was correct—indeed it's a macabre understatement—to say the Nazis on trial in Kharkov were "political enemies" of the Soviet Union. It was a semantic point as irrelevant to the larger point as her geography lesson. The legal pretext for the Kharkov trial of the Nazis was less important than their alleged crimes. For the victims, dead was dead.

I asked Fagin if she would change or add anything if she were writing history for the memorial today. "I don't know," she said. "I have not seen the recent research. I no longer teach history. I am now teaching morality."

Ukraine's standing, until quite recently, as a distant, dark planet in the universe of the Holocaust knowledge—very much a self-imposed isolation by the secretive Kremlin masters—was evident in the itinerary of a 57-member commission President Carter appointed in 1979 to prepare a report that laid the foundation for the U.S. Holocaust museum in Washington, D.C. The commission's first stop on a fourteen-day fact-finding mission was Poland, where it visited the site of the Warsaw Ghetto, the death camps at Treblinka and Auschwitz, a Jewish cemetery in Warsaw, and was given a tour of Polish archives pertaining to the war. The commission, led by Elie Wiesel, met with a host of government and cultural ministers, viewed Polish documentaries about the Holocaust, and attended a performance at a Jewish theater in Warsaw.

The next stop, in the Soviet Union, was comparatively brief. The only Holocaust site the commission visited was Babi Yar, where the members—many of them distinguished scholars and authors of Holocaust books—were "shocked" to find no acknowledgement that nearly all the victims of the massacre had been Jewish—an indication of just how little was still known, even by experts, about this far-flung flashpoint of the Holocaust. In Moscow the commission met with various ministers and the chief Soviet prosecutor at Nuremberg, and laid a wreath at the Tomb of the Unknown Soldier. Then it was off to Denmark.

The twenty years since Ukraine went from being a closed Soviet republic to an open, independent state has seen a profusion of literature, scholarship, and journalism about the Holocaust and its aftermath in Ukraine, but people are resistant to change and thinking outside the box; they love their fixed paradigms and rusty icons. It will take time for "news" and revelation from the Ukraine to penetrate the public's holy trinity of Anne Frank, Auschwitz, and *Schindler's List*. There is a lag—to borrow Wiesel's formulation—between public "information" and the public's "knowledge," or awareness.

The glacial progress was evident in two state-of-the-art world history textbooks I examined which are used in the Orange County (Fla.) school system, one of the largest in the U.S. The Ukraine is not mentioned directly in the chapter on the Holocaust. It is encouraging that the *Einsatzgruppen* killings are included, but they are described, vaguely, as having occurred "in eastern Europe." To revisit my own analogy, can you imagine a textbook today saying that on Dec. 7, 1941, the Japanese attacked a U.S. naval base "in the Pacific"?

But the textbook writers are not so far behind the historical curve or cultural *Zeitgeist*, judging by story selection in the *New York Times*, which not only reports on the

Zeitgeist, but is itself a part of it. On April 20, 2009, Holocaust Remembrance Day, I found a story about Ukraine on page 6A, with two photos, which took up half the page under the headline "New Looks at the Fields of Death for Jews"—graphic testimony to the time warp from which the Holocaust in Ukraine is just now emerging.

"People know of Auschwitz and Bergen-Belsen," wrote Ethan Bronner. "Many have heard of the tens of thousands shot dead in the Ukrainian ravine of Babi Yar. But little has been known about the hundreds, perhaps thousands, of smaller killing fields across the former Soviet Union where some 1.5 million Jews met their deaths."

The story ran on the same day the Yad Vashem Holocaust museum and research center in Jerusalem made public on its Web site new information about Nazi killing sites in a host of smaller towns and villages in Ukraine, Belarus, Lithuania, and Latvia. "In many cases, locals played a key role in the murders, probably by a ratio of 10 locals to every one German," said the head researcher. "We are trying to understand the man who played soccer with his Jewish neighbor one day and turned to kill him the next."

It is likely that my mother's family was betrayed the same way, by friends, or at least acquaintances, in the building on Katsarskaya Street in Kharkov where they lived in December 1941 when the Nazis rounded up all the Jews—the ones who had not fled east—on the pretext of marching them to a labor camp. My mother and her sister escaped the march—my mother by her father's bribe, and Frina by unknown means (she has never spoken of it to anyone, to my knowledge, except possibly her husband). The rest were murdered just after New Year's at Drobitsky Yar, a larger cousin of the killing fields, which are still being discovered today in Ukraine, even as denier Web sites proliferate in cyberspace.

I had always regarded Holocaust deniers as the looniest of the lunatic fringes, peddlers of a theory so laughably, patently false that it made alien-abduction and telepathic spoon-bending look like good science. The notion that the Holocaust did not happen wasn't worth my attention or acknowledgement, much less my concern five years ago. That all changed after *Hiding in the Spotlight* was published and I discovered the great void in common knowledge about the Holocaust in Ukraine. There were many more open, malleable minds up for grabs than I had ever imagined possible—targets for the deluded demagogues and sociopathic liars from Denial Land. And hadn't we heard from the forefathers of these fabulists before—in Germany in the 1930s? I saw the opportunity to provide an antidote.

Hiding in the Spotlight took me to numerous middle schools and the most achingly vulnerable minds of all, soft clay waiting to be shaped—or misshapened. Nowhere was the response to my mother's story so sharp or personal as it was in these classrooms, perhaps because it was about someone the same age as the students themselves. It could be *their* story.

A couple of weeks after a middle-school talk, we always received a large envelope with individual thank-you notes from the students. They were portraits of minds and sensibilities in uneasy transition from childhood to adult consciousness. The rainbow lettering, squiggly lines, block-letter THANK YOU's and purple hearts on the front often belied a darker message inside.

"I learned so much. I never knew about the holes people got shot into. So sad.—Rachel."

"Your mom's story is the most earth-shattering thing I ever heard. I did not know about the killing fields. I only knew about the death camps, and to hear about what your mom went through just really hit me.—Lauren."

"You taught me so much. I hardly knew anything about the Holocaust before you came to our school. Now I know way more than enough.—Drew."

"I can't imagine what it would be like living in Germany at that time. Never knowing if the Nazis will barge into your house, hearing screams for mercy when you are trying to sleep. You have changed how I look at the normal everyday things I have. I'm more grateful and thankful. I can't wait until I get to share all I know about the Holocaust with my friends.—Katie."

The words were different, but I think all four were saying the same thing: Never again.

CHAPTER FIVE

I realized this book needed a brief primer on Ukraine the day a neighbor, Ted, told me he thought Moscow was west of Ukraine. In fact, it's the reverse. Most of Ukraine lies west of Moscow. Ted also thought that Moscow was south of Ukraine—again, quite the opposite.

In our small Orlando neighborhood of people smarter than me, Ted may be the smartest. He is a retired military man who tutors honors students headed for elite colleges. He does Soduku in his sleep, is a voracious reader, and would be my first pick when choosing teams for a neighborhood Jeopardy tournament. If Ted is confused about Ukraine, I decided, the general public is in deep trouble. This was final confirmation of a realization that had dawned on me in the course of my experience promoting *Hiding in the Spotlight*.

While there usually, but not always, were exceptions in every room, what I found was that even these reasonably well-informed Americans could not come within a thousand miles of finding Ukraine on an unmarked map. In part, you can blame America's historic obliviousness to the rest of the world, separated as we are from most of it by two oceans. Our splendid isolation and relatively secure borders have made us blithely geo-phobic (and arrogantly monolingual). No doubt there are many other places Americans can't find on that unmarked map.

But Ukraine poses a special challenge because of its history. For those of us who grew up in the fifties and sixties, Ukraine for all practical purposes did not exist. It was invisible—a neat trick for a place nearly the size of Texas. There was only the enormous and forbidding Soviet Union, which most people including our teachers referred to as Russia. We had no more idea—probably less—that the Soviet Union was made up of republics such as the Ukraine and Belarus and Azerbaijan than an average Soviet student did that America was a collection of states like Idaho and Arkansas and Delaware.

In this monolithic yet nebulous "Russia" there was Moscow, and everything else was "Siberia" (thank you, *Doctor Zhivago*). Cold War rhetoric deepened our confusion by making the "the Iron Curtain countries"—Rumania, Czechoslovakia, Hungary, et al.—synonymous with the Soviet Union, as if they, too, were part of "Russia." So, given

nearly a half century of misinformation and missed information, I was surprised but not shocked when Ted guessed
that Ukraine was somewhere east of the Ural Mountains,
where Siberia starts and unknown lands begin.

I was just as disoriented before writing my mother's
story. She spoke often about "Russia" when I was growing
up, but I recall almost no mention of Ukraine. Her persona
is best described as a proud Russian who happened to have
been born in Ukraine—rather like the slogan "American
by birth, Southern by the grace of God" found on bumper
stickers. Her self-identifying as Russian is natural since
the Ukraine was a dot in the vast pointillist tapestry of the
Russian Empire long before the Soviet Union in which she
came of age, and did not become its own country until
1991—fifty years after she was ripped from the arms of
her Mother Russia by the Nazis. The first research I did
for the book was to get out a map and find my mother's
hometown of Berdyansk on the Sea of Azov in southeastern
Ukraine, just north of the Black Sea. She spent her middle
childhood before the war in Kharkov in northeast Ukraine,
420 miles due south of Moscow, nowhere near the Arctic
Circle. Old impressions die hard. When I told friends I
was going to Ukraine in December 2010, they gave me the
"Siberia" look, but Chicago and New York certainly had
much tougher winters.

As puzzling as it is, Ukraine's geographic location is
a day at a Black Sea beach next to its political history, a

stupefying phantasmagoria of cultures, influences, princes, and nations stretching back to the ninth century and the Kievan Rus, a precursor to the Russian Empire, which for a time in the eleventh century was the largest state in Europe, with Kiev as the capital. For Ukraine as much as any place on Earth, situated at the intersection of Europe, Russia, and Asia, geography has been destiny—eternally traversed, invaded, settled, and abandoned. I've seen no better capsule biography of Ukraine than this from George Friedman, CEO of Stratfor, a Texas-based geopolitical think tank, who has written extensively about the country where his grandfather was born:

"The name 'Ukraine' literally translates as 'on the edge.' It is a country on the edge of other countries, sometimes part of one, sometimes part of another, and more frequently divided. In the seventeenth and eighteenth centuries it was divided among Russia, Poland, and the Ottoman Empire. In the nineteenth century it was divided between Russia and Austria-Hungary. And in the twentieth century, save for a short period of independence after World War I, it became part of the Soviet Union. Ukraine has been on the edge of empires for centuries."[1]

Such constant fluctuation is difficult to fathom for Americans who grew up in states with borders which have never changed and never been breached by a foreign army. In our lifetime, Ukraine's longest period of geographic and political "stability"—some might call it arrested development—was as a captive republic of the Soviet Union. After the implosion of the USSR in 1991, the Ukraine declared independence, ditched the "the" and became, simply, Ukraine. At the same time it was gaining independence, Ukraine was regaining its stolen identity after years of anonymity as a Soviet cipher.

Many Americans probably first took notice while watching the opening ceremonies of the 1994 Winter Olympics in Lillehammer, Norway. The tortoise-paced procession of costumed delegations with their distinctive national flags has traditionally served as a handy, color-coded refresher course on the rest of the world for American TV viewers every four years (every two since the winter and summer games were staggered) For half a century the Cold War was fought on the playing fields and ice rinks of the Olympics. We became accustomed to the sight of the vast Soviet delegation marching stolidly into the stadium under the red hammer and sickle, then soaking up a lion's share of medals during the games. Disappearance of the Soviet "team" was dramatic visible proof to Americans that the Cold War was over. Ukraine marched under its own blue-and-gold flag for the first time at Lillehammer. A decade later in the winter of 2004–05, the famously short American attention span was riveted by the spectacle of the Orange Revolution in Independence Square in Kiev, even if the average viewer did not know Yushchenko from Yanukovych.

One price of independence for Ukraine has been the revival—or continuation—of an ancient identity crisis. Ukraine can still be found at the intersection of gravitational forces, pondering its fate. As Friedman notes, the western third leans toward Europe, the eastern third toward Russia, and the remaining third in the center is pulled in both directions, with Kiev the capital of indecision. Should it tilt west and join the European Union? Or pay homage to its historic ties to Russia, so intimate and intertwined as to be familial?

"There are endless arguments over whether Ukraine created Russia or vice versa," Friedman wrote. "Suffice it to say, they developed together." And it seems they are destined to move forward together, separate yet indivisible like separated Siamese twins. Meanwhile, as Ukraine is pulled east and west into the future, it is subject to another powerful gravitational force—the past.

Before leaving Orlando for Ukraine, I made the acquaintance online of Victor Melikhov, a seventy-year-old Ukrainian who teaches English to university students in Kharkov. Ukrainian history is Victor's hobby. In Kharkov we met at my hotel for pots of tea and a mini-seminar in his favorite subject. Is life better for him in independent Ukraine than it was in the Soviet Union?

"If life is just food and pleasure, maybe not," Victor laughed. "Vodka and sausage were cheap in those days. But if life is reading good books popular in the world, not just what somebody in the Kremlin wants me to read, then I say we are on the right way. The difficult way."

The "difficult way" includes facing historical truths about the Holocaust that were distorted and suppressed by Soviet authorities, with the connivance of anti-Semitic elements in Ukraine. Victor's tutorial was illuminating about the primacy and the persistence of the past. When the Nazis learned that archaeologists had found bones of Goths—Germanic people—from 300 to 500 A.D. in Ukraine, he said, Hitler ordered a special exhibit to prove to his troops that this land—this fresh *Lebensraum*—had always belonged to Germany. They were merely taking back what was theirs. They failed, leaving the Russians and Ukrainians to resume their curious co-dependent dance.

"The last two centuries, the territory of northeastern Ukraine, especially the Kharkov region, was under strong Russian domination in politics, economics and culture," Victor said. "The population of this region consisted of 60% Ukrainians and 40% Russians, but these Ukrainians were and are completely Russified. You see that the Russian language is still common in Kharkov. During World War II some Ukrainian and Russian political groups and leaders— and some common people—collaborated with the Nazis. And now in Russian and Ukrainian societies there is a very active and noisy discussion about this painful theme."

Victor is a master of understatement. Collaboration of "some" Ukrainians was vital to the Nazi campaign, especially in the early stages of Operation Barbarossa when the invading Germans were greeted with bread and salt and flowers. People in the towns and villages of western Ukraine welcomed the Nazis as their liberators from the tyranny of Stalin, with his purges and punitive famines that killed millions in the 1930s. At the same time, Nazi propaganda making Jews the primary agents of Stalin and Bolshevism unleashed the anti-Semitism that was never far below the surface in Ukraine. The Germans became puppet masters of "spontaneous" pogroms by Ukrainians, many of them nationalists who saw the moment as a pathway to independence.

How many Ukrainians collaborated? Enough that the Germans had a word for those who donned uniforms and took up rifles against their fellow Ukrainians: *Schutzmannschaften.* By 1942 more than 100,000 Ukrainians had volunteered to take orders from the Nazi occupiers.

"Basic anti-communist and nationalistic feelings and anti-Semitism, which were common to the majority of those who volunteered, served as fertile soil for the anti-Jewish indoctrination they received during their service," wrote historian Yitzhak Arad. "They not only carried out orders from their German superiors but they also demonstrated initiative in hunting down and killing Jews. . . . The indigenous police forces became an essential tool for the implementation of the Final Solution in the occupied territories of the Soviet Union."[2]

Even *before* the Nazis had formalized a "Final Solution" at the Wannsee Conference in January 1942, it should be added.

A hundred and forty-six years after the end of the American Civil War, there are still bitter debates about flying the Confederate flag at state capitols and football stadiums in the South. Is it any wonder, then, that only seventy years after *Schutzmannschaften* were hunting down and murdering their fellow Ukrainians, that this unspeakably dark chapter remains an open wound? Healing is slowed by the variety of wartime experiences within Ukraine—Ukrainians, Jews, Crimean Tatars, Poles, and others—observed Anatoly Podolsky, director of the Ukrainian Center for Holocaust Studies in Kiev. "Remembrance culture in Ukraine has reached a dead end," he wrote in 2008. "Unconnected, isolated histories lead to the expression of memories that are isolated from one another. Each is in itself biased. The risk that aggression and intolerance in Ukrainian society will increase is considerable. The only solution is to accept history responsibly and to promote the exchange and reconciliation of competing narratives."[3]

Ukraine will be searching for its soul, for reconciliation with itself and with its troubled history, as well as its place in the world—long after my friend Ted has found its place on the map.

CHAPTER SIX

I f the answer on *Jeopardy!* was "He sparked the Protestant Reformation of the Roman Catholic Church in the
sixteenth century when he nailed his Ninety-Five Theses
to the door of a church in Wittenberg, Germany," there
is no doubt Alex Trebek would accept this as the correct
question:

"Who was Martin Luther?"

And Martin Luther *was* that man, a figure I remember
in heroic silhouette, if not great detail, from the course on
the Reformation that I took in college in the sixties. I
closed the book on Luther after that and did not open it
again until 2010, when I began work on this book. While
researching the roots of anti-Semitism in Germany, I ran
across this same man and decided that there must be
some mistake. Here are some of his words about Jews,
written in 1543:

GREG DAWSON

"They are thirsty bloodhounds and murderers of all Christendom with full intent, now for more than fourteen hundred years, and indeed they were often burned to death upon the accusation that they had poisoned water and wells, stolen children, and torn and hacked them apart in order to cool their temper secretly with Christian blood."

It went on.

"They hold us Christians captive in our country. They let us work in the sweat of our noses, to earn money and property for them, while they sit behind the oven, lazy, let off gas, bake pears, eat, drink, live softly and well from our wealth. They have captured us and our goods through their accursed usury; mock us and spit on us, because we work and permit them to be lazy squires who own us and our realm."

And on.

"It is more than fourteen hundred years since Jerusalem was destroyed, and at this time it is almost three hundred years since we Christians have been tortured and persecuted by Jews all over the world, so that we might well complain that they had now captured and killed us all, which is the open truth. We do not know to this day which devil has brought them here into our country; we did not look for them in Jerusalem."

I was in disbelief to discover that the name on this collection of virulent, operatic anti-Semitism, *About the Jews and Their Lies*, was Martin Luther—the same Martin

74

Luther of my hagiographic undergraduate memory. There was no mistake—Raul Hilberg did not make mistakes about this. Even in the pantheon of Holocaust scholars the late Hilberg has no peer. His masterwork, *The Destruction of the European Jews,* is to the Holocaust what *On the Origin of Species* is to evolution.

Hilberg put Luther in the first pages of his three-volume, 1,388-page opus as the Johnny Appleseed of German anti-Semitism, quoting widely from his vile 65,000-word treatise. Yet this "other" Martin Luther basically does not exist today. He can be found, but only if you know where to look by Googling "Martin Luther and anti-Semitism" or "Martin Luther and Hitler." A clueless middle-school student in search of a quick reference is likely to encounter only the sanitized Martin Luther.

The American Heritage College Dictionary says simply "German theologian and leader of the Reformation." The online *Encyclopedia Brittanica* offers a 19-line capsule summary of Luther's life without a hint of his anti-Semitic obsession, and it's barely mentioned in a long article below the summary. Wikipedia gives the issue similar treatment and states vaguely that Luther was "a controversial figure among many historians and religious scholars." To non-historians, Luther is a bland one-dimensional figure in a funny hat.

History is replete with anti-Semites and their malignant vituperations. Why dwell on Luther? Because, as Hilberg shows, Luther's anti-Semitism was not just a personality tic or the evanescent ranting of an old man that was interred with his bones. It became the philosophical foundation for the great edifice of Nazi anti-Semitism and near extermination of the Jews. "The Nazi destruction process did not come out of a void," Hilberg wrote. "It was the culmination of a cyclical trend . . . The Nazis did not discard the past, they built upon it. They did not begin a development, they completed it."[1] And they were especially shrewd in manipulating the age-old anti-Semitism in places like Poland, Slovakia, and Ukraine.

Like most Americans, I had internalized the simplistic idea that the Holocaust did indeed "come out of a void" as a unique event, an aberration, an original cancer with shallow roots in Hitler's hatred of the Jews, his lust for power, and a unique set of socioeconomic conditions in the 1930s which lowered the Germans' resistance to the poisonous prescriptions of a mesmerizing megalomaniac. There was no place in that tidy view for the more disturbing idea that Hitler represented something endemic in German culture—that Nazism was a continuation of an ancient contagion.

Coming of age, the only Martin Luther on my radar screen was Martin Luther King, Jr., and I never thought about his name. Now that I know its provenance, the irony is mind-boggling. King carried the name of a man who espoused views inimical to all that he stood and died for. Like his father Martin Luther King, Sr., a Baptist minister, Martin Luther King, Jr. was born Michael King. When Michael was five, his father changed both their names in honor of the German priest he admired for his civil disobedience against Rome. The catalyst for that change elevates the story from ironic to macabre.

In 1934, Michael King joined ten other Baptist ministers on a trip to the Holy Land and Europe, including Berlin, for the Fifth Baptist World Alliance Congress. It was held at the Sportpalast, a favored venue for Hitler speeches, where the large hall was festooned with Nazi banners and Christian crosses for the Baptist event. By then, copies of *About the Jews and Their Lies* were being displayed in glass cases at the epic Nuremberg rallies glorified by filmmaker Leni Riefenstahl in *Triumph of the Will*, filmed the same year the Baptists gathered in Berlin.

It's highly unlikely that Rev. King from Atlanta was aware of the rallies or knew of Luther's repellent 400-year-old calumny. It was two years before Hitler would preside at the Summer Olympics in Berlin, four years before *Kristallnacht* shattered illusions about the Nazis once and for all. Moreover, Baptists at the Congress liked the fact that Hitler and his minions did not smoke or drink. Back home in Georgia, inspired by his visit to the homeland of Martin Luther, Michael King decided that from then on he and his son would carry the name of the great theologian. If only he had known then what most of us still don't know today about Luther.

Hitler did. He praised Luther as one of the greatest reformers in history, and he was not referring to the priest's crusade against indulgences in the Catholic Church. "He saw the Jew as we are only beginning to see him today," Hitler said. Whether or not *Kristallnacht*—November 9–10, 1938—was actually dedicated to Luther's birthday on November 10 as many suggest, it certainly fulfilled his marching orders to Christians four centuries earlier.

"Set fire to their synagogues or schools," Luther had said. "Destroy their homes, confiscate all Jewish holy books, forbid rabbis to teach, force Jews to do physical labor, abolish their right to safe conduct on the highways, confiscate all Jewish money and gold so they cannot practice usury." If necessary, Luther said, expel the Jews. "These anti-Semitic ravings were not peripheral jottings of Luther's," said Jewish writer Joseph Telushkin. "They became well-known throughout Germany."

In 1895 a notorious anti-Semite, Hammner Ahlwardt, was debating a fellow Reichstag deputy who opposed his idea to expel all Jews from Germany. There are not enough Jews in Germany to cause trouble, the other deputy argued.

"Yes, gentlemen, Deputy Rickert would be right, if it were a matter of fighting with honest weapons against an honest enemy," Ahlwardt retorted. "Then it would be a matter of course that the Germans would not fear a handful of such people. But the Jews, who operate like parasites, are a different kind of problem. Mr. Rickert, who is not as tall as I am, is afraid of a single cholera germ—and gentlemen, the Jews are cholera germs. It is the infectiousness and exploitive power of Jewry which is involved."

Hilberg observes, "It is remarkable that two men, separated by a span of three hundred and fifty years, can still speak the same language. Ahlwardt's picture of the Jews is in its basic features a replica of the Lutheran portrait. The Jew is still (1) an enemy who has accomplished what no external enemy has accomplished—he has driven the people of Frankfurt into the suburbs. (2) a criminal, a thug, a beast of prey who commits so many crimes that his elimination would enable the Reichstag to cut the criminal code in half. (3) a plague, or more precisely, a cholera germ. Under the Nazi regime these conceptions of the Jew were expounded and repeated in an almost endless flow of speeches, posters, letters, and memoranda."[2]

Julius Streicher was editor of the Nazi newspaper *Der Sturmer* and among the most obstreperous and vehement anti-Semites in Hitler's inner circle. It was a proud moment for Streicher when the city of Nuremberg presented him a first edition of *On the Jews and Their Lies*. In 1935, he addressed the Hitler Youth about Jews.

"This people has wandered about the world for centuries and millennia, marked with the sign of Cain. Boys and girls, even if they say that the Jews were once the chosen people, do not believe it. A chosen people does not go into the world to make others work for them, to suck blood. It does not go among the people to chase the peasants from the land. It does not go among the people to make your fathers poor and drive them to despair. A chosen people does not slay and torture animals to death. Boys and girls, for you we have always suffered. For you we had to accept mockery and insult, and became fighters against the Jewish people, against that organized body of world criminals against whom already Christ had fought, the greatest anti-Semite of all times."

Streicher probably would have put Martin Luther at No. 2—though it would have been a tough call for him between Luther and the Führer. Testifying in his trial at Nuremberg, Streicher used Luther as a sort of celebrity witness *in absentia* to rationalize his actions. "Dr. Martin Luther would very probably sit in my place in the defendants' dock today, if this book (*On the Jews and Their Lies*) had been taken into consideration by the prosecution."

A prominent Anglican cleric and writer, Rev. William Ralph Inge, made the same argument from outside the dock in 1944. "If you wish to find a scapegoat on whose shoulders we may lay the miseries which Germany has brought upon the world, I am more and more convinced that the worst evil genius of that country is not Hitler or Bismarck or Frederick the Great, but Martin Luther."[3]

After the war the memory of the "worst evil genius" and his seminal screed against the Jews vanished from public consciousness like the SS officers and death camp guards who escaped capture and melted into anonymity in places like Brazil and Cleveland. Some eventually were brought to justice; not so the muse of their unprecedented crimes.

It's a terrible poetic injustice that our collective ignorance about the "other" Martin Luther allows him, like a vampire bathed in moonlight, to benefit fraudulently from the reflected glory of Martin Luther King, Jr., with whom he is not worthy to share his own name. Fifteen hundred fifty-eight years after *On the Jews and Their Lies* was published, sixty-six years after Auschwitz and Dachau and Sobibor were liberated, it's past time for a new *Jeopardy!* answer:

"He was a sixteenth-century German theologian and reformer whose anti-Semitic writings were quoted by Hitler and other Nazis to justify the extermination of six million Jews in the Holocaust."

Who was Martin Luther? At last we know.

CHAPTER SEVEN

Even if Joe Public's knowledge of World War II derives mostly from old movies and dimly remembered history classes, odds are he knows about the Kamikaze pilots, approximately 2,800 Japanese airmen who spectacularly crashed their planes into U.S. ships in the Pacific on suicide missions, sinking 34 ships and killing approximately 4,900 sailors. But odds are even greater—almost a sure thing—that Mr. Public knows nothing about the 3,000 German soldiers who fired the first shots of the Holocaust and murdered over a million Jews.

In his book *Masters of Death*, historian Richard Rhodes says of these men, the *Einsatzgruppen*, "No more sinister phalanx was ever loosed on the world." *Ever?* At first blush it seems an extravagant claim, considering the multitude of sinister phalanxes over thousands of years of recorded human depravity. The rest of the book's title also feels like overreach: *The SS-Einsatzgruppen and the Invention of the Holocaust*. However, check the record and you will discover that what sounds like hyperbole turns out to be simple statement of fact.

Before Auschwitz and Sobibor and Treblinka, there were the killing fields of Ukraine. The *Einsatzgruppen* were the exterminators, bullets their chosen tool. But the shooting and disposing of scores of men, women, and children every day proved so public, labor-intensive, and horrific that the Nazis decided there had to be a better way—less draining for the killers. Perhaps . . . behind closed doors, using gas? Perverse necessity became the mother of satanic invention. After the wretchedly bloody and inefficient carnage in Ukraine, the Holocaust realized a sanitized and orderly perfection in the gas chambers of Poland and Germany.

"It is impossible to understand how the Holocaust unfolded without knowing this part of the story, because the *Einsatzgruppen* massacres preceded the invention of the death camps and significantly influenced their development," Rhodes wrote.[1]

The German army, the *Wehrmacht*, was built to fight battles, take prisoners, and conquer and occupy countries. The *Einsatzgruppen* had but one purpose: to kill Jews— though they willingly, even eagerly, killed others along the way. Absent Hitler's goal of a *Judenfrei* Europe, the forming of the *Einsatzgruppen* in the spring of 1941 makes no sense. Indeed, given his stated intentions for Operation Barbarossa, they were inevitable.

Hitler did not seek merely to conquer territory, as he had in Poland, France, Belgium, and elsewhere across Europe. He intended to eradicate the people and institutions of Judeo-Bolshevism in the Soviet Union, which he regarded as an alien ideology and spoke of almost as if it were a living virus. He once described Jews as "a racial tuberculosis of the people." In a speech to hundreds of officers three months before the invasion, Hitler called Bolshevism "the equivalent of social delinquency" and said Barbarossa would be "a war of extermination."

Historians have searched in vain for a written "Declaration of Extermination" signed by Hitler, sealing the Jews' fate. As historians have noted, that was not the Führer's management style. If Hitler's aggressive, grandiloquent oratory was opera, his management and decision-making style was jazz—teasing, improvisational, illusive. Pinning down the Führer was like trying to nail Jell-O to the wall. From the podium Hitler issued sweeping prophecies and left his lieutenants to divine his true intent and transform it into action. "This elicited all sort of initiatives, all sorts of plans," observed historian Christopher Browning. "Sometimes he said, 'No, you didn't read me right.' Sometimes he put up a red light. Sometimes he flashed a yellow light—'not ready yet'—and sometimes he shone a green light and gave approval to go ahead. You can't go to a single document or a single meeting and say, 'Here is where something was decided.'"[2]

Hitler's instinct to camouflage trickled down the chain of command. Even early in the war, before the prospect of defeat gave the Nazis cause to conceal their crimes, they were careful to cover their tracks by employing a host of euphemisms for murder such as "special tasks" and "executive measures." Jews were "rendered harmless," "got rid of," "appropriately treated," "finished off." Ample evidence of Hitler's intentions and verbal orders is found in statements of subordinates. Less than a week before the launch of Barbarossa, *Einsatzgruppen* commanders were summoned to the Berlin office of Reinhard Heydrich, chief of the Reich Security Main Office (RSHA).

One commander in the room, Dr. Walter Blume, recalled in his trial testimony Heydrich's warning that "in the imminent war with Russia, partisan warfare has to be anticipated, and that the region had a large Jewish population which must be liquidated. He added that the Jews of Eastern Europe—as the germ-cell of world Jewry—must be exterminated." At Nuremberg the *Einsatzgruppen* commanders pleaded not guilty, arguing they were following an order from Hitler (known as the *Fuhrerbefehl*) to murder the Soviet Jews. Consistent with Hitler's method, no document was ever produced with a *Fuhrerbefehl*. Otto Ohlendorf, the first to testify, claimed the order was orally conveyed to him by RSHA personnel chief Bruno Streckenbach before

Operation Barbarossa, and other commanders eagerly parroted him on the stand. Streckenbach, of course, was only the messenger from Heydrich or Himmler, who were reading the Führer's tea leaves from above. By the end of the trial, the prosecutors had proven beyond a reasonable doubt that Hitler was the impetus and inspiration for extermination of the Jews in Ukraine and the East.

The four "action groups" (*Einsatzgruppen*) that would form the leading edge of the Holocaust were recruited and trained with breathtaking haste—about a month. By comparison, basic training for a U.S. Marine is thirteen weeks minimum. Physical training was perfunctory, and not really necessary for their upcoming tasks. There was time on a firing range, and "terrain exercises" which amounted to little more than paintball without the paint. Mostly, the *Einsatz* recruits sat and listened to lectures that instilled a simple, murderous syllogism: Bolshevism was the enemy that must be eliminated. All Jews were Bolshevist. Thus, all Jews must be eliminated. This included Jewish women and children, who carried the seeds of future enemies.

The enduring conundrum of the Holocaust is the bestial/celestial duality of the German soul, capable of soaring to infinite heights and burrowing to unimaginable depths. This duality was personified by the *Einsatzgruppen* commanders—the few, the proud, the depraved—who also represented the best and brightest of German society. "In any society, people with proven track records are frequently selected to carry out important tasks," wrote historian Hilary Earl. "In the case of the *Einsatzgruppen* leaders, almost certainly they would have attained important jobs even if the Nazis had never seized power, because they were the elite of their generation."[3]

This was the image of Germans that my grandfather acquired as a young man and clung to until it was too late. Dmitri Arshansky had befriended Yiddish-speaking German soldiers during their relatively benign occupation of his hometown, Poltava, in World War I. To Dmitri, an amateur violinist who imported a German-made Bechstein piano for his budding prodigies, Zhanna and Frina, Germany represented the pinnacle of musical culture.

Waldemar Klingelhofer matched the image in Dmitri's mind of German refinement, and also embodied its cursed duality. After graduating from the Wilhelm Classical Gymnasium, young Waldemar worked in a bank to pay for voice lessons and ultimately achieved his dream of touring Germany as a professional opera singer. In another life, Klingelhofer, the artist, and Dmitri, the patron, might have come together one day in a concert hall—Dmitri with his daughters in tow, eager for them to experience firsthand the epitome of musical achievement. In this life, they were destined to come together only as ciphers on opposite sides of a war that would consume them both.

Klingelhofer's opera career was cut short by an injury to his voice. His best career option in 1935—at the suggestion

TOP: Kharkov under Nazi rule. Seventy percent of the city was destroyed during the Germans' 22-month occupation. BOTTOM: Shell-shocked Hotel Krasnaya in Kharkov. Krasnaya is Russian for red—or beautiful.

ABOVE TOP: Downtown Kharkov buildings that escaped massive damage during German bombing and shelling. ABOVE BOTTOM: Dzerzhinsky Square in Kharkov during the war—five times larger than Red Square in Moscow—renamed Freedom Square after Ukraine declared independence. OPPOSITE: Kharkov church ravaged by German attacks. Nazis targeted cultural, educational, and religious institutions no less than military installations in an attempt to eviscerate existing society in Kharkov.

TOP: Gosprom—government buildings circling Dzerzhinsky Square—were the first high-rise buildings in Ukraine constructed of ferro-concrete and survived sustained German attacks. BOTTOM: German reconnaisance photo of unnamed facility, possibly agricultural, near Kharkov.

TOP: Life goes in Nazi-occupied Kharkov. BOTTOM: Dispirited citizens in the Kharkov marketplace. An estimated 100,000 residents died of hunger during German occupation.

TOP: Portrait of Hitler in a Kharkov store window. In the first weeks of the war in western Ukraine, the Führer was hailed for liberating Ukraine from the tyranny of Stalin. BOTTOM: A German soldier directing "traffic" in central Kharkov.

TOP: Anti-Semitic Nazi propaganda in a Kharkov store window. Most Jews fled east to the Urals before the Nazis arrived. Those who stayed—some 16,000—were killed at Drobitsky Yar. BOTTOM: Boys inspect a German tank in downtown Kharkov.

Geman attacks devastated the infrastructure of Kharkov, destroying most bridges, the railway junction, power stations, telephone and telegraph connections, and fifty industrial plants.

of a friend—was to join the SD (*Sicherheitsdienst,* or Security Service). Two years later he was promoted from clerk to head of the Department of Culture in the SD, which suited his musical training and language skills (he was fluent in Russian). There was no indication that Klingelhofer yearned for a more adventurous mission than administering culture from a desk. But in May 1941, he was among the SD members summoned for duty in the *Einsatzgruppen,* and that's when the music died for Waldemar Klingelhofer. The same voice that caressed Mozart and Puccini and Wagner would soon be barking orders to shoot Jews.

The *Einsatzgruppen* training, such as it was, took place in Pretzsch, a town about fifty miles southwest of Berlin. The several thousand recruits came from various elements of the Nazi security edifice: Gestapo, SD, SS, Waffen SS, Order Police, and local police. They were organized into four *Einsatzgruppen*—A, B, C, D—ranging from 800 to 1,200 men. These were subdivided into smaller units known as *Sonderkommandos, Einsatzkommandos,* and *Teilkommandos.* The top echelon of *Einsatzgruppen* commanders was top-heavy with lawyers, economists, academics (nearly a third held doctorates), and even the odd theologian, musician, and architect. Heinz Schubert, an officer in this "elite" corps, though not a musician, was a direct descendant of the composer Franz Schubert.

The four *Einsatzgruppen* formed for Operation Barbarossa were larger versions of *Einsatzgruppen* that

accompanied the *Wehrmacht* when Germany invaded
Poland in 1939. Working with Order Police, Waffen SS, and
other forces, the *Einsatzgruppen* participated in the murder
of Polish citizens, including many Christians. A harbinger
of the *Einsatzgruppe* mission and method in the Soviet
Union is glimpsed in this eyewitness account of executions
in one Polish town: "The first victims of the campaign were
a number of Boy Scouts, from twelve to sixteen years of
age, who were set up in the marketplace against a wall and
shot. No reason was given. A devoted priest who rushed to
administer the Last Sacrament was shot too."

The career officers of the *Wehrmacht*, the German
National Army, were not pleased with aspects of the
Einsatzgruppe performance in Poland—drunken killing
sprees and gratuitous brutality violated their old-school
code—and they protested to Himmler and Heydrich.
Not a problem! To minimize friction and preempt
jurisdictional disputes in Operation Barbarossa, Hitler
drafted a provision giving the *Einsatzgruppen*—his
surrogate id—a blank check for mayhem in the Soviet
Union, not answerable to the *Wehrmacht*, the rapidly
atrophying superego separating Nazi war-making from
pure criminality.

"The *Reichsführer-SS* (Himmler) assumes on behalf
of the Führer special tasks which arise from the necessity finally to settle the conflict between two opposing
political systems," stated Hitler's addendum to Directive

21 (Barbarossa). "Within the framework of these duties the *Reichsführer-SS* acts independently and on his own responsibility." Translation: the SS was now free to move about the country without their *Wehrmacht* chaperones, murdering at will, with special attention to communists and Bolshevists—both code words for Jews.

Another key provision of the agreement allowed the killing squads to operate not only in rear areas, as it followed the army, but also on the front lines. "This concession was of great importance, for the Jews were to be caught as quickly as possible," wrote Hilberg. "They were to be given no warning and no chance to escape." In this manner, "several hundred thousand Jews could be killed like sleeping flies" in the early stages of the operation.[4]

Once German soldiers and tanks crossed the Soviet border on June 22, 1941, and began to roar east unopposed, all pretense of civilized restraint vanished in an intoxicating cloud of Teutonic id that obliterated the fine line between military and ideological warfare. The military goals of the *Wehrmacht* and the genocidal goal of the *Einsatzgruppen* merged into one vast criminal enterprise, each justifying the other.

The legal brilliance, and dramatic power, of American prosecutor Ben Ferencz's case against 24 *Einsatzgruppen* commanders at Nuremberg is that it was based entirely on the defendants' own words—thousands of field reports written by *Einsatz* commanders and sent to Berlin. In the end, Teutonic barbarism was undone by German efficiency.

"Two large-scale actions were carried out by the platoon in Krupka and Sholopaniche, 912 Jews being liquidated in the former and 822 in the latter," read one typical report. "*Einsatzkommando* 5 took care of 506 Bolsheviks and Jews in the course of 14 days," echoed another. Jews were considered "useless eaters," reflected in this field report from central Ukraine. "It was impossible to supply food to the Jews as well as the children and subsequently there was an ever-increasing danger of epidemics. To put an end to these conditions, 1,107 Jewish adults were shot by Kommando 4a, and 561 by the Ukrainian militia."

The careful litany of slaughter goes on page after page. The magnitude of the homicide is even more difficult to grasp than its depravity.

"One million corpses is a concept too bizarre and too fantastical for normal mental comprehension," Ferencz said at Nuremberg. "To the average brain one million is more a symbol than a quantitative measure. However, if one reads through the reports of the *Einsatzgruppen* and observes the small numbers getting larger, climbing into ten thousand, tens of thousands, a hundred thousand and beyond, then one can at least believe that this actually happened—the cold-blooded, premeditated killing of one million human beings."

Our resident opera-star turned SS Major Waldemar Klingelhofer was no Otto Ohlendorf, the suave, handsome prince of the Nazi red tide who blithely admitted at Nuremberg to supervising the murder of 90,000 Jews as commander of *Einsatzgruppen* D. Though a minor spear carrier to Ohlendorf's malignant Wotan, Klingelhofer did his part as leader of a *Vorkommando* to drive up the death count. The trial established that he ordered and supervised the murder of thousands, and in his pre-trial affidavit Klingelhofer admitted shooting 30 Jews, including three women to whom he extended a unique brand of Nazi mercy. "He had them blindfolded for the execution and then ordered that they be given a separate grave," the prosecution at Nuremberg stated.

My mother never encountered Waldemar Klingelhofer in her four-year masquerade as a non-Jewish piano prodigy, performing for unwitting German soldiers and officers. He was posted near Moscow, and she was in Ukraine and later Germany. But everywhere there were Klingelhofer *doppelgangers*, exemplars of the bestial/celestial dichotomy. During their time in German-occupied Kremenchug in east-central Ukraine, my mother and her sister often were summoned to dine with Gestapo and *Wehrmacht* officers, and afterward ordered to perform. They sat on a piano bench side by side and played Chopin, Schubert, Beethoven, Brahms. The men in uniform were an appreciative audience.

"They were very serious people, a wonderful audience," my mother recalled. "They kept saying, 'Noch einmal!'— once more!—over and over."

The next day the music lovers would return to their work of murdering Jews.

Noch einmal—over and over.

CHAPTER EIGHT

H itler took Poland first, then France and the remainder of Western Europe, but all that was mere prelude to the war on Russia. This was the war he had long prophesied and for which he had been arming Germany—in violation of the Versailles Treaty—and diabolically indoctrinating the German people since he seized dictatorial powers in 1933.

Western Europe and Britain were military objectives. Russia was Hitler's obsession, his great white whale. Only by conquering Russia—he never used the sterile term "Soviet Union"—could Hitler satisfy his twin obsessions of gaining *Lebensraum*—living space—for a greater German empire, and eradicating Judeo-Bolshevism, which he considered a disease in the guise of ideology. His writings and speeches, from *Mein Kampf* on, provide a road map of his megalomania leading ineluctably East.

"We stop the endless German movement to the south and west, and turn our gaze towards the land in the east," Hitler stated in *Mein Kampf,* dictated from his jail cell in 1924 and published in two volumes the following two years. "If we speak of soil in Europe today, we can primarily have in mind only Russia and her vassal border states."

Lebensraum in the east was not just Germany's destiny, Hitler wrote, it was her cosmic duty. His vision was painted in the primary colors of apocalypse and Armageddon, with himself and Germany on the side of the angels.

"We must regard Russian Bolshevism as Jewry's attempt to achieve world rule in the twentieth century. Should the Jew triumph over nations of this world by means of his Marxist creed, his crown will be mankind's dance of death; and this planet will move through space devoid of man, as it did millions of years ago. Thus, I believe myself to be acting in the sense of the Almighty creator: by defending myself against the Jew, I fight for the Lord's work."

In a 1931 interview with a German newspaper editor made public after the war, Hitler said, "The menace to western civilization was never so great. Even before we assume power we must make clear . . . that sooner or later we shall be forced to conduct a crusade against Bolshevism." In 1938, nine months before the *Kristallnacht* terrorizing of German Jews, Hitler warned, "More than ever, we regard Bolshevism as the incarnation of the human destructive impulse."

The symphony of lies, canards, false grievances, and atavistic anti-Semitism which Hitler had been orchestrating and rehearsing for half a dozen years reached a crescendo near the end of a speech to the Reichstag in January 1939.

"In my life I have often been a prophet, and most of the time I have been laughed at. During the period of my struggle for power, it was the Jewish people that received with laughter my prophecies that some day I would take over leadership of the state, and that among other things I would solve the Jewish problem. The laughter of Jews that resounded then is now choking in their throats. Today I want to be a prophet once more: If international-finance Jewry inside and outside of Europe should succeed once more in plunging nations into another world war, the consequence will not be the Bolshevization of the Earth and victory of Jewry, but the annihilation of the Jewish race in Europe."

These were no longer just the febrile, grandiloquent scribblings of an imprisoned zealot.

"Hitler was not only a propagandist but also a head of state," wrote Hilberg. "He had power not only to speak but also to act. Hitler was a man who had a tremendous urge—one could almost say a compulsion—to carry out his threats. He 'prophesied.' With words he committed himself to action."[1]

On June 22, 1941, Hitler acted, sending three million men and more than three thousand tanks across the Soviet border. The invasion was named Operation Barbarossa in tribute to a German king who waged war on the Slavs in the twelfth century. Months before the invasion, Hitler had addressed a gathering of his generals about the coming conflict in terms that left many of them appalled, even mutinous.

"The war against Russia will be such that it cannot be conducted in a knightly fashion," the Führer said. "This struggle is one of ideologies and racial differences and will have to be conducted with unprecedented, merciless, and unrelenting harshness. I know that the necessity for such means of waging war is beyond the comprehension of you generals . . . but I insist absolutely that my orders be executed without contradiction."

Hitler ordered that Soviet commissars and officials— agents of the Bolshevist disease—were to be considered criminals, not prisoners of war, and were to be shot upon capture as if they were rabid dogs. Such disregard for traditional laws of war violated the soldierly rectitude of the generals, who sent word to the High Command that they could never carry out such orders.

Ultimately, of course, there was no mutiny. But like Captain Ahab dragged to the bottom of the sea by the wounded whale, Hitler would be destroyed in the end by his obsession with Judeo-Bolshevism—his dream of a Thousand-Year Reich lost in a sea of blood in Ukraine where he could not stop killing, even in retreat after he had lost.

How to convey—to make real—the scale and horror of Nazi destruction in Ukraine to readers in a country whose wars have been fought on distant shores in other people's back yards? Are there any historical analogues that literally hit home and tap our common ground as Americans? There are two—the Civil War and the 9/11 terrorist attack—but even they fall short of this existential challenge.

Before laying siege to Atlanta in 1864, Gen. William Tecumseh Sherman, considered a practitioner of "total war," famously warned city leaders that "war is hell" and ordered civilians to leave the city. He then proceeded to burn down much of Atlanta in a conflagration immortalized in *Gone with the Wind,* not targeting private homes or civilians, but not sparing them either. Sherman's army then marched to the sea, ravaging and plundering the land, and though civilians died, once again they were—as we would say today—collateral damage.

Terrible as it was, if this was "hell" we need a different word—a fresh hell—for what Hitler's armies and mobile killing units did to Ukraine. Take civilian casualties. Civilians were not collateral damage, but the direct target and focus of this invasion. Historian Alexander Kruglov says that in the second half of 1941 alone, after the Nazi invasion of the Soviet Union, the Germans and their allies killed more than 500,000 Ukrainian Jews, including at least 16,000 in Kharkov. This is more than the total U.S. dead (405,000) for the entire war. In contemporary terms, it's the equivalent of a 9/11 inferno every day for six months. And the Nazi killing machine was just warming up.

At the time of the Nazi invasion in 1941, some 2.7 million Jews lived in the area that is now Ukraine. By 1945, about 60 percent—1.6 million—had perished. Roughly 900,000 Jews fled east to the Ural Mountains and Siberia ahead of the Germans, heeding rumors of Nazi atrocities at Babi Yar and points in western Ukraine where residents had little or no warning of the Nazi onslaught, and where in places there was near total extermination of Jews. Lviv had a pre-war Jewish population of 260,000 and lost an estimated 215,000, nearly 83 percent. In Ternopil, slightly to the east, an estimated 132,000 Jews were murdered—a staggering 97 percent of the population. Elsewhere, 100,000 survived the occupation in hiding or in Nazi camps and ghettos. Though Jewish life in Ukraine survived, shtetls did not. Thousands of the Jewish villages and agricultural settlements, a unique phenomenon for generations in eastern Europe, were swept away forever in the Nazi storm. They survive only in memory and in productions like the musical *Fiddler on the Roof,* set in a fictional Russian shtetl.

Because it is faceless, the physical destruction wreaked by German forces is perhaps even more difficult to fathom than the human loss. At the Nuremberg trials, chief Soviet prosecutor Roman Rudenko presented a statistical summary of the destruction in all Soviet territories, and it is difficult to conjure images which do justice to his words and numbers. As I write this in March 2011, the TV screen is filled with images of total devastation from the earthquake and tsunami in Japan. Imagine across Russia the wreckage of a thousand tsunamis.

"The German fascist invaders completely or partially destroyed or burned 1,710 cities and more than 70,000 villages and hamlets," Rudenko told the Nuremburg court. "They burned or destroyed over six million buildings and rendered some twenty-five million persons homeless.

"The Germano-fascist invaders destroyed 31,850 industrial establishments employing some four million workers; they destroyed or removed from the country 239,000 electric motors and 175,000 metal cutting machines. The Germans destroyed 65,000 kilometers of railway tracks; 4,100 railway stations, 36,000 post and telegraph offices, telephone exchanges, and other installations for communications.

"The Germans destroyed or devastated 40,000 hospitals and other medical institutions, 84,000 schools, technical colleges, universities, institutes for scientific research, and 43,000 public libraries. The Hitlerites destroyed and looted 98,000 collective farms, 1,876 state farms, and 2,890 machine and tractor stations. They slaughtered, seized, or drove into Germany 7 million horses, 17 million head of horned cattle, 20 million pigs, 27 million sheep and goats, and 110 million head of poultry."

In addition to everything in Rudenko's litany, there was the flooding of mines and the poisoning of wells by the Nazis. The special commission of dignitaries and citizens, which gathered the evidence, estimated total damage to the Soviet economy, including loss of workers shipped to slave labor camps in Germany, to be 679 billion rubles. As Arad notes, at the time the ruble was worth more than the dollar.

Sherman's conduct of war seems genteel by comparison. Here are excerpts from his Special Field Orders, No. 120, issued before his notorious March to the Sea, from Atlanta to Savannah.

"Soldiers must not enter the dwellings of inhabitants, or commit any trespass, but during a halt or a camp they may be permitted to gather turnips, potatoes, and other vegetables, and to drive stock to their camp. To army commanders alone is entrusted the power to destroy mills, houses, cotton gins, etc., for them this general principle is laid down: In districts and neighborhoods where the army is unmolested, no destruction of such property should be permitted. In all foraging, of whatever kind, the parties engaged will refrain from abusive or threatening language, and may, where the officer in command thinks proper, give written certificates of the facts, but no receipts, and they will endeavor to leave with each family a reasonable portion for their maintenance."

Reading this, I thought of the night German soldiers stormed into my mother's home in Kharkov in 1941, screaming "dirty Jews!", slamming her mother Sara against the wall and holding a gun to her head, demanding gold from her father, which he did not have. The enraged looters tried to take the family's Bechstein piano but could not maneuver it out the door. They settled for Dmitri Arshansky's beloved violin. The Germans did not provide a "certificate of fact" for taking what my mother called "the fifth member of our family."

To be sure, the Union army would never be mistaken for the Peace Corps. Soldiers often ignored Sherman's stated restrictions on foraging, wrote historian Anne Bailey for *The New Georgia Encyclopedia*. "His men had destroyed all sources of food . . . and left behind a hungry and demoralized people. Although he did not level any towns, he did destroy buildings in places where there was resistance." Bailey notes that "physical attacks on white civilians were few."

In sum, this was war waged by a man who at least *had* a moral compass and occasionally checked it. In contrast, Himmler, chief implementer and rationalizer of Hitler's genocidal vision in the East, displayed an aggressive contempt for anything resembling conventional morality or rules of war. In his topsy-turvy universe, the greatest virtue was being "hard" enough to embrace evil when others blinked. Many Germans speak favorably of eliminating the Jews, he said, but they do not have the strength to act on their beliefs.

"Of all those who talk this way, not one has seen it happen, not one has been through it," Himmler told an assembly of *Gruppenfuhrers* (SS leaders) in 1943. "Most of you know what it means when a hundred corpses lie side by side, when five hundred lie there or when a thousand lie there. To have gone through this and to have remained decent—that has made us hard. This is a glorious page in our history."

The record is thick with stories of men who seemed eager to share that glory and earn Himmler's badge of honor by remaining "hard" and not succumbing to "weakness." Consider the testimony of a captured German soldier, a private first class, in *The Black Book*, considered the Torah of Nazi atrocities in the Soviet Union. The machinegunning of three hundred men, women, and children into open graves is the least horrific part of his story of the carnage in one village.

"Little children were picked up by their feet and their heads smashed against a rock. One young girl had hidden in a barn behind a beam. When the SS men found her, one of them climbed up into the loft while the others formed a circle below with fixed bayonets. The girl was stabbed with a bayonet until she had no choice but to jump down. She was then literally run through with bayonets. When I asked the SS man in charge why such horrible things were being done, he said, 'We kicked the Jews out of Germany, and now we have to do away with them here too.' In the end all the livestock from the village was herded together and driven off, and the village was burned to the last house."[2]

One fundamental way in which Sherman's mission differed from Hitler's is that he was making war to free slaves—Hitler wanted to make millions of *new* slaves. Himmler urged his *Gruppenfuhrers* to remember that it was their sacred, patriotic duty as Germans to subjugate these mongrel populations.

"Whether other races live well or die of hunger is only of interest to me insofar as we need them as slaves for our culture. Whether ten thousand Russian women collapse from exhaustion in building a tank ditch is of interest to me only insofar as the tank ditches are finished for Germany. We Germans, the only ones in the world with a decent attitude toward animals, will also adopt a decent attitude with regards to these human animals, but it is a sin against our own blood to worry about them and give them ideals.

"When somebody comes to me and says, 'I can't build tank ditches with children or women—that's inhumane, they'll die doing it,' then I must say: 'You are a murderer of your own blood, because if the tank ditches aren't built, then German soldiers will die, and they are the sons of German mothers. That is our blood.' Everything else is froth, a fraud against our own people, and an obstacle to earlier victory in the war."

Himmler's rhetoric did not fall on deaf ears. It was echoed in marching orders issued by commanders of the hydra-head Nazi killing machine from the *Einsatzgruppen* mobile murder squads and regular troops of the *Wehrmacht* to the *Feldgendarmerie* (military police), *Geheime Feldpolizei* (Secret Field Police), and *Ordnungspolizei* (Order Police). Taking his cue from a document titled "Guidelines for the Behavior of Troops in Russia," General Erich Hoepner issued this directive to the troops of Armored Group 4 in May 1941, a month before Operation Barbarossa.

"The war against Russia is the old fight of the Germans against the Slavs—the defense of European culture against the Muscovite-Asiatic flood, the repulsion of Jewish Bolshevism. The goal of this fight must be the destruction of contemporary Russia and therefore must be conducted with enormous violence. Every combat action, in its conception and conduct, must be governed by an iron will to pitiless and complete annihilation of the enemy."

Despite his best and most strenuous efforts, Himmler was not able to erase the conscience of all German soldiers and officers, who were men first and Nazis second. Some retained enough basic decency to have moral qualms about the unspeakable things they witnessed and were ordered to do.

In August 1941 in the village of Byelaya Tserkov, about fifty miles from Kiev, the Germans and their local henchmen shot several hundred Jewish men and women at a firing range near the village. Before the shootings, children of the condemned Jews were locked in a building nearby without food or water or toilets. A German soldier who heard loud crying and whimpering alerted two military chaplains who entered the building and filed a report.

"We entered the house and found in two rooms some ninety children, from a few months to five, six, or seven years old. There was no kind of supervision. The rooms were in a filthy state. Children lay or sat on the floor, which was covered in their feces. There were flies on the legs and abdomens of most of the children, some of whom were only half dressed. Some of the bigger children were scratching the mortar from the wall and eating it. The stench was terrible. The visiting soldiers were shaken, as we were, by these unbelievable conditions and expressed their outrage over them. One of them said that he himself had children at home."[3]

Afterward, the chaplains learned that other children had been taken from the building earlier and shot, and that those who remained soon would share the same fate. The chaplains' report on conditions in the building and their plea for mercy for the children went to the Catholic divisional chaplain, who sent it up the line to Sixth Army Field Marshal von Reichenau, who essentially washed his hands of the matter. "It would have been far better if the report had not been written at all," he wrote.

Col. Paul Blobel, the *Einsatzgruppen* commander who later supervised the massacre at Babi Yar, ordered *SS-Obersturmfuhrer* August Hafner to carry out the death sentence which von Reichenau had refused to lift. Hafner objected, noting that many of his men had small children. It was decided that Ukrainian militia would do the job. The children were taken to the edge of the village near some woods.

"They were lined up along the top of the grave and shot so that they fell into it. The Ukrainians did not aim at any particular part of the body. Many children were hit four or five times before they died. The wailing was indescribable. I shall never forget the scene throughout my life. I particularly remember a small fair-haired girl who took me by the hand. She, too, was shot later."[4]

A key weapon in the first weeks of the Nazi push into Ukraine was the igniting of pogroms by Ukrainians against Jews in their midst, especially in western Ukraine areas annexed by the Soviets in 1939, where there were centuries-old traditions of pogroms sparked by hardly anything at all. Some Ukrainians were acting on long-festering anti-Semitism that had roots as old as Luther in Germany; others had swallowed propaganda and saw Jews as agents of Bolshevism and the hated Stalin, who had inflicted mass starvation on Ukraine in the 1930s as punishment for resistance to his new system of collective farming. Sometimes the Germans covertly organized killing parties; often they simply stepped aside and allowed human nature, and historical precedence, to take its grisly course.

For sheer savagery, if not scale, nothing exceeded the scene at the garage complex of an agricultural center in Kovno, a Lithuanian border village in the direct path of the Nazi invasion. A German officer described the events, witnessed by a large crowd of men, women, and children from the village.

"A blond man of medium height, age about twenty-five, stood leaning on a wooden club, resting. The club was as thick as his arm and came up to his chest. At his feet lay about fifteen or twenty dead or dying people. Water flowed continuously from a hose washing blood away into the drainage gully. Just a few steps behind this man some twenty men, guarded by armed civilians, stood waiting their execution. In response to a cursory wave the next man stepped forward silently and was beaten to death with the wooden club, each blow accompanied by enthusiastic shouts from the audience."[5]

Earlier I wrote that Sherman "famously" warned Atlanta leaders that "war is hell." Famously—but not actually. Sherman "probably never said these words, and if he did, he certainly didn't while in Atlanta," Marc Wortman wrote in *The Bonfire: The Siege and Burning of Atlanta*. The clarion aphorism has become part of the myth that Sherman alone razed Atlanta, though Confederate defenders also lit a "monumental bonfire," he wrote.

What Sherman actually said in a letter to the mayor and city council denying their plea to lift his expulsion order for civilians was this: "You cannot qualify war in harsher terms than I will. War is cruelty, and you cannot refine it." Yet he did. In the same letter, he offered his "services" to make the exodus of civilians out of harm's way "as easy and comfortable as possible." And he concluded, "My dear sirs, when peace does come, you may call on me for anything. Then I will share with you the last cracker, and watch with you to shield your homes and families against danger from every quarter."

In September 1943, Himmler ordered the retreating German army "to leave behind in Ukraine not a single person, no cattle, not a ton of grain, not a railroad track. The enemy must find a country totally burned and destroyed."

Not a single cracker.

By "refine," Sherman meant to make more gentle and civilized, or at least less barbaric and violent. But refine can have an alternate meaning: to polish and perfect— removing all flaws and impurities. Even the faintest gesture of mercy or restraint—a cracker for the vanquished—would be regarded by Himmler as a soft, corrupting flaw in the waging of total war.

One Confederate soldier called Sherman's assault on Atlanta "a grand holocaust of death." Across the ocean, stirring in the belly of Germany, was a far grander holocaust—a hard, diamond-like refinement of war free of the impurities of mercy and conscience that stop a man from smashing the head of a child against a rock or running it through with a bayonet.

> *And what rough beast, its hour come round at last,*
> *Slouches towards Bethlehem to be born?*

The demon impulse had been gestating for centuries in Germany since the time of Luther. Now the day was drawing near when the belly would disgorge its little prince upon the "blood-dimmed tide" of Yeats's dystopian vision and reawaken the same devil within other lands.

CHAPTER NINE

T he German military was guilty of more than a million counts of first-degree murder in Ukraine. But that's a rather one-dimensional picture. A complete, 360-degree view of the havoc wreaked by Hitler's minions must also include vandalism and armed robbery on an epic scale. Ukraine was not a mere war zone—it was the largest and most varied crime scene in history, bearing the fingerprints of an army of Charles Mansons, Sopranos, and Alex DeLarge and his marauding, nihilistic mates in *A Clockwork Orange*.

Hitler aimed not just to kill the Jews and enslave the rest of Ukraine's population, he intended to eradicate their history and culture—to scrape the earth clear of Slavic fungus for the transplanting and flowering of German civilization. Eliminating the people but leaving remnants of their culture would be like chopping the tops off weeds and leaving the roots.

GREG DAWSON

At Nuremberg, the assistant prosecutor for the Soviets told the court: "The Hitlerite conspirators considered culture of the mind and of humanity an obstacle to the fulfillment of their monstrous designs. In working out their insane plans for world domination, they prepared a campaign against world culture. They dreamed of turning Europe back to the days of her domination by the Huns and Teutons. Destruction of the national culture was a fundamental part of the plan for world domination established by Hitler's conspirators. It is difficult to determine whether destruction or plunder was the more prevalent factor in these plans. But there is no disputing that both plunder and destruction were aimed at one goal—extermination—and this extermination was carried out everywhere, in all territories occupied by the Germans, on an enormous scale."

In Hitler's and Himmler's vision of a colonized East, the conquered Slavic natives—whom they regarded as subhuman—would become a permanent, semi-literate servant class. These modern-day serfs would be allowed only enough education to read their names and sign documents. Over time, the memory of their once-great cultures would wither and finally die. In this way the subject Ukrainians would be like the violently deracinated Africans brought to America to become slaves, but without ever leaving their back yards. In the summer of 1942, the Nazis were well on the way to implementing this pillar of their mission in the *Reichskommissariat Ukraine*—six administrative districts covering most of Ukraine—second in urgency only to eradicating the Jews.

"We are like slaves," wrote a Ukrainian woman in her diary in July 1942. "Often the book *Uncle Tom's Cabin* comes to mind. Once we shed tears over those Negroes— now we ourselves are experiencing the same thing."

This came as a bitter disappointment to the many Ukrainians, especially in the west, who had greeted the Germans as liberators and hoped that life in the *Reichskommissariat Ukraine* would be better than it had been under the Soviet thumb. They were quickly disabused of their fantasy. Peasants were shocked when the Nazis ordered them back to the hated collective farms they had abandoned in celebration of the invasion. The Germans engineered a famine in Kiev as part of their goal to cripple Ukrainian industry and create an exodus of city dwellers to rural areas. There were massive forced deportations to Germany. Between starvation, deportation, and shootings by Nazi authorities who ran the city like a concentration camp, the official population of Kiev shrank by 57,000 people from spring 1942 to the summer of 1943.

"Almost all Jews and Roma were killed," historian Karel Berkhoff wrote about life in the *Reichskommissariat Ukraine*. "For the others, there were seemingly ceaseless daily humiliations, most notably public beatings, and a permanent sense of danger." Nazi Ukraine was actually worse than a slave society, she noted. "Slaves, after all, were supposed to be used as servants—not to be disabled, let alone killed."[1] The captive Ukrainians were even more dehumanized than African slaves in the Confederacy, whose owners at least understood the importance of maintaining their valuable "property."

In December 1943, as the Nazis were retreating and the ebb tide was revealing the full, nearly unfathomable extent of their crimes, the Soviet Academy of Scientists sent a cable—really an S.O.S.—to the Faraday Society, fellow scientists in Britain. The cable described the slaughter of citizens—"beyond all effort of the imagination"—and also enumerated the systematic destruction of cultural and scientific institutions. What follows is just a small swatch from the vast tapestry of Nazi depredations in the Soviet Union as described in the cable:

"When they retreated from Smolensk, the Germans burned down the teaching, nutritional, and agricultural institutes, railway technical institutes, and the institute of telegraph and telephone communications. They blew up buildings devoted to museums, art, and history, and ruined almost all the churches—fine, old monuments of Russian architecture. In the town of Staline the Germans wrecked the medical institute and burned down all the buildings of the industrial institute where 15,000 students studied. They looted all the Kiev museums, libraries, archives, laboratories, and research institutions. Professor Alexander Brodsky, member of the Ukrainian Academy of Sciences, bears witness that the Germans blew up and burned the mining institute, with its huge library, at the University Institute of Applied Chemistry, and they looted and destroyed a number of other research institutes at Dnepropetrovsk. At Poltava, Zaporozhye, Chernigov, and other towns that have been liberated from the Germans, we found colleges, libraries, and schools destroyed."

The British scientists responded to the plea of their beleaguered brothers with evident but ultimately impotent horror. "The Faraday Society will do its utmost to bring this to the notice of all scientists and intellectuals of the united (allied) nations, to the end that civilization shall be protected and justice meted out to the barbarians."

The apocalyptic scale of Nazi ruination beggars the imagination; it mocks the capacity of words to make it real. Only art can express the existential truth of such carnage, as Picasso did in *Guernica*. If the bombing of one Spanish village could inspire abstract horror, what would Picasso have made from the rubble of a thousand villages, the ruins of a hundred libraries, the bones of a million and a half Jews?

The Nazi plundering of Mother Russia had a deeply primordial quality, like the Romans' burning of the Great Library at Alexandria and the salting of the fields at Carthage. But unlike those ancient stories, which exist in a netherworld between fact and myth, the looting of Russia was meticulously documented—by the looters.

The Nazis formed a unit for the express purpose of conducting the plunder. Special Staff Rosenberg—under the direction of Alfred Rosenberg, Minister for Eastern Territories—was responsible for confiscating the cultural and artistic assets owned by the Soviet government (i.e., art in state museums), as well as privately held Jewish assets. Special Staff Rosenberg claimed that it surveyed and looted the contents of 2,265 museums, libraries, churches, synagogues, and university archives in the occupied Soviet territories.

"The material collected underwent preliminary sorting with the help of local employees. It was then decided which material would be transferred to Germany and which would remain or be sent to paper factories for recycling," Yitzhak Arad writes. Based on the reports of Dr. Johann Pohl, an expert on Judaism who supervised the sorting of stolen books, Arad estimates that "hundreds of thousands" of volumes were sent to Germany. "A similar, or even larger, number of books were sent to paper mills for recycling."[2]

So it was that Jews and their books suffered much the same fate. Could it be they were recycled together in Himmler's private collection of books with covers made of Jewish skin? Not likely, but such macabre, seemingly fantastic extrapolation enters the realm of possibility, given credible accounts by visitors to Himmler's home. The Nazis were always one unthinkable idea ahead of the crowd. And the meticulousness with which such deeds were carried out never ceases to amaze.

The Nazis engaged in two sorts of looting—micro and macro. Individual German soldiers indulged in the spontaneous, all-you-can-carry micro-looting practiced by invading armies throughout time, bursting into homes and taking whatever they could find. The organized macro-looting by Nazi authorities was more like the methodical harvesting of human organs and siphoning of Earth's water supply by aliens in a sci-fi horror movie. In 1938, Orson Welles simulated Armageddon on the radio with *The War of the Worlds*. Three years later in Russia, something close to it was happening for real.

Special Staff Rosenberg had three central offices—in Riga, Minsk, and Kiev—working in tandem with German Army groups North, Center, and South. All had branches in the main cities of the occupied territories, staffed by German academics and locals. After the winnowing process at these locations, the chosen items were shipped to Germany for further classification before transfer to the central library in Berlin or the Institute for the Research of the Jewish Question in Frankfurt. Some of the material was used to mount exhibitions "proving" the link between Jews and Bolshevism.

It took Soviet prosecutors at Nuremberg in 1946 many hours to detail the Nazi search-and-destroy-and-plunder operation. Most of the evidence they presented was gathered by the Extraordinary State Commission for the Investigation of Atrocities Committed on Soviet Territory by the German-Fascist Invaders and their Accomplices. Much like the Warren Commission which studied the assassination of President Kennedy, the Extraordinary Commission was made up of eminences from academia, politics, law, and the military. The ten-member Commission included an agronomist, the father of Russian neurosurgery, and one of the first female pilots in the Soviet air force.

The Commission, which was formed in November 1942, engaged a small army—some 32,000 people—for the task of gathering evidence, not surprising considering the vastness of the country and the scope of the destruction. The result was a staggering volume of evidence: 54,000 affidavits and 250,000 depositions about killing and torture, and four million affidavits relating to material damage. According to the Commission, in Soviet territories the Nazis destroyed, severely damaged, and/or plundered:

- 1,710 cities and more than 70,000 villages and hamlets
- 87,000 industrial buildings belonging to cooperatives, trade unions, and other social organizations
- 427 museums
- 1,670 Greek Orthodox churches, 532 synagogues, 237 Roman Catholic churches,

69 chapels, and 254 other buildings for religious worship
- 44,000 theaters and clubs
- 46 pioneer camps and children's convalescent institutions
- 605 scientific research institutes
- 334 colleges and 82,000 elementary and secondary schools
- 6,000 hospitals, 33,000 clinics, dispensaries and out-patient departments, 976 sanatoriums, and 656 rest homes.

The mind's eye glazes over at the magnitude of such cataclysmic mayhem. It is easier and more instructive to focus on an abbreviated summary of the horror visited on just one place, Kiev:

"Before the German invasion, Kiev possessed 150 secondary and elementary schools. Of this number, 77 were used by the Germans as military barracks. Nine served as warehouses and workshops, and eight were turned into stables. During their retreat from Kiev, the German barbarians destroyed 140 schools. They burned and blew up one of the most ancient centers of Ukrainian culture, the T.G. Shevchenko State University.

"They burned down the building of the Red Army Dramatic Theater, the Theatrical Institute, and the Academy of Music where the instruments were burned together with the library. They blew up the beautiful circus building; burned down the M. Gorki Theater for Juvenile Audiences, and destroyed the Jewish Theater.

"They burned the archives of Kiev's Psychiatric Hospital, priceless from a scientific point of view, and destroyed the magnificent hospital library of 20,000 volumes. The Uspenski Cathedral, built in 1075–89 by the order of Grand Duke Svjatoslav, with murals painted in 1897 by the famous painter V.V. Vereshchiagin, was blown up by the Germans on Nov. 3, 1941."

The Nazis had acquired a taste for stolen art in 1940 after conquering France and taking control of the world's finest collections. Many works ended up in the private collection of Luftwaffe chief Hermann Göring; others were reserved for a *Fuhrermuseum*, a grandiose complex of galleries and museums which the failed art student turned mass murderer hoped to build in Linz, Austria, his home city. Hitler put Rosenberg in charge of looting, with the active cooperation of Göring and General Keitel. Working in tandem with Rosenberg's units were three "Ribbentrop Battalions," under the aegis of Foreign Minister Ribbentrop, which followed the German army into eastern territories. At the peak of plundering, forty to fifty freight cars of loot a month were being sent back to Germany, wrote historian Peter Petropoulous.

In testimony at Nuremberg, *Obersturmfuhrer* Norman Paul Forster described the activities of the Ribbentrop Battalion to which he was attached in Ukraine.

"We reaped a rich harvest in the library of the Ukrainian Academy of Science, the rarest manuscripts of Persian, Abyssinian, and Chinese literature, first edition books printed by the first Russian printer, Ivan Fyodorov, and rare editions of works of Shevchenko, Mickiewicz, and Ivan Franko. From the central Shevchenko museum, portraits by Repin, canvases by Vereschagin, Fedetoff, and Goe, sculptures by Antokolsky and other masterpieces of Russian and Ukrainian painters and sculptors were dispatched to Berlin.

"In Kharkov several thousand valuable books in deluxe editions were seized from the Korolenko library and sent to Berlin. The remaining books were destroyed. From the Kharkov picture gallery several hundred pictures were secured, including fourteen by Aivasovsky, works by Repin and many paintings by Polienov, Schischkin, and others. Antique sculptures and the entire scientific archive of the museum were also taken away. Embroideries, carpets, Gobelin tapestries, and other exhibits were appropriated by the German soldiers."

Apparently, the Nazis found the artistry of the "subhuman" Slavs much to their liking. The Germans' fastidiousness in "preserving" (i.e., stealing) works of art belied the barbarism always lurking just beneath the surface, frequently erupting in orgies of desecration it would be unfair to call animalistic—unfair to animals, whose bestiality is unconscious, and who are not capable of sadism and do not possess the urge to humiliate and defile. The "Hitler-ites" turned museum spaces into chicken coops, stables, and latrines, the Extraordinary Commission reported. They used portraits for target practice. One museum was used as a garage for motorcycles, heated by fires fueled by manuscripts, books, and other museum exhibits. They used rare books as paving stones in the mud to ease passage of German military vehicles. The invaders kept dogs and horses in churches. One church was used as a slaughter-house for cattle.

These Germans, representatives of the culture of Beethoven and Brahms, Goethe and Mann, sought out and trashed the homes of Chekhov and Tolstoy, Rimsky-Korsakov and Tchaikovsky. My mother has always told me that no writer expresses the Russian soul more truly and sublimely than Pushkin. The Nazis seemed to sense that and saved a special fury for the destruction of the poet's estate, Mikhailovskoye.

"Mikhailovskoye was very dear to the Russian people," the Extraordinary Commission said. "Here Pushkin fin-ished the third, fourth, fifth, and sixth chapters of *Eugen Onegin*. Here, too, he finished his poem *Gypsies*, and wrote the drama *Boris Godunov*, plus a large number of epic and lyrical poems. In July 1941, the Hitlerites forced their way into the Pushkin reservation. For three years they made themselves at home and ruined everything. Prior to their retreat from Mikhailovskoye, the Germans completed the destruction and desecration of the Pushkin estate. The German vandals put three bullets in the large portrait of Pushkin hanging in an archway at the entrance to Mikhailovskoye, then they destroyed the archway. The sacrileges perpetrated by the Germans against the national sanctuaries of the Russian people are best demonstrated by the desecration of Pushkin's tomb. It was found completely covered with refuse. Both stairways leading down to the grave were destroyed. The platform surrounding the grave was covered with refuse, rubble, wooden fragments of ikons, and pieces of sheet metal."

It's as if an invading enemy had systematically destroyed Robert Frost's home in Vermont and Carl Sandburg's in Illinois, burned the contents of the New York City Library, looted the Metropolitan Museum of Art, smashed the Liberty Bell in Philadelphia, and trashed the Smithsonian in Washington, D.C. Just for starters.

"Even though it be possible, by a tremendous effort, to rebuild the cities and villages destroyed by the Hitlerites, even though it be possible to restore the factories and plants blown up or burned down by them, mankind has lost for all time the irreplaceable art treasures which the Hitlerites so ruthlessly destroyed, as it has lost forever the millions of human beings sent to their death in Auschwitz, Treblinka, Babi Yar or Kerch," said the Extraordinary Commission.

"The modern Huns have surpassed, in cruelty and vandalism, the darkest pages of history. While arrogantly

challenging the future of mankind, they trampled under-
foot the finest heritage of mankind's past. Themselves
without faith or ideals, they sacrilegiously destroyed both
the churches and the relics of the saints. But in this unpar-
alleled struggle between civilization and barbarism, culture
and civilization prevailed."

Nearly seventy years after that victory, the Nazi barbarism in Ukraine and across Mother Russia still awaits a
Picasso and its own *Guernica*.

CHAPTER TEN

U nlike Hitler and Göring, who coveted looted paintings from the East for their own collections, SS Chief Heinrich Himmler was not an aficionado of fine art. According to one visitor to his home, Himmler's taste ran to books bound in human skin and furniture made of the bones of his victims. But in his own mind at least, Himmler was not without compassion for his fellow man, including the Jews he worked so hard to eliminate from the human gene pool.

The "better angels" of Himmler's nature spread their wings in August 1941 on a visit to Minsk, less than two months after the *Einsatzgruppen* had begun the mass murder of Jews as *coup de grâce* of the Nazi invasion of the Soviet Union. Eager to know how the mission was going, Himmler told the local *Einsatzgruppen* commander that he would like to witness an execution. The next day he was taken to a forest outside the city where two pits had been dug. More than a hundred prisoners, including two women, had been chosen to face a twelve-man firing squad for Himmler's viewing pleasure.

As the gunmen took aim at one group of victims, Himmler stepped in and walked up to a young man with light hair and eyes.

"Are you a Jew?" Himmler asked.

"Yes."

"Are both your parents Jews?"

"Yes."

"Do you have any ancestors who were not Jews?"

"No."

"Then even I can't help you," Himmler said, his compassion thwarted.

The Reichsführer's great empathy for the victims did not end there. When the shooting began, his face turned white and he looked down. And when the gunmen shot wildly and managed only to wound two female targets, Himmler was horrified, recalled an SS officer at the scene. "Himmler jumped up and screamed at the squad commander: 'Don't torture these women! Fire! Hurry up and kill them!'"

Afterward, the SS officer suggested to the rattled Himmler that he rethink the idea of murdering all the Jews in this fashion.

"*Reichsfuhrer*, that was only a hundred."

"What do you mean by that?"

"Look at the men, how deeply shaken they are! Such men are finished for the rest of their lives. What kind of followers are we creating? Either neurotics or savages!"

Apparently conscience-stricken, Himmler ordered that a "more humane" method of exterminating the Jews be found, one that did not take such a grievous emotional toll on the shooters. The immediate answer was gas—not the state-of-the-art gas chambers of Auschwitz, yet to be built—rather, mobile gas chambers, large trucks customized to pipe carbon monoxide into hermetically sealed compartments holding dozens of victims. The *gaswagens* were an outgrowth of Operation Euthanasia, a Nazi program under which 70,000 mental patients were killed with the aid of gas. Since the institutions doing the killing had crematoriums to burn the bodies, the program could have been a rehearsal for Auschwitz.

"The men in charge of the *Einsatzgruppen* in the East were increasingly complaining that the firing squads could not cope with the psychological and moral stress of the mass shootings indefinitely," said Dr. August Becker, who worked on development of the *gaswagens*. "I know that a number of members of these squads were themselves committed to mental asylums, and for this reason a new and better method of killing had to be found." Something less intimate than what was being done all over Ukraine, including Kharkov where use of the *gaswagens* to kill thousands of Jews would be a focal point of the first trial of Germans for their wartime crimes.

No doubt there were cases of soldiers buckling under the strain of repeated up-close-and-personal shooting of Jews, but it should be noted that there is ample documentation of killers who not only tolerated their shooting assignment, they reveled in it. Some saw it as a series of Kodak moments.

"The soldiers not only killed and watched but took pictures, wrote letters, and talked about the shootings until the news spread in the occupied territory and in Germany,"[1] wrote historian Nora Levin. When I first interviewed my mother in 2000 for *Hiding in the Spotlight,* the memory of being humiliated by Germans on the death march to Drobitsky Yar was still an open wound.

The most painful thing was not the hunger, not the cold, not the fear. It was the way we were disgraced by the Germans. They were laughing at us while we marched, taking photographs to send home to proudly show future generations how they led unarmed people in freezing conditions to their extermination.

The *Einsatzgruppen* troops became inured to "excesses," Levin wrote. "They lived in a world perforated by acts of killing and the sight of bleeding, quivering corpses—a world in which murder was a civic duty. They got used to their work with the help of ever larger doses of alcohol."[2]

Himmler's order to find a more humane, hands-off method of execution led to an experiment with the help of a chemist from an institute of technology. Some thirty mental patients were locked in a sealed room and carbon monoxide was pumped in from a car exhaust. Five minutes of that seemed to have no effect on the trapped patients. The chemist concluded that the car exhaust was not sufficiently lethal, so a second hose was connected to a truck. That did the trick—in five minutes the patients were unconscious. The successful test was reported to Berlin, and development began on a mobile gas chamber.

The technical department of the Reich Security Head Office, under the leadership of Obersturmbanfuhrer Walter Rauff, produced two rolling death houses: a Saurer truck that could accommodate fifty to sixty people, and a Diamond, made to hold twenty-five to thirty passengers. They resembled ordinary delivery trucks and had lights to illuminate the interior. The first experiment of the new vehicle was in Germany using thirty Soviet prisoners of war. It was a huge success. After a thirty-minute drive, all the prisoners were dead. Cause of death was carbon monoxide poisoning, the effects of which were vividly described by Soviet medical experts who examined the bodies of gas wagon victims exhumed in Ukraine: "The skin, skeletal muscles and mucous membranes of lips, stomach, intestines, pericardium, and peritoneum were either a pale pink, or bright cherry color, also noted in some cases in sections of internal organs such as the kidneys, lungs, and heart."

By December 1941 (or a month or two earlier—accounts differ), the gas vans were rolling in Ukraine and other occupied areas. They were also used in the Chelmno concentration camp. However, euphoria over the successful road test in Germany soon faded as reports filtered in from the field where the vans were proving to be more trouble than they were worth. There were equipment problems, weather problems, operator errors.

"The uneven surfaces and road conditions are causing the nails to come loose from the seals and joints," Dr. Becker reported after an inspection trip to Ukraine. "The brakes of the Saurer van which I took from Taganrog to Simferopol were damaged on the way. When I reached Stalino and Gorlovka a few days later, the drivers of the vans there complained of the same trouble. The gassing is generally not carried out correctly. In order to get the *Aktion* finished as quickly as possible, the driver presses down on the accelerator as far as it will go. As a result, the persons to be executed die of suffocation and do not doze off as was planned."

Dr. Becker noted that despite his best efforts at masquerade, no one was fooled about the true mission of the wagons. "I have had the vans disguised as house trailers, by having a single window shutter fixed to each side of the small vans, and on the large vans two shutters, such as one

JUDGMENT BEFORE NUREMBERG

sees on farmhouses in the country. The vans had become so well known that not only the authorities but the civilian population referred to them as 'Death Vans.' In my opinion the vans cannot be kept secret for any length of time even if they are camouflaged."

But even worse, and most ironically, the gas vans were producing a more grotesque horror show than the shootings they were designed to replace. A citizen forced by Germans to help unload the vans gave this account:

"A dark gray vehicle, looking like an ambulance, arrived in the clearing a number of times. When the back door was opened, human bodies fell out—men, women, and children. The bodies were joined together, as if linked by a convulsive embrace in distorted postures, with faces bitten away. I saw one man's teeth sunk in another's jaw. Some had their noses bitten off, some their fingers. Many were holding their hands in a convulsive grip—they must have been members of the same family. These corpses we were told to separate by force. When it could not be done, we were ordered to hack them, cut off hands, legs, and other parts."

Paul Blobel, leader of a *Sonderkommando* unit and ruthless orchestrator of the Babi Yar massacre, was driven to drink by the gas wagon horrors. His driver describes taking Blobel to an unloading site for the wagons. "Jews who were still alive unloaded the bodies that had not fallen out when the doors were opened. The bodies were covered with vomit and excrement. It was a terrible sight. Blobel looked, then looked away, and we drove off. On such occasions Blobel always drank schnapps, sometimes even in the car."

The *gaswagens* became the Edsel of the Nazi motor pool. The leader of *Einsatzgruppe* B said thanks, but no thanks, sending his allotment on to *Einsatzgruppen* C and D. Though they never became the high-volume killing machines Himmler hoped for, the *gaswagens* were used to murder thousands of Jews, mostly women and children. In Crimea, the non-Jewish nurses in a convalescent home betrayed fifty-two children who were then killed in *gaswagens*. The identical scenario occurred at Minsk Children's Home No. 1 where thirty Jewish children were betrayed by the manager and driven away in a gas wagon—out of sight and out of mind.

The primary responsibility of Bulanov, the collaborator who stood trial with three Nazis in Kharkov, was driving a gas wagon. Ukrainians called it *dushohubka*—the destroyer of the soul. Bulanov said the wagon he drove was "a huge two-axled truck of approximately five to seven tons capacity. It was painted gray and had a six-cylinder engine. The body of this machine had folding doors which closed hermetically. It was evidently made airtight by means of the rubber lining of the door." Bulanov described a typical pickup, this one from a hospital in Kharkov.

"Gestapo men began to lead out patients dressed only in their underwear, and load them into the trucks.

After loading, I drove the truck to the shooting site under German escort. The place was approximately four kilometers from the city. When we arrived at the shooting site, screams and sobs of patients who were already being shot filled the air. The Germans shot them in front of the other patients. Some begged for mercy and fell down naked in the cold mud, but the Germans pushed them into the pits and then shot them."

How fortunate for Himmler, with his tender sensibilities and compassion for both shooters and victims—on display at Minsk—that he was not present at this piteous display.

"Himmler wanted his victims to be killed without bloodshed and his SS men to be just like other workers, which is the fundamental reason he switched the method of killing from *Einsatzgruppen* executions to gas vans and gas chambers,"[3] said Richard Rhodes. As Levin wrote, this switch served the larger purpose of hiding the Nazi crimes by destroying the evidence. "The fear that the world would know what was happening even deep within Russia and the need for swift annihilation led the Nazis to contrive the technical improvements at the gassing camps where the secrecy of mass exterminations could be guarded more easily."[4]

Himmler's dream of an antiseptic Holocaust in which there was no blood and bones, no screams of wounded women, no corpses covered with vomit and excrement, a

Holocaust in which the dead did not pile up at his feet but instead disappeared into the sky as ashes—that Holocaust came to fruition at Auschwitz. Observing an extermination with Zyklon-B at the camp in July 1942, with the wind at the Nazis' back across Europe, Himmler surely felt fulfilled. That messy, awkward day in Minsk could be forgotten.

"Now he could watch a crowd of people murdered without batting an eye and go on to an evening of *Gemutlichkeit* with Hoss, the local Gauleiter, and their wives, even allowing himself to smoke a few cigarettes and drink a glass of wine," Rhodes wrote.

The *Reichsführer* was savoring the fruits of his hard labor in the east to produce a "more humane" path to the goal of a *Judenfrei* Europe. The greatest attempted coverup in human history had begun.

CHAPTER ELEVEN

M adagascar is the title of a 2005 animated movie about New York zoo animals suddenly and unexpectedly transported to the island of Madagascar off the east coast of Africa. Madagascar is also the name of a 1940 Nazi plan to suddenly and unexpectedly transport four million European Jews to the same island. The movie is much more believable—and entertaining—than the Nazi fantasy, which never got beyond what in Hollywood is called the development stage.

But the fact that the cockamamie Madagascar plan was mulled, albeit briefly, as a viable option speaks volumes about the pathology of the Nazi neuroses which found their full and inevitable expression in the slaughter of the Jews, who were transported no farther than Auschwitz, if they weren't killed in their own back yards in Ukraine.

I ran across the Madagascar plan in reading about *lebensraum*, the additional "living space"—i.e., other people's land—Hitler deemed necessary for expansion of Germany, which he believed could not achieve its true destiny within its ample existing borders. Of course, it wasn't enough to take other people's land, the people themselves must be removed to make room—*lebensraum*—for German colonists. There were only two ways to do this: kill them or relocate them.

Enter Adolf Eichmann, former traveling salesman for the Vacuum Oil Company, who bumbled his way up the byzantine Nazi hierarchy to become the *logisticsfuhrer* responsible for relocating millions of Jews inconveniently occupying the Germans' new living space. Raul Hilberg said the Holocaust advanced inexorably from expulsion to concentration to extermination. Eichmann was a participant in all three stages, beginning in 1938 when he engineered the "forced emigration" of 150,000 Jews from Austria. Eichmann, who insisted he had nothing against the Jews "personally," even visited Palestine before the war to study the possibility of Jewish emigration out of Nazi Germany.

Eichmann was a relentless careerist with a taste for harebrained schemes that he thought might pretty up his resume. In 1939, he and his Vienna superior, *Brigadefuhrer* Franz Stahlecker, hatched the idea of carving a Jewish protectorate out of Polish territory newly occupied by the

Germans. They found an area near the Russian border, and a few thousand Jews, mostly from Austria, were hustled into a place with few buildings and little drinkable water. The idea rapidly dissolved in chaos, incompetence, and bureaucratic in-fighting.

The spectacular failure of the so-called "Nisko" project did not cure Eichmann of his weakness for dubious ventures with a high degree of improbability. So when the Madagascar plan landed in his to-do box in the summer of 1940 with the imprimatur of his boss, Reinhard Heydrich, Eichmann not only embraced the chimerical notion, he would later attempt to claim authorship. I believe that Hannah Arendt, in *Eichmann in Jerusalem*, her psychoanalytical account of Eichmann's 1961 trial, got it right. "The Madagascar plan was always meant to serve as a cloak under which preparations for the physical extermination of all the Jews of Western Europe could be carried forward."

Arendt, of course, was writing in the dark ages of Holocaust research before the discovery of Nazi files showing that the Madagascar plan was not a fig leaf, but rather an actual—if utterly fantastic—plan. Though she may have been factually wrong, Arendt's psychological insight was inadvertently acute: Madagascar was hatched by minds not in full touch with reality.

"That anybody except Eichmann and some other lesser luminaries ever took the whole thing seriously seems unlikely, for—apart from the fact that the territory was known to be unsuitable, not to mention the fact that it was, after all, a French possession—the plan would have required shipping space for four million in the midst of a war and at a moment when the British Navy was in control of the Atlantic,"[1] Arendt wrote.

One truism I discovered about the Holocaust is that what "seems unlikely" often is true. The idea that soldiers from the country of Bach and Beethoven and Brahms were moving across Ukraine in 1941 slaughtering Jews seemed unlikely to my grandfather, who apprehended his misjudgment only when his family was marching to the killing field at Drobitsky Yar. Unlikely as it seems, Madagascar was taken seriously not just by "lesser luminaries" but indeed by the leading lights of the Nazi high command.

In a paper presented at the United States Holocaust Museum in 2003, Holocaust historian Christopher Browning traced the genesis of Madagascar and its odyssey through the Nazi bureaucracy. "In May 1940, Himmler presented Hitler with a memorandum concerning his thoughts on the treatment of alien populations in Eastern Europe," Browning said. "He revived his vision for revolutionizing the demographic structure of Eastern Europe through massive ethnic cleansing, and proposed expelling the Jews from Europe altogether, perhaps to some country in Africa."

Hitler gave Himmler the okay to pursue the idea, noting that Africa was an appropriate destination for the

Jews because it would "expose them to a climate which diminishes every person's ability to offer resistance to us." At the same time, an underling in the Foreign Office was mulling ways to use recently conquered French territories and decided that Madagascar would be a good place to put the Jews—not Africa but close enough. Next stop for the plan was Foreign Minister Ribbentrop and then *back* to Hitler, who mentioned to Mussolini in a June meeting that Madagascar was to become a Jewish "reservation," Browning said.

Hitler's use of "reservation," which conjures for Americans the shameful images of our own forced resettlement of indigenous peoples, was not accidental or casual. Hitler studied American history and adduced the white European settlers' brutal expulsion and imprisonment of Indians as historical imprimatur for clearing the East of Jews and Slavs to make room for Germans.

Over the next two months both the Foreign Office and Heydrich's Reich Security Main Office tinkered with the "script" for Madagascar. This is the point at which Eichmann, Heydrich's main adviser on Jewish affairs, glommed onto the plan and tried to make it his own, though he kept confusing Madagascar with Uganda, Arendt wrote.

Madagascar had sufficient high-level interest to percolate through the Nazi ranks even to local commanders in occupied Poland. However, as Browning noted, the plan assumed Germany would conquer Britain and gain control of the seas and its merchant marine, necessary for the shipping of four million Jews, assuming Moses was not available to part the waters of the South Atlantic. When the Brits repelled the Nazis in the Battle of Britain, the Madagascar plan was put aside and ultimately forgotten. Much later, it would become a tool of Holocaust deniers such as David Irving because it provides a faux "ah-ha!" moment showing that Hitler's original preference was to relocate the Jews, not murder them, and that the Holocaust just sort of *happened,* a plan B that got out of hand.

In 2004, prior to publication of *The Origins of the Final Solution,* Browning was interviewed in the pages of *The Atlantic Monthly,* which did its earnest liberal duty by providing space for an opposing view from David Irving, the world's only "certified" Holocaust denier as a result of his courtroom defeat to historian Deborah Lipstadt, whom he sued for libel for calling him a denier. Irving was in a chesty I-told-you-so mood in his comments to *The Atlantic.*

"So Browning finally comes around to the solution that I first proposed in *Hitler's War*—that Hitler was largely in the dark about what is now called the Holocaust, and certainly issued no order for the systematic extermination of the Jews," Irving sniffed. "The Madagascar Plan was not aborted in the summer of 1940. Hitler was still referring to it as a likely outcome in his table talk in July 1942. That was six clear months after the Wannsee Conference where—so conformist wisdom has it—Hitler's decision to exterminate was announced."

To which the proper response is: So what? Irving is playing a silly game of semantic *gotcha* that ignores the fact that by July 1942, upwards of a million Ukrainian Jews, including my grandparents and great-grandparents, already were dead, murdered by the *Einsatzgruppen* and their Ukrainian helpers. What difference does it make what Hitler was talking about over his sauerbraten and potato pancakes?

In his deluded certitude, Irving reminds me of the paranoid-schizophrenic math genius John Nash (Russell Crowe) in *A Beautiful Mind* who fills up walls and notebooks with manic scribbling, codes and equations that supposedly provide proof of a vast, unspecified government conspiracy. But no matter how frantically Irving and other deniers spin their sophistical formulas, the result will forever be the same: six million dead. Arendt, whose moral imagination was as capacious as Irving's is cramped, saw clearly the invisible writing on the wall spelling out the ineluctable logic of the Nazi neurosis. Hitler's flirtation with the undoable—Madagascar—was laying the groundwork for doing the unspeakable.

"When the Madagascar project was declared to have become 'obsolete,' everybody was psychologically, or rather, logically prepared for the next step: since there existed no territory to which one could 'evacuate,' the only 'solution' was extermination,"[2] Arendt wrote. A week before the invasion of the Soviet Union, Himmler addressed his top SS and police leaders. "It is a question of existence . . . a racial struggle of pitiless severity, in the course of which twenty to thirty million Slavs and Jews will perish through military actions and crises of food supply."

Further research has shown that the Madagascar plan was merely a whimsical detour in what had been Hitler's plan from almost the beginning. The visionary Führer had foreseen *Lebensraum*-through-extermination as early as 1931. In comments to a German newspaper editor which became public after the war, Hitler said, "We must colonize the East ruthlessly. We intend to introduce a great resettlement policy. Think of the biblical deportations and the massacres of the Middle Ages—and remember the extermination of the Armenians. One eventually reaches the conclusion that masses of men are mere biological modeling clay."

Hitler and Himmler aimed to create a "Garden of Eden" in the East once it was cleared—one way or the other—of undesirables. "Hitler dreamed of the Crimea as the future German Riviera," wrote historian Wendy Lower. Though *Lebensraum* was an article of faith for both men, for Himmler it was fulfillment of a youthful dream to become a "warrior-farmer" in the East. "Some day I will live my life in the East and fight my battles as a German far from beautiful Germany," Himmler told his diary at age nineteen. He earned a degree in agronomy, but ultimately chose to leave the actual farming to others while he concentrated on warring.

Unveiled in April 1942, Himmler's Edenic blueprint, *Generalplan Ost*, called for removal of thirty million people from Poland and the Soviet Union to make room for the migration of Germans and ethnic-Germans, including German-Americans who would be forcibly repatriated to the Fatherland after Hitler triumphantly marched up Pennsylvania Avenue with the Nazi flag flying over the U.S. Capitol—a grand encore to his stroll up the Champs-Elysees after conquering France.

In the spring of 1942—with more than half a million Ukrainian Jews in the ground, with the death camps at Belzec and Auschwitz and Sobibor "processing" thousands more a day from across Europe—all things seemed possible for Hitler, even a monstrous grandiosity like his plan to colonize the East, *Generalplan Ost*. He was still sailing on a cloud of "victory euphoria," as Browning called it, untethered from reality on the ground. "He felt he could be more uninhibited, that he could give greater rein to turning his fantasies into reality," Browning told *The Atlantic*.

Hitler's "Garden of Eden" fantasy reached an abortive zenith in the fall of 1942 when nearly 100,000 *Volksdeutsche* (Germans and German-speaking Ukrainians) were moved from the barren north to fertile lands of Poland and Ukraine which had been cleared of Jews and other inhabitants. The

Jews, of course, had been and continued to be murdered in "yars" throughout the region. The Ukrainian peasants occupying the target area were displaced en masse, a hundred miles or more to areas east of the Dnieper River. (They were more fortunate than the 1.5 million Ukrainians who were forcibly deported to Germany to perform hard labor or to serve as domestic servants.) The signature *Generalplan Ost* colony was Hegewald, situated near Himmler's headquarters at Zhytomyr, where the farmer-turned-warrior could watch others toiling in the fields. It did not take long for the fantasy to collapse under the weight of its own sheer implausibility and incompetent management.

SS and regional Nazi officials "found that they could not feed and care for the ethnic Germans, especially for the hundreds of kidnapped children who had been placed in makeshift orphanages," wrote Lower. "Soviet partisans attacked the *Volksdeutsche* settlers and raided their food supplies. The defeat of Hitler's forces by the Red Army and mounting partisan warfare behind the lines cut short Nazi colonization plans. Yet, regional leaders realized early in the campaign that developing productive colonies was a far more difficult task than destroying 'non-Aryan' populations and cultures."[3]

Or shipping them to Madagascar. Had the technology been available, someone deep in a Berlin think tank surely would have proposed "relocating" the Jews to the moon, a climate that would permanently diminish their ability to offer resistance, while sparing Nazis on Earth the trauma of murdering them and disposing of the evidence, which in zero gravity would simply float off into space. Eichmann no doubt would have claimed ownership of the ingenious "lunar solution" to the Jewish problem.

After the withering of his "garden" in the East and the German defeat at Stalingrad, Hitler could take solace in pursuing his overarching goal—extermination of the Jews— which "must be ruthlessly implemented and endured to the end," he told Himmler. "Murdering the Jews, in Hitler's eyes, was the equivalent to winning the war," Rhodes wrote.

Madagascar, Nisko, and Hegewald were all just mile markers on the same road: This way lay madness.

CHAPTER TWELVE

I suppose the same instinct that makes me tolerant of the death penalty when fairly applied—say, for Adolf Eichmann—allowed me to enjoy *Inglourious Basterds*, Quentin Tarantino's glorious revenge fantasy about the Holocaust, without guilt. Well, maybe a trace. After all, my mother is Jewish and my father was Catholic. Those groups practically invented guilt.

I admit I did feel a twinge of guilt when reading reviews suggesting that the vengeance gleefully wreaked on Hitler and other Nazis with guns, knives, and baseball bats, as only Tarantino can, was moral pornography—that it made Jewish-American avengers, such as Mr. Louisville Slugger (my nickname for one character), no better than the Nazis themselves. "Tarantino indulges this taste for vengeful violence by, well, turning Jews into Nazis," wrote author and critic Daniel Mendelsohn.

Having indulged so heartily in Tarantino's all-you-can-watch revenge buffet, had I, well, turned into a Nazi? This crisis of conscience did not last long. Soon I was rooting for a Nazi to win an Academy Award. Okay, so technically I was rooting for an actor *playing* a Nazi, but Christoph Waltz did win for his mesmerizing portrayal of SS Colonel Hans Landa, a charming, sophisticated, cold-blooded executioner. David Denby of *The New Yorker* praised Waltz but still slammed the movie. "The film is skillfully made, but it's too silly to be enjoyed, even as a joke."

I don't know what to call *Inglourious Basterds*—all Tarantino's work defies categorization—but it is no joke. It's a very serious movie in satirical garb. You can't watch *Basterds*, in particular the brilliant colloquies between Col. Landa and whoever is sitting across the table, and not wonder on some level about the anatomy of good and evil. When you leave the theater, Col. Landa and his cold stare and smirk leave with you. This is more than can be said for most non-fiction on the subject.

Basic "awareness" of the Holocaust is at an all-time high, but so is the number of Holocaust deniers, who have discovered in the Internet the ideal delivery vehicle for their vile fantasies. Survivors, scholars, and journalists rebut the fantasies with fact, as well they should. Holocaust fact is, indeed, stranger than fiction. But at some point the sheer quantity of facts, the magnitude of the Nazis' crimes becomes unfathomable, like a federal debt of a trillion dollars. The mind can't compute the number and eventually shuts down and refuses to accept more data.

"Just the facts, ma'am" was fine for Det. Jack Webb investigating bank robberies on *Dragnet.* The Holocaust, not so much. Art—high and low—can reach people in places and at depths inaccessible to simple fact, no matter how compellingly presented.

In *Life is Beautiful,* another fantasy, a Jewish Italian father persuades his young son that their life in a Nazi concentration camp is just a big game staged for his amusement—a leap of imagination too great for some critics who were not amused and dismissed the movie as a forgettable trifle. Roberto Benigni won Academy Awards for actor and screenplay, leaping and climbing over seats to reach the stage to get his Oscars. I've never forgotten Benigni's leap of imagination—or the eyes of the little boy as American tanks rumble into the liberated camp—while the estimable but linear and didactic *Schindler's List* has faded to a mental footnote.

One reason I feel so strongly about the need for fantasy to supplement and animate fact, to expand the boundaries of imagination, is that I see the need in myself. In August 1943, U.S. Supreme Court Justice Felix Frankfurter was in a group of American dignitaries who met with Jan Karski, a Pole who provided graphic descriptions of what he had seen in the Warsaw ghetto and Belzec death camp. "I know what you say is true," Frankfurter said, "I just don't believe it." Nearly seventy years later, I found myself suffering the same failure of imagination—at the very scene of the crime, no less.

It happened at the Chichikov Hotel in Kharkov, where I met for tea and conversation with Victor Melikhov, the English instructor and amateur historian who gave me a two-hour crash course on the sprawling arabesque that is Russian-Ukrainian history. He began with a pithy truism from Russian writer-satirist Mikhail Zadornov: "Russia is a great country with an unpredictable past." My inability to make the leap of imagination came near the end of the tutorial when, in the most casual way, Victor said something astonishing. In the town of Artyomovsk in southeastern Ukraine, he said, the Nazis had herded thousands of Jews into wine cellars and bricked up the openings, leaving them to die the slowest death possible—by suffocation.

I knew that what Victor said must be true—I just didn't believe it.

I had read and heard countless stories of Nazi atrocities in Ukraine, including the shooting and bayoneting of babies. But there was something so medieval, so *theatrically* sadistic about entombing people in a cave with bricks— even for Nazis—that it just wouldn't register as real in my brain.

Back home in Orlando, still in disbelief and expecting little, I Googled "Artyomovsk" and "wine cellars" and "Nazis." Not much popped up—but just enough: a wine lover's blog featuring Artyomovsk Winery. I had to scroll down past many photos of wine bottles, arched tunnels lined with colorful murals, stainless steel vats, rooms full of wine, more tunnels, more vats, more racks of wine, and the winery cat prowling the tunnels, before finally finding this entry under the heading, "The weeping wall—memorial to a massacre."

"The Artyomovsk underground quarry was the scene of a particularly horrible mass murder during World War II. The Germans arrived in the town in October 1941 and drove more than 3,000 people believed to be Jews to the underground, bricking them in alive in one of the galleries (tunnels) after taking their belongings. The Soviet Army liberated the area in September 1943 and a memorial was later built at the entry of the gallery where the crime took place. The 'weeping wall' is the name of the memorial and it happens to be the only place in the underground mine where some water comes out in tiny drops from the wall. It is said that these water drops are the tears of the victims. After this solemn meditation in front of this wall, the visitors are invited to a more cheerful experience—tasting of several wines."

Above the blog entry was a photo of the quite beautiful memorial: a white brick wall maybe thirty feet long and twelve feet high with cut-outs for tall candles, and in the center, a jagged opening and two mournful, bowed figures carved in white stone. I now "believed" what Victor told me, but I still could not feel it—the enormity of such an act. Was there an inscription on the Weeping Wall? The blogger did not say. There is no mention of the memorial on the Artyomovsk Winery Web site, or on a tourism Web site for Donetsk, the largest nearby city, though it does hail the winery as "our national pride . . . the largest East European facility producing exquisite bottled sparkling wines." It seems that sparkling wine does not go well with the Holocaust.

After much online surfing and trawling, I was able to find a bit more information. There were gypsum mines and an alabaster plant at Artyomovsk when the Germans arrived in 1941 and decided that the tunnels, 230 feet below the surface, would make an excellent living grave for the Jews of the town. After the war, the Stalin government converted the mines to a massive wine-storage facility, and erected the Weeping Wall memorial. Artyomovsk Winery was established in 1950 and now holds 30 million bottles of wine. None of these facts gave me any sense, any visceral knowledge, of what occurred at Artyomovsk in October 1941—of how it was for the Jews as the Nazis entombed them brick by brick.

The only reference I had for this sort of scenario in my imagination was a dimly remembered short story from high-school lit class by Edgar Allan Poe in which a man seals an adversary in a wall with bricks. Refreshing my memory from a Poe collection on the shelf, I was startled to discover that the scenario in *The Cask of Amontillado* was even closer than I had recalled to the events at Artyomovsk. The narrator of Poe's story, Montresor, encased his erstwhile friend, Fortunato, not in a wall but the wine cellar of his palazzo, luring him there with the prospect of a bottle of Amontillado, a prized sherry. He shackled the drunken Fortunato in a niche deep in the cellar among the catacombs. Reading on, I felt for the first time stirrings of the horror at Artyomovsk.

"I soon uncovered a quantity of building stone and mortar," Montresor says. "With these materials and with the aid of my trowel, I began vigorously to wall up the entrance of the niche. I had scarcely laid the first tier of the masonry when I discovered that the intoxication of Fortunato had in a great measure worn off. The earliest indication was a low moaning cry from the depth of the recess. I laid the second tier, and the third, and the fourth; and then I heard furious vibrations of the chain. The noise lasted for several minutes. That I might hearken to it with more satisfaction, I ceased my labors and sat down upon the bones.

"When at last the clanking subsided, I resumed the trowel, and finished without interruption the fifth, the sixth, and the seventh tier. The wall was now nearly upon a level with my breast. I again paused, and holding the flambeaux over the mason work, threw a few feeble rays upon the figure within. A succession of loud and shrill screams, bursting suddenly from the throat of the chained form, seemed to thrust me violently back. I thrust a torch through the remaining aperture and let it fall within. There came forth in return only a jingling of the bells. My heart grew sick; it was the dampness of the catacombs that made it so. I hastened to make an end to my labor. I forced the last stone into its position. I plastered it up. Against the new masonry I re-erected the old rampart of bones. For the half of a century no mortal has disturbed them. *In pace requiescat!"*

After the region was liberated in late 1943, Soviet investigators examined the quarry at Artyomovsk. "The cave was full of human corpses, pressed up against each other with their backs to the tunnel's entrance," they reported. "The corpses were pressed so close to each other that they appeared at first glance to be a single solid form. Due to the unique conditions in the cave (dry air, steady low temperatures) the corpses had undergone a mummification process and most of them had been excellently preserved. It was possible to see on most of the corpses a white arm band on which a Star of David had been painted or stitched around the left sleeve of their coats."

The Germans could have murdered the Jews of Artyomovsk in the same manner they did most Jews in Ukraine— by bullets, at the edge of a ravine. A leap of imagination was required to bypass routine. What manner of mind, of cold-blooded efficiency crossed with a perverted flair for the dramatic, would eschew bullets for the final solution at Artyomovsk?

Yes, the mind of our fictional doppelganger Col. Hans Landa. It is easy to imagine Landa as the commanding officer at Artyomovsk, observing with giddy aesthetic pleasure as soldiers applied mortar to the final bricks of the wall entombing the three thousand Jews, and exclaiming with delight, as he did in *Inglourious Basterds:*

"Ooh, that's a bingo!"

CHAPTER THIRTEEN

When I set out in 2000 to do research for my mother's biography, *Hiding in the Spotlight*, I could count on one hand the high-profile Nazis in my mental Holocaust file: Hitler, Himmler, Göring, Goebbels, Rommel—who thanks to James Mason in *Desert Rats* didn't even seem like a Nazi—and maybe Heydrich or Keitel on the other hand if I also included the History Channel.

The first name I encountered outside this circle of usual suspects was Paul Blobel. It wasn't random. I had gone looking for the men who murdered my grandparents and great-grandparents. Blobel was leader of *Sonderkommando* 4a, a unit of *Einsatzgruppe* C, one of four mobile-killing squads that followed in the path of the *Wehrmacht* across the Soviet Union shooting Jews. Blobel's unit was assigned to northern Ukraine, including Kharkov, where my mother lived.

Sonderkommando 4a arrived in Kharkov on October 21, 1941, and promptly began public hangings—from lamp posts, trees, balconies, statues—116 in the first two weeks, according to Yuri Radchenko, a young Holocaust historian I met in Kharkov who showed me the landmarks of Nazi occupation. Two months later, elements of Blobel's unit, aided by German Special Order Police and Ukrainian collaborators, marched 16,000 Kharkov Jews to the killing fields of Drobitsky Yar, my mother, her sister, and her parents and grandparents included.

While Blobel had special significance for me personally, he is worth examining more closely for other reasons. There were *Einsatzgruppe* commanders guilty of killing more Jews—Otto Ohlendorf freely confessed to 90,000— and others with more interesting and paradoxical backgrounds: before signing up to commit mass murder, the aforementioned Waldemar Klingelhofer made his living as an opera singer, while another, Ernest Biberstein, had been an ordained Protestant minister.

Blobel is intriguing because he was the Zelig of *Einsatzgruppe* commanders, present at the two most important events—both real and symbolic—of the Holocaust in Ukraine. Indeed, together they express both the full destructive fury and the deluded, self-immolating futility of the entire Nazi enterprise in a way that the gas chambers of Auschwitz and Sobibor and Treblinka do not. Those gated abattoirs, after all, were created in large measure as alternatives to the open-air slaughter and highly public crime scenes in Ukraine.

In September 1941, Blobel supervised the murder of 34,000 Jews in just two days at Babi Yar outside Kiev—the most iconic massacre of the Holocaust that did not use gas, and the largest to that date in the war. Babi Yar is the only Ukrainian place name from the Holocaust that's a household word in some American homes, thanks to the 1961 poem of the same name by Yevgeny Yevtushenko. Blobel's other claim to infamy was, arguably, the most gruesome task given to any German officer during the war. As the Germans were retreating from Ukraine in 1943, and the Soviet press began to report the discovery of mass killing sites in areas liberated by the Red Army, Blobel was put in charge of "Aktion 1005"—an attempt to destroy the evidence of Nazi genocidal crimes by digging up and burning the bodies, a million corpses in thousands of graves across a country the size of Texas, a task to make Sisyphus grateful for his rock and his hill. Whether by design or accident, the man and the mission were perfectly matched: both were nearly insane.

In January 1942, Blobel had been relieved of his *Sonderkommando* duties by *SS-Obergruppenfuhrer* Heydrich and sent to Kiev to await reassignment. A Catholic priest who dined with Blobel shortly before his dismissal said Blobel was "entirely exhausted, to the point where he was no longer competent." He also seemed to be nurturing

GREG DAWSON

a ghoulish satisfaction with his recent commanding of the blood bath at Babi Yar. Riding past the ravine with the same priest, Blobel smiled and made a sweeping gesture with his arm: "Here live my thirty thousand Jews." At Blobel's trial after the war, his adjutant said Blobel suffered a nervous breakdown in July 1941 after the slaughter of three thousand Jews in Zhitomyr. "He was talking confusedly. He was saying it was not possible to shoot so many Jews and that what was needed was a plough to plough them into the ground. He had completely lost his mind."

With his beard, gaunt face, and feral eyes, Blobel stood out from his clean-shaven, robust, and neatly coiffed *Einsatz* comrades who out of uniform resembled a group of bankers or importers-exporters. As historian Hilary Earl noted, Blobel was the only defendant who seemed to physically personify the evil he committed. Judge Michael Musmanno noted that Blobel "sat in the front row in the defendants' dock with his square red beard jutting out ahead like the prow of a piratical ship commanded by himself. His blood-shot eyes glared with the penetrating intensity of a wild animal at bay."[1]

On the other hand, Blobel knew quite well where the bodies were buried in Ukraine—34,000 of them at least—and the massacre at Babi Yar he directed was so expeditiously completed that Heydrich had nominated Blobel for a War Service Cross. "It's almost impossible to imagine what nerves of steel it took to carry out that dirty work down there," said a witness at the ravine. "It was horrible." So perhaps Blobel's solid resume as an efficient killer allowed Heydrich to overlook the recent emotional meltdown and the chronic drunkenness and to give Blobel a task that not even the most diabolical sorcerer could accomplish. And he was hardly that.

Blobel's deposition for the war crime trial in Nuremberg is the melancholy self-portrait of a quintessential cipher, an ineffectual drifter through life whose failures led him to the Nazi party and ultimately the power of life and death over tens of thousands. This is his journey, in abbreviated form:

"I was born in Potsdam on 13 August 1894. I attended grammar school and vocational school until 1912. Until the outbreak of the First World War, I worked as a carpenter. I served as an engineer at the front and was discharged with the rank of staff sergeant. Until 1919, I was unemployed. I attended the school of architecture in Barmen and established myself as an independent architect in Solingen. During the bad times in Germany, I did not get any orders and was on unemployment relief from 1930 to 1933. After that I was employed for office work with the city. I became a member of the NSDAP in 1931 . . . the SS in 1932. In June 1935, I came to SD headquarters in Dusseldorf, where I remained until May 1941. Finally I was section leader for Dusseldorf. In June 1941, I became chief of *Sonderkommando* 4a. In January 1942, I was removed from the post and transferred to Berlin for disciplinary reasons. There I had no assignment for a time."

In May 1942, Heydrich called Blobel into his office in Berlin. After mocking him for developing a belly—"you're a soft person"—Heydrich told the unemployed and unstable Blobel, "I'll stick your nose very much deeper into it," meaning the *Einsatzgruppen* massacre in Ukraine. In June, Blobel met with Gestapo chief Heinrich Müller to get his marching orders. "This order was top secret, and *Gruppenfuhrer* Muller decreed that, owing to the strict secrecy of this task, no written correspondence of any kind was to be carried on," Blobel told the court.

The Nazi high command was so profoundly myopic that it could not see the patent absurdity of trying to keep such an operation—the unearthing and burning of a million corpses in open fields—"top secret." Or that in the end the very attempt to cover up the crimes would only confirm them. By the way, Himmler told Blobel, raising the degree of impossibility to lunatic heights, make sure you leave no ashes.

There was a hint of dark farce as Blobel searched for methods to accomplish his grisly task. He tried dynamite, experimenting with corpses exhumed at the Chelmno death camp, but that only created a bigger mess. He devised a machine for grinding human bones into fine particles that could be easily disposed of. His final solution—the one employed throughout the occupied territories—reflected his architectural training: "Pharonic tombs" which alternated rail track, wooden planks, and human bodies to create towering pyres which were drenched with gasoline and set on fire. Like the original murders, the unearthing and burning was conducted with characteristic Nazi flair for order and job titles. As with the Jewish "barbers" and "dentists" at Treblinka who were kept alive for a while to perform dirty work, it was Jews from nearby concentration camps who were given the horrific task of digging up and burning the bodies. Sometimes they were assisted by Soviet prisoners of war.

Historian Yitzhak Arad described a dig-and-burn operation at a concentration camp near Lvov. About 120 Jewish prisoners dug and burned under the close supervision of German forces. To maintain secrecy, no Ukrainian police were allowed to observe the operation.

"One group of Jews was employed in opening the graves and exhuming the bodies while another group carried the bodies off and threw them onto a giant bonfire. The bonfire was supervised by a prisoner know as 'Brandmeister' (fire chief), whose job was to keep fueling the fire with blocks of wood and gasoline and to give instructions as to which part of the bonfire needed more corpses thrown on it. They were also responsible for removing the remaining bones for crushing. Next to the bonfire stood a prisoner known as 'Zahler,' who was in charge of counting the bodies as they were thrown on the bonfire. Another group of prisoners, known as 'Aschkolonne' (ash team) dealt with crushing the burned bones and sieving the ashes for any gold (teeth, rings, etc.) and other valuables left on the cremated bodies. At first the burned bones were crushed manually, but later a special machine which resembled a cement mixer was brought to the site for this purpose. About 2,000 corpses were burned each day."[2]

Blobel kicked off his fool's errand, aptly enough, by unearthing the bodies he had put in the ground at Babi Yar. "I personally reviewed the burning of bodies in the mass grave near Babi Yar," he reported. "It took about two days for the whole grave to burn. Afterwards, the grave was covered and the evidence was destroyed."

The two *Sonderkommando* units assigned to "Aktion 1005" fanned out across Ukraine and beyond to Belorussia, Latvia, and Estonia, burning 3,000 corpses here, 7,000 there. As the military tide began to turn against the German army in 1943, the Nazi washing of hands became more frantic and irrational. At the same time that evidence was being destroyed, new evidence was being created with the shooting of still more Jews throughout the western Soviet Union—those the Nazis may have missed on the way in during Operation Barbarossa in 1941. On the same day the Germans finally withdrew from Estonia— September 19, 1944—they murdered 2,500 Jews in a labor camp at Klooga in northern Estonia. The Germans were in such a hurry to get out of town that they didn't have time to burn all the bodies. Soviet forces found pyres of bodies that were never torched.

Most of the Jews and other prisoners forced to assist in burning and disposing of the "evidence" were subsequently killed, some while trying to escape into nearby fields and forests. But enough miraculously survived to tell the story of "Aktion 1005," which was studiously *un*documented by the normally record-happy Nazis. Although "hundreds of thousands, certainly, possibly even millions" of corpses were destroyed, Arad wrote, millions were left in the ground untouched, including those at Drobitsky Yar where my mother's family perished. Blobel seemed to take the failure of his impossible mission in stride, blaming lack of time. "My duties should have covered the entire area in which the *Ein-satzgruppen* were employed. However, owing to the retreat from Russia, I did not totally carry out my orders."

Blobel was remorseless to the end, proclaiming his innocence and conceding nothing in courtroom collo-quies with prosecution attorneys. Did he believe that the reported murder of 1,160 Jews in retaliation for the killing of ten German soldiers was justified? "I don't know," Blobel answered. "I am not a militarist, you see." Earl wrote that Blobel "seems to have been universally hated as a malicious and cowardly man. Blobel was so reviled that he was one of the few defendants who had difficulty securing affidavits from fellow SS and SD men attesting to his strength of character."[3]

But then, how much is a character reference from a fellow mass murderer really worth? In the months leading up to the execution of the convicted killers, there had been a flurry of petitions requesting clemency for the many defendants at Nuremberg. No one petitioned on behalf of Blobel. Americans concluded he was "friendless."

Blobel and four other *Einsatz* commanders were hanged at Landsberg prison near Munich on June 7, 1951. He was in good company, if not among friends.

CHAPTER FOURTEEN

Ours is a curious age of narcissism and self-flagellation, an excuse culture of exhibitionists in which the high priests—Oprah and Dr. Phil—invite us to advertise our sins and remorse in the klieg lights of their studio confessionals. The essence of this public ethos is found in words not coined but made famous by the Rev. Oprah: "Denial is not just a river in Egypt."

With our supreme self-absorption comes historical myopia. We think we *invented* denial. This same vanity, crossed with savvy marketing and contempt for history, produced the ludicrous notion of a "greatest generation"—and a bestseller for Tom Brokaw. With a straight face, Brokaw suggested that the soldiers who fought in World War II represented a generation of Americans somehow superior to those who stood with Washington at Valley Forge, with Lee and Grant in Virginia, nobler than the doughboys who died in Flanders fields—worthier than the generation of Americans who marched with King, were beaten and jailed for registering voters in the South, and gave lives and limbs to a misbegotten task in Vietnam.

That is some pretty audacious nonsense, but Brokaw and other contemporary peddlers of altered reality must bow before the perpetrators of the Holocaust—the architects and true masters of denial. Hitler's Thousand-Year Reich lasted only twelve years. He dreamed of a "Garden of Eden" in the East, free of Jews, and left a desert littered with skulls. The Führer also left behind accomplices—from the high command in Berlin to distant command posts in Ukraine—who in courtrooms in Kharkov and Nuremberg produced the greatest exercise in collective denial ever recorded.

The Nazi killers were nothing if not creative. Their denial was expressed to different degrees, on a variety of levels, from simple denial of documented physical facts to tortured denial of legal principle and philosophical truth.

For example, at one darkly comic extreme—the Sgt. Schultz "I know *nothing*" position—was Walter Haensch, an *Einsatzgruppe* commander who claimed that he first learned of the mass murder of Jews in 1947 when he was told by an interrogator at Nuremberg. Never mind that the *Einsatzgruppe's* own field reports placed Haensch at sites in Russia where 3,400 people were shot between

Jan. 16 and Feb. 14, 1942. Haensch blithely insisted he was in Berlin at the time for a birthday party and dental appointment.

At the opposite extreme was Otto Ohlendorf, the charismatic, intellectually combative commander of *Einsatzgruppe* D who admitted to supervising the murder of 90,000 Jews, and welcomed the opportunity to adamantly deny legal guilt. Killing violated his personal beliefs, Ohlendorf said, but duty required him to follow orders from a superior. In a display of mental gymnastics worthy of a perfect 10, Ohlendorf argued that killing Jews was an act of war, not a crime against humanity (genocide), because Hitler's military plan called for wiping out Judeo-Bolshevism, not Jews per se.

"Killing children was militarily necessary, too, he claimed, because they posed a possible security risk, especially when they reached adulthood and could avenge the death of their parents," historian Hilary Earl wrote.

Ohlendorf also hoped to mitigate his crimes in the eyes of the court by noting that "My mission was to see to it that this general order for executions would be carried out as humanely as conditions would permit." It was strictly forbidden to mistreat victims before they were shot. Taking personal possessions from victims or forcing them to undress was not permitted (so we're to conclude the tons of luggage, clothing, and shoes were "donated" by victims?). Any shooter found to be enjoying the experience would be barred from participating in future executions—the Nazis' idea of tough love. Alas, Ohlendorf's "humane" executions went unappreciated by the court and he was sentenced to death.

The judges at Nuremberg were regularly driven to distraction by the fictions and prevarications of the defendants. *Einsatzgruppe* commander Paul Blobel, who appeared to have been separated at birth from Rasputin, oversaw the epic slaughter at Babi Yar—34,000 persons, mostly Jews, shot in two days. He offered a fantastical rationale which was met with cold outrage by Judge Michael Musmanno, the seventh of eight children born to Italian immigrants in a small town near Pittsburgh.

> **Blobel:** All the German people know, your Honor, that an order was given by General Eisenhower that for every one American killed, two hundred Germans are to be shot.

> **Musmanno:** Do you say that every German and every defense counsel here knew of such an order?

> **Blobel:** I am convinced that many of the defense counsel knew of this order.

There were many Germans in the courtroom. Musmanno asked Blobel to find one who would confirm the

Eisenhower story. Not a single hand went up. Musmanno demanded that Blobel apologize for besmirching the good name of General Eisenhower, who had earned the respect of friends and foes alike. Blobel meekly complied.

Musmanno had a similarly testy exchange, at a higher level of intellection, with Ohlendorf over his unquestioning acceptance of an order to murder—just because it was an order. Would he question the morality of an order to kill his own sister, Musmanno asked. Ohlendorf at first refused to answer what he considered a trick question. But since his defense was based on strict obedience to orders, Ohlendorf finally said that, yes, he would have murdered his sister if ordered.

Musmanno also engaged in a mini-Socratic dialogue with *Einsatzgruppe* commander Willy Seibert, also sentenced to death.

> **Musmanno:** Let us suppose you received an order directly from Hitler that you were to execute the chief of the *Einsatzgruppen*. Would you execute that order?

> **Seibert:** No, I would not have carried it out.

> **Musmanno:** Well, then, suppose you received an order to shoot a twelve-year-old Jew? Would you shoot him?

Seibert: I cannot say.

I think we, as outside observers, can say that both Ohlendorf and Seibert were lying. The scenario presented to Ohlendorf of course was theoretical, but would a man who took pride in "humanely" murdering Jews pull the trigger on his own sister? Not likely. As for Seibert, it's hard to understand his indecision—or perhaps poor memory. The point-blank shooting of Jewish children was quite common. You don't get to six million by sparing twelve-year-olds.

Because his trial in Jerusalem was held nearly fifteen years after Nuremberg and was covered extensively by the now widespread medium of television, Adolf Eichmann became—and remains—the Nazi poster boy for the "just following orders" defense. Eichmann testified about the Wannsee conference outside Berlin in January 1942, at which the Nazi High Command decided on the total annihilation of European Jews by gas (half a million Jews already had been shot in Ukraine). Finally having all the Nazi elites "on board" the death train was a great relief to the outranked Eichmann, who served as recording secretary at the conference.

"At that moment, I sensed a kind of Pontius Pilate feeling, for I was free of all guilt," he testified. "Who was I to judge? Who was I to have my own thoughts in this matter?"

The "following orders" mantra was used like table salt on potato pancakes from the top to the bottom of the Nazi war machine, starting with the three mid-level officers chosen by the Soviets for the first war crimes trial in Kharkov in 1943. Later, at Nuremberg, the German generals were asked why they so blindly followed Hitler's orders to commit acts they knew to be war crimes. General Alfred Jodl said it was "not the task of a soldier to act as judge over his supreme commander. Let history do that or God in Heaven." Far down the line of command, at the level of sergeant in American terms, *Unteroffizier* Peter Maiguart, a circus acrobat before the war, repeated the company line, but with more lurid details:

"Our rifles were pointed at the back of the Jews' heads. I had to shoot a young teenage girl. In German she said to me, 'How can you murder people?' I answered, 'Orders.' Then I shot her. Altogether I shot twenty-four people that day, maybe more. Others shot more."

It has been argued that soldiers such as Maiguart followed orders to murder because refusal to do so would mean their own execution or exile to a concentration camp. However, there is a very basic flaw in this argument, noted historian Christopher Browning.

"In the past 45 years no defense attorney or defendant in any of the hundreds of postwar trials has been able to document a single case in which refusal to obey an order to kill unarmed civilians resulted in the allegedly inevitable dire punishment," Browning wrote in *Ordinary Men*, his 1992 study of German Reserve Police Battalions which performed many of the same killing tasks as the *Wehrmacht* and *Einsatzgruppen*.

To the contrary, Browning and other historians have documented many cases in which German soldiers and officers refused or begged off orders to murder and were given a pass. Sometimes they did not even have to ask. Browning tells the story of conscience-stricken Major Wilhelm Trapp, leader of Reserve Police Battalion 101 sent to execute the Jews of a small Polish village.

"The male Jews of working age were to be separated and taken to a work camp. The remaining Jews—the women, children, and elderly—were to be shot on the spot by the battalion," Browning wrote. "Having explained what awaited his men, Trapp then made an extraordinary offer: if any of the older men among them did not feel up to the task that lay before him, he could step out."[1]

Only one man stepped out. The rest carried out the bloody orders that day and on many subsequent days, giving the lie to "putative duress," the notion heard repeatedly from Germans in the dock that they followed criminal orders out of reasonable expectation of punishment if they refused. As Browning notes, after Major Trapp's tearful offer of immunity, "putative duress did not exist in the battalion"—yet the killing went on without any shortage of killers.

Major Wilhelm was not alone in offering immunity to his men. In her study of auxiliary police units in the Soviet Union, Meredith Meehan writes: "Despite the common misconception that executioners were often 'ordered to shoot or be shot,' there is almost no evidence to support this allegation. In fact, one auxiliary noted that, 'It was made clear to us that we could refuse to obey an order to participate in *Sonderaktionen* (special actions) without adverse consequences."[2] This reflected growing awareness in Berlin that point-blank executions were exacting a crippling psychological toll on the shooters. Why else, in planning consummation of the Final Solution, would they switch from bullets in Ukraine to gas in Germany and Poland?

Exemptions were issued from the earliest days of the Nazi Holocaust in Soviet territories. The first traceable killing order of Operation Barbarossa, writes historian Konrad Kwiet, was issued on June 23 or 24, 1941, in Berlin by Heinrich Müller, head of the Gestapo, to SS-Major Hans-Joachim Böhme, head of an *Einsatzkommando* unit in the East Prussian city of Tilsit. Ultimately, the unit conducted some six thousand executions. Not a single member of the unit hesitated to shoot Jewish men, Kwiet writes, but some drew the line at women and children.

"In late summer of 1941, after a bestial murder of women and children, a police officer declared, 'I am not doing that again in the future.' Böhme responded: 'You will be put in an SS uniform, and you will receive an official order,' adding later, 'Fine, you can leave, you do not have to do this—you have a wife and children.' No one who protested against the murder of Jews or who disobeyed a killing order was ever sentenced to death by the special SS and Police courts. As a rule, such persons were demoted, transferred, or dismissed."

A prominent example was Erwin Schulz, an *Einsatzgruppe* commander in Ukraine who asked to be relieved of his duties in the summer of 1941 after receiving orders to increase executions, which might require Schulz himself to kill. The word came down from Himmler that all Jews not engaged in work were to be executed, including women and children. "I was shattered when I heard this piece of news and I had absolutely no doubt that I could never carry out such an order," Schulz said years later in court. He was released from his duties without penalty.

The true face of the *Einsatzgruppen* was not the anguished Erwin Schulz but rather the smugly remorseless Ernst Biberstein, a Protestant minister before the war. When asked by the president of the tribunal why—as a professed man of God—he did not provide spiritual balm to those about to be executed, Biberstein replied without hesitation, "Mr. President, one does not cast pearls before swine."

By the same token, it would be wrong to conclude from examples of the Nazi version of conscientious objection—refusal to quicken the *pace* of executions—that the German military was rife with reluctant killers. There are many more stories of soldiers who not only followed orders to kill but relished the task, sometimes creatively as with the wine cellars of Artyomovsk. They were guilty of a crime not in the books: *aggravated* genocide.

"Most men accepted their orders automatically and soon got used to the work," concluded the editors of *The Good Old Days.* "Some were positively addicted to it and 'could not get enough of it.' Ordinary soldiers of the *Wehrmacht* who came to watch would sometimes ask to join in, borrowing guns to share in the sport, shooting Jewish children as they ran like hares."[3] A witness to a mass execution in Minsk said the shooters "seemed merry while sitting on top of the execution pits with machine guns and behaved as if they were at a wedding party."

The willing, even enthusiastic, participation by ordinary soldiers and mid-level officers was instrumental to smooth operation of the Nazi killing machine. "It quickly became apparent that even at the lowest levels in the chain of command there would be no resistance to the shooting orders," wrote Konrad Kwiet. "On the contrary, the rank and file of the murderous apparatus offered through their actions the clearest evidence of the feasibility of the Final Solution."[4]

Himmler unwittingly helped lay the foundation for post-war denial in December 1941 when he ordered that massacres during the day were to be followed by *gemüt-lich* evenings—social gatherings—which amounted to brainwashing, or conscience-cleansing, sessions. Psychiatrists would have had a field day with Himmler had he not committed suicide shortly after being captured by Allied troops in 1945. While the after-parties ostensibly were intended to foster bonding and loyalty among officers, Himmler appeared to be addressing, perhaps subconsciously, his own oft-stated revulsion for the slaughters. He became agitated and turned "white as cheese" while witnessing the shooting of Jews at Minsk early in Operation Barbarossa. At least in word, Himmler seemed more repulsed than many of the men who carried out his orders.

"It is the holy duty of senior leaders and commanders *personally* to ensure that none of our men who have to fulfill this burdensome duty should ever be brutalized or suffer damage to their spirit and character in doing so," he stated in his *gemütlich* order, adding that it was "impermissible" to discuss "facts and related numbers" from the day's events at such gatherings. "It should be an evening on which they sit and eat at table in the best German domestic style, and music, lectures, and introductions to the beauties of German intellectual and emotional life occupy the hours."

This exactly describes the gatherings to which my Jewish mother and her sister were often summoned during the year they spent in Nazi-occupied Kremenchug in central Ukraine. Masquerading as non-Jews after escaping the ravines of Drobitsky Yar near their home in Kharkov, Zhanna and Frina made their way west to Kremenchug, where they served in a troupe of locals organized by Nazi commanders to keep their troops entertained. Some evenings, they were "invited" to dine with *Wehrmacht* field officers and Gestapo in their private quarters, and then to play for them—Bach, Beethoven, Chopin.

There were other practices and events that aided the killers in building emotional armor to deflect pangs of conscience or actual accountability for their crimes. One was the concept of *Blutkitt*, or "blood cement," the result of group involvement in crimes such as shootings. The family that killed together stayed together. If everyone was guilty, *no one* was guilty. Physical as well as emotional distance from the crime made the Nazi conscience grow fonder of denial.

"The physical retreat from the Eastern occupied territories enabled the perpetrators to disassociate themselves psychologically from their crimes and facilitated their more or less smooth integration . . . into postwar German society," wrote historian Jürgen Matthäus. "Even decades after the war, few of those former SS and policemen who became suspects or defendants in court cases displayed signs grasping the significance of what they had done in the East."⁵

For those who ended up in the dock at Nuremberg, denial *was* just a river in Egypt. Their emotional armor could protect the killers from themselves—their own demons and consciences, if they had not totally atrophied from disuse—but not from the blunt force of law that pierced the armor and exposed their specious rationalizing about obedience to orders.

"The Charter of this tribunal recognizes that one who has committed criminal acts may not take refuge in superior orders nor in the doctrine that his crimes were acts of states," said Robert Jackson, chief U.S. counsel, in his opening statement at Nuremberg. If those dodges were allowed, Jackson added, it would result in "immunity for practically everyone concerned in the really great crimes against peace and mankind."

In a lovely *coup de grâce* of karmic justice—of what goes around and comes around—the final nail in the Germans' legal coffin came from their own military code.

"If the execution of a military order in the course of duty violates the criminal law, then the superior officer giving the order will bear the sole responsibility," Jackson said, quoting from the German code. He continued: "However, the obeying subordinate will share the punishment . . . if he has exceeded the order given to him, or if it was within his knowledge that the order of his superior officer concerned an act by which it was intended to commit a civil or military crime or transgression."

The German Military Code thus effectively indicted every German soldier who had shot an unarmed Jew, slammed a Jewish baby against a rock, or filled a synagogue with the sick and insane and set it ablaze. But it was the officers who sent them to kill—on orders from Hitler, they reminded everyone in court—who faced justice at Nuremberg. Jackson made it clear the buck stopped with them. "Their responsibility is correspondingly great and may not be shifted to that fictional being, 'the state,' which cannot be produced for trial, cannot testify, and cannot be sentenced."

The defendants, however, could be tried and sentenced—and they were. In the end, both their crimes and their guilt were—undeniable.

TOP: Kharkov citizens exult at the hanging of four convicted war criminals—three Germans and a Russian traitor—on Dec. 19, 1943. BOTTOM: The crowd surges toward the gallows of fresh-cut wood erected on the grounds of a market burned down by the Nazis. Journalists estimated 40,000 to 50,000 onlookers.

TOP: The makeshift courtroom in the Opera House, illuminated with klieg lights for the filming of movies and newsreels. *Photo courtesy of Yad Vashem.*
BOTTOM: Military Tribunal of the 4th Ukrainian Front. Presiding judge (center), Major General Miasnikov. *Photo courtesy of Yad Vashem.*

TOP: Defendants Bulanov, Ritz, Reinhard, Langheld in the courtroom. Captain Langheld was the only German to maintain his military bearing, even on the gallows. *Photo courtesy of Yad Vashem.* BOTTOM: SS Lt. Ritz standing before the court, perhaps pleading for mercy before the judges retire to decide the sentences. *Photo courtesy of Yad Vashem.*

TOP: Russian writers Konstantin Simonov and Ilya Ehrenburg (co-editor with Vassily Grossman of *The Black Book*) observing at the Kharkov trial. *Photo courtesy of the U.S. Holocaust Museum.* BOTTOM: Reinhard Retzlaff, corporal in the German Secret Police, testifies at the trial. *Photo courtesy of Yad Vashem.*

The defendants. Clockwise, starting at lower left: Mikhail Bulanov,
Hans Ritz, Reinhard Retzlaff, William Langheld.
Photos courtesy of Sovfoto.

OPPOSITE TOP: Russian soldiers memorialized at Sokolniky Park outside Kharkov, which exchanged hands four times during the war. OPPOSITE BOTTOM: Memorial at Drobitsky Yar near Kharkov where 16,000 Jews were murdered and buried in ravines by Germans. ABOVE: Two of four tablets at Drobitsky Yar memorial engraved with the admonition "Thou Shalt Not Kill," in myriad languages.

TOP: Markers at the site of the tractor factory on the outskirts of Kharkov that served as a temporary ghetto for Jews on the way to the killing field at Drobitsky Yar. Monument to left honors Righteous Gentiles who hid Jews from the Nazis. BOTTOM: Entrance pathway leading to the Motherland statue at Sokolinky Park near Kharkov.

CHAPTER FIFTEEN

C oming of age in the sixties, the child of classical musicians on the faculty of a liberal arts university in the Midwest, I probably was destined to grow up liberal. My father was raised a Roman Catholic in Charlottesville, Va., no enclave of raging liberal thought in the early 1920s, but a prodigious talent for violin sent him at age fourteen to the Juilliard School of Music in New York where he absorbed the culture and progressive politics and became, in my mother's words, "the best 'Jew' I ever knew." He was against the Vietnam War before I was.

If anything, my mother was even more liberal. This made her a rare bird among Russian immigrants of her generation who as a group could be found holed up at the far right end of the American political spectrum. In some cases this no doubt was a reaction to harsh experiences in the Soviet Union. Others may have decided that adopting the views and rhetoric of Cold Warriors such as Barry Goldwater and Ronald Reagan was the best way of proving their bona fides as patriotic Americans. A desire to accommodate and fit in was not part of my mother's DNA, to put it mildly.

I don't remember my mother talking politics very much. She expressed her view on Vietnam by obtaining a letter from a renowned Indianapolis doctor stating that a congenital hip defect made me unfit for military purposes (among many other reasons). The letter resulted in a military classification similar to some of my college report cards: 4-F.

Her maternal instinct to keep her son safe aside, my mother's liberalism was most evident in a powerful affinity and admiration for the oppressed and dispossessed, African-Americans in particular. In the sixties, she befriended leaders of the Black Student Union at IU and invited them to our home. Because of the troubles they've seen and survived, my mother regarded blacks as the most exemplary Americans. At the time, I knew nothing about her Holocaust experience, but now I better understand her visceral bond with the descendants of slaves and those forced to endure humiliation and insult at the whim of society.

For me the most the most surprising plank of my mother's strict orthodox liberalism was an unswerving opposition to capital punishment. Conversely, this was the only liberal issue on which I was an apostate, and I could not account for it. There were no dots connecting the rest of my fundamentalist lefty agenda to a tolerance, if not embrace, of the death penalty. There was nothing in my life—no rape or murder of a family member—that would have given me a taste for eye-for-an-eye justice. At least nothing I was aware of on a conscious level. From time to time over the years, after I learned of her Holocaust experience, I did ask my mother if she would have opposed the death penalty even for Hitler. Yes, she said every time, killing an unarmed person was a cowardly, bestial act, no matter the person's crime. I wonder, in this instance, if her hatred for Hitler was trumped by an instinctive solidarity with those whose great crime was simply being Jewish or black.

In November 2010, as I prepared for my trip to Ukraine to do research for this book, I was startled to detect a crack in the great wall of my mother's opposition to capital punishment. Looking back now, I should not have been so surprised. For the first time in her life, she was reading an account of the Holocaust—not including my telling of her story, *Hiding in the Spotlight*, which she read in manuscript at my request, making annotations. She had not read Anne Frank's diary or *Night*—though she revered Eli Wiesel— much less a psychological horrorscape like *Sophie's Choice*. She had not seen *Schindler's List*, *The Pianist*, or the TV miniseries *Holocaust*. Nor had she ever visited a Holocaust museum, even though a fine one, the Breman, is ten minutes from her Atlanta condo. I guess she saw no reason to go out of her way to revisit a nightmare.

It was against this backdrop that a friend in Ukraine sent her a 120-page article, in Russian, about the Nazi occupation of Kharkov and the subsequent trial. There was a name on the article, but it wasn't clear if it was a student paper, the work of a scholar, or the report of an amateur historian. Knowing no more, I asked my mother if she could read it and translate any parts she thought would be helpful in my research. Neither of us suspected it would be a transformative experience.

A few days later, November 28, I received an ecstatic e-mail from Atlanta. "The translation is moving along well, very well, and no use trying to imagine what's in it," my mother wrote. "It's so much more dramatic than we can guess. But what a thriller! I am going back to it in a minute."

By the next morning, her mood had darkened. "I am staying astounded the entire time while translating. My mind cannot cope with the German brilliance of invention—how to kill the most people in the shortest time and the cheapest price. I now have basic aversion toward the country of great music. I want to take all the leftover butchers, put them on the verge of a high & steep hill, put them on the edge of it & then start the automatic guns. Not a tear would be lost by me."

She dispatched Dick, her dear friend and condo mate of twenty years, to Office Depot to fax me page after page of her translation in longhand. It was immediately apparent to me that the article was written by someone with deep knowledge of the subject.

"The Nazis broke into the city of Kharkov on Oct. 24, 1941. They were equipped with the most terrifying weaponry. In no time they had black swastikas over a large building and on the wall a sign stating, 'Death for appearing on a street from 8 p.m. until 5 a.m. Death for opposing occupying power. Death for hiding partisans.' Dangling from ropes in the wind were bodies totally frozen and stiff."

At the end of one fax, after translating another numbing litany of Nazi brutality and sadism visited on the residents of Kharkov, my mother took a deep breath. Something new was stirring in her, a voice I had never heard, of bitterness and joyful revenge.

"The next are my words," she wrote. "Now I am sure I understand why they invaded Russia twice and I can guarantee that they are getting ready for the next time. Himmler said the Slavs would only need to know how to sign their names, otherwise they do not need to learn anything because the Germans are the only people that deserve to be taught more than that. But let's look at these supermen and their gaswagens. What did they win? They cannot hide any longer their lowdown motives. Hello, supermenches, how superior do you feel after losing to Russia *twice*? Rotz of ruck, Fritzes!"

Is it possible for a Holocaust survivor to lose her innocence at 83? I read it in my mother's e-mail on December 2, 2010, telling me she could not go on with the translation.

"Someone else, maybe in Kharkov, will have to translate the pages which describe Drobitsky Yar. I cannot go over that horror again because I think that I am reading about my parents & grandparents. It's just that I lose my emotional balance and cannot control the hate I feel toward all the world that was supportive of the Germanic mentality. They hated and kept destroying Ukraine because they never expected what was going to happen there. Good heavens, a trial of the greatest race on Earth by the people of Kharkov? Yup! Your mother wants to go back and have them rebuild Russia, the whole place including Siberia, and then get ready for the last step—throwing them all alive on the bottom of Drobitsky Yar. Sorry, I am not anymore against capital punishment."

The next e-mail I received was on the morning of December 8, the day before my departure for Ukraine. I had sent a review of the French translation of *Hiding in the Spotlight* and she was unable to open the file.

"I can stand anything but more stories about the Germans in Russia," she wrote. "I now know at least something, but none of it like anything I ever suspected. I imagine by now you have read your share about Germans who were saved by great many supporters all over the globe and maybe even some Russians. I still want to write some for you because you have to be up on this story somehow. I just hope that you will not have to give speeches or be visible in Ukraine because I know that the Germans will never stop preparing for the next round of their beloved occupation, and a lot of Russian land is good in many ways. Kharkov is terrific. I mean it was. I will let you work now. I am watching my screen here for news."

The "news"—of deliverance and justice for the people of Kharkov and Ukraine, of condign punishment at the end of a rope for their tormentors—was to be found in my mother's own handwriting deep in one of many faxed pages of the translated article by her countryman.

"In the nightmarish hell of concentration camps, on top of burned towns, by freshly buried graves, came belief about the inevitability and righteousness of such a trial, the kind of trial that will not only disclose unimaginable butchery of the German military but also stand as a warning to anyone else."

CHAPTER SIXTEEN

A sharp unmelodic jangle pierced my sleep, jolting me awake but disoriented in total darkness. The phone! I scrambled out of bed to a small desk and grabbed the offending receiver.

"Good morning, Mr. Dawson, this is Victor at the front desk. You asked to be called at 5:45 A.M."

"Da, da—spasiba," I said.

It was December 15, 2010. This was the day I had been dreading. It was also the reason I had come to Kharkov. Sixty-nine Decembers ago my mother, her sister, and her parents and paternal grandparents awoke on this day to an unimaginable fate. The day before, December 14, 1941, the occupying Nazis had posted notices across Kharkov ordering all Jews to report the next day to public squares for transport to an abandoned tractor factory southeast of the city. The blind hope of Dmitri Arshansky and others was that they were being sent to a camp to serve as slave laborers until the war ended, victoriously, and they could return home. My mother had darker premonitions.

We knew it could mean only two things: they would make us laborers in a concentration camp, or it meant the end of our lives.

At noon under a powder-blue sky that belied intense cold, 16,000 Jews began the eight-mile trek to the factory. The streets were coated with fresh snow. Whip-wielding German soldiers and *Schutzmannschaften*—Ukrainian collaborators—patrolled the sea of marchers, some pulling carts or sleds with belongings, as it flowed glacially on Moscow Avenue out of the city. When darkness fell, the procession was still well short of the factory. By morning, the roadside and surrounding fields were littered with the bodies of marchers dead from exposure. The Arshanskys had survived by huddling together for warmth in a tiny shed Dmitri found.

The living, those who made it to the factory, would soon envy the dead. The buildings at the complex had no heat or running water; a galaxy of broken windows produced conditions of a giant meat locker. The captives were given no food (some had brought scraps from home) and the only "water" was a filthy liquid more likely to cause diarrhea than to slake thirst. The women's "toilet" was a shed with three holes in the ground. It was a sight my mother could never forget, or forgive.

It was inhuman. The sight of women the age of my mother and grandmother made me shake in shame for the Germans. I wanted to put those who created this hell in the same place as these women. That's where I wanted Hitler and Himmler and Goebbels.

After two weeks in this fresh circle of hell, after hundreds had frozen or starved or died of disease, after the German soldiers had taken a day off from killing to celebrate Christmas and then the New Year, the surviving Jews were ordered to relinquish all their valuables and prepare once again for transport. Their destination was not a labor camp in Poltava as they had repeatedly been told. Poltava was to the south, and they were being marched in a different direction. The scales at last had fallen from Dmitri Arshansky's eyes. He did not know where it would end, but he knew instinctively it was a final journey. Perhaps he also sensed that they were now less than two miles from a place with no exit.

As the throng of doomed Jews—organized in rows of six, the size of the Arshansky family—crept toward their fate, Dmitri reached deep into a pocket of his winter coat and pulled out a gold watch he had managed to conceal when the Nazis were confiscating property. He flashed it at a young *Schutzmannschaften* walking alongside. "Look at me," Dmitri said quietly, "you can see that I am not a Jew. Please just turn your eyes away and let my little girl go." The guard snatched the watch. "Let her go and I will pretend not to see."

Zhanna, walking next to Dmitri, heard the exchange. Moments later, she saw her opportunity up ahead—two babushkas by the side of the road watching the march. Next to them on the ground was a mass of unraveled barbed wire. She would leap from the line and pretend to become entangled in the wires, just another observer. Her father slipped his coat over fourteen-year-old Zhanna's slender shoulders, and she was gone.

I became one of the gray women, just watching the column. I saw a German looking straight at me, and I thought he would stop and grab me, but he kept going.

So did her family. Zhanna watched them disappear over the horizon. Frina is the only one she would ever see again. They found each other days later in Kharkov, but Frina has refused to reveal how she escaped. Maybe she dashed out of line as Zhanna did, or she reached Drobitsky Yar with her parents and grandparents and miraculously dodged their horrible fate at the bottom of the ravine. I suspect we will never know.

I had come to Kharkov to make that final journey, to walk the same route from the tractor factory to Drobitsky Yar. And this time, unlike my first visit in 2006, I would not stop at the precipice. This time I would go to the depths of the yawning ravine that swallowed the 16,000 human sacrifices to Hitler's *Judenfrei* fantasies. In 2006, I'd been there on a cloudless September day when the ravine and graves and monuments to horror were bathed in a sunny, narcotizing glow. This time I would be walking in the same punishing cold as December 15, 1941.

I was no martyr to my mission, however. I did not intend to freeze. The forecast called for a high of 15 degrees, and I planned to walk in the morning before the mercury shot up to double digits. This was tough for a guy from Florida who does not retain heat well to begin with. For the first time in my life, I put on a pair of long johns, black and form-fitting. Looking in the mirror, I felt like the lead in an AARP production of *Spider-Man*. To that layer I added a shirt and a padded vest. For my feet, three pairs of heavy-duty socks and instant-heat insoles from the hunting-gear aisle at Outdoor World. My neighbor had loaned me a pair of hiking boots suitable for Grizzly Adams. I had gloves the label said were made for "extreme cold," but I had tested them in downtown Kharkov and my fingertips were freezing in 15 minutes. Watching Ukrainians passing by, I figured out their secret to warm hands: *keep them in your pockets.* I had a scarf to cover my face and a stocking cap to keep the heat from escaping through my head. Finally, a puffy new coat made of a poly-synthetic, wind-resistant material—a gift from my mother on my last visit to see her before the trip. I already had a good winter coat, but she was insistent.

"You will need this," she said. "I do not want you to be cold."

Those words were so familiar. They seemed almost ritualistic, an incantation. My mother was in the habit of presenting winter coats to me and my brother Bill and other family as gifts. They were given with love, but also with a measure of passion and urgency not usually attached to an article of clothing. Not until that morning in my hotel room in Ukraine, as I dressed for the walk to Drobitsky Yar, did I stop to wonder: Every time my mother insistently handed me a new coat, was she unconsciously reliving the moment her father had placed his coat on her shoulders before she escaped the death march?

I fortified myself for the journey with a breakfast of eggs, cheese, baked cabbage and peppers, black bread with honey and apple preserves, and strong coffee in the lovely Hotel Chichikov dining room where, per widespread local custom, smoking is still allowed—and enjoyed. The young English-speaking desk staff had called a cab for me, explaining my destination to the driver who spoke even less English than I do Russian. Of the thirty or so random words I retained from my bilingual childhood, most are not survival words for a tourist, unless you need information about a dog, pencil, room, housefly, movie, or herring.

I settled my Michelin Man shape into the back seat of the cab and exchanged smiles across the language barrier with the twenty-something driver.

"Dobray ootra (good morning)," I said, clearly surprising him.

"Dobray ootra!"

"Drobitsky Yar?" I said hopefully.

"Da, da."

In fact, I was not going all the way to Drobitsky Yar. I was getting out at the site of the tractor factory, the temporary ghetto, and then walking the final distance to the ravine. I had been to the ghetto site in 2006 and had passed it just the day before when I traveled by bus with a large group to a commemorative service at Drobitsky Yar. We would end up hopelessly lost in translation if I tried to explain all this to the driver. I would just have to point as we approached the ghetto site.

From the Chichikov we wended through side streets to downtown and then to Moscow Prospect. In 1941 it was a rutted rural road suitable for donkey carts. Today it's a major four-lane thoroughfare lined with a hodgepodge of commercial development and the occasional factory and apartment complex. It's no place for pedestrians, but development thins after a few miles and the countryside creeps closer to the pavement. I could see the ghetto site coming up on the right. The wooded acreage is enclosed by a forest-green, corrugated-metal security fence that stood out against the wintry tableau.

I motioned for the driver to pull over, and he gave me a quizzical look. "Drobitsky Yar," he insisted, pointing straight ahead.

I motioned again for him to pull over, more dramatically this time, and he decided not to mess with the crazy American. Once we were stopped, I tried to explain that I was going to walk the rest of the way.

"Drobitsky Yar," I said, pointing to myself and doing the international sign language for walking with two fingers.

"Ah! Da-da," he said, and then pulled out his arsenal of English. "Seven kilometers."

I had assumed the old ghetto site was closed off because it is sacred/profane ground. That was overly sentimental on my part. In fact, the security fence surrounds a building site, or would-be building site. Mounted at the top of the fence is a colorful conceptual drawing of a high-rise residential development that's never gotten off the ground. Jewish leaders in Kharkov, including the Chief Rabbi, have vigorously protested the project, noting the presence of memorials marking the ghetto as a way station to Drobitsky Yar. Nevertheless, the fate of this sacred real estate remains an issue in post-Soviet Ukraine, where "private" and "profit" are no longer heretical notions.

Just outside the fence are two monuments side by side. "The Wall of Sorrow" is a flat, brick-colored slab, about ten feet high and eight feet long, with square and rectangular cutouts. Flowers had spilled out these openings when I last visited on that balmy September day in 2006. On this December day they were just stark holes in a wall, windows in a prison. A plaque on the memorial, erected fifty-one years after the fact in 1992, says, "In 1941 there was a Jewish ghetto here. Its prisoners were executed in Drobitsky Yar." To the left of the wall on the ground is a boulder with a plaque reading, "To Rescuers—Righteous Gentiles. Grateful Jews of Kharkov."

My mother was an insatiable—her parents would say incorrigible—explorer as a young child, pushing through doors and boundaries in her hometown of Berdyansk on the Sea of Azov in southeastern Ukraine. Maybe it was an inherited instinct to breach barriers, married to the moment, but I was seized by a need to go over the fence and stand on that ground, to see and feel what was there. But it was too high and slick to climb, and I found no place where I could squeeze through. Still unsatisfied, I am left with a snapshot of trees and a snowy field taken through a narrow opening where two sides of the fence meet.

I pressed on toward Drobitsky Yar, dodging piles of dirty snow on the roadside, too close to the passing traffic for comfort. I was relieved to encounter a footpath running parallel to the highway a few feet below the pavement. It was packed with snow and lined by tall trees. The 9 A.M. sun was a pale silver circle cold as a full moon over the fields. The deserted footpath stretched out before me. I opened my cell phone and found a text message from my wife Candy in Orlando where it was just after 2 A.M. "Thinking of you, walking with you every step of the way. Be safe and know I love you."

The footpath ended and I was back on the main road. I passed a gas station, a man selling oranges out of his trunk, and a jumble of shops that we would call a strip mall in the U.S., except these were ramshackle and more jammed together. I saw two women standing outside a flower shop smoking, watching—and I realized it was in this stretch, in the final kilometers before Drobitsky Yar, that my mother bolted out of line and became one of the gray women on the side of the road. And somewhere near here, the escapee was taken in and given shelter for the night by Ukrainians, who risked their lives by harboring a Jew, before continuing her perilous journey back to Kharkov.

We exchanged glances, and one of the women shouted something in Russian I didn't understand. "Amerikanski!" I said, shrugging my shoulders and turning my palms up. They smiled broadly and waved for me to come inside. "Nyet, spasiba (no thank you)!" I shouted, and marched on.

Another canopied footpath led me along more open fields and then back to the road and a bridge over train tracks. The traffic was accelerating. The highway began to diverge, with exits to other places. None led to Poltava.

When he saw the trucks go north, my father knew they were going to kill us because there was nothing to the north. It was the road to nowhere.

Over the next hill, on the left, I spotted a bus shelter. It looked freshly painted in robin-egg blue and brilliant red blooms on the back wall. A sign across the roofline announced the name of this stop. It was in Russian, but I could read it: Drobitsky Yar.

A few hundred yards beyond the shelter away from the highway was the outline of a menorah. At the base of the menorah is a plaque that says, "This is the place where the dead teach the living ones." This was my stop.

CHAPTER SEVENTEEN

As I was preparing for this visit to Ukraine, I came across *The Time of the Assassins*, a novel by Godfrey Blunden, an Australian journalist who covered World War II from the Battle of Britain to the battles for Stalingrad and Kharkov. Published in 1952, *Assassins* is about the alliances, betrayals, and butcheries of Nazi-occupied Kharkov. Like *Inglourious Basterds* and *Life is Beautiful*, *Assassins* is fiction that pays tribute to fact by giving it life in our imaginations.

Near the end of the novel, a Russian collaborator, Dr. Karandash, visits a place outside Kharkov clearly modeled on Drobitsky Yar. One winter day, an SS officer named Müller takes him to a "tractor factory" and then "a small ravine some distance from the factory . . . to see the work that was being done." Karandash likens the frozen ravine to an oil barge—"It began in shape like the bow of a ship"—with a deck stretching hundreds of yards.

"And down the middle of the deck, so to speak, there was this path, like the catwalk on a big tanker. . . . What we were walking on, even though its even white cover made it look like a huge tarpaulin-covered deck, was in actual fact ice."

Karandash and Müller step off the catwalk onto the ice, which cracks and opens up under them. They go tumbling like two Alices down a rabbit hole—"sliding, grappling at the side of the crevasse, plunging finally in a metallic shower of ice to the bottom of the abyss"—which deposits them not in a Wonderland but a chamber of horrors.

"We had fallen into one of their disposal pits. The ravine was full of bodies. How many? How can I guess? What does it matter? Does a mathematical symbol have reality? I have heard since that there are fifty thousand bodies there. It is not improbable. Below the snow-covered decks of that huge tank-barge there was a cargo of dead . . . legs and arms and bodies interlocked like the links of a sheet of chain mail, the snow sifting through the chinks of the mass, thawing and then freezing hard, joining it all into one flesh as hard as iron and as brittle as glass. . . . We saw bodies all around us, some ruddy, wax-like . . . others white as marble . . . tall and short, old and young, people of all cultures, men, women, and children. At our feet at the bottom of the crevasse there was the head of an old man. In our fall, one of us had fallen on the old man's head and under the sudden weight it had snapped off, as clean as a carrot, and as raw, and now it rested at our feet, staring up at us through frosty spectacles."

The image pulsed in my mind's eye as I turned off the Kharkov-Rostov road and began the long walk from the highway and bus stop past the black menorah down a winding road to the ravine. At first glance from this distance the snow-covered ravine is just one benign element of a pastoral landscape, a Ukrainian Currier & Ives idyll. Then on the horizon the eye catches the shape of a flame, the pale stone beacon of the Drobitsky Yar memorial, shattering the momentary illusion. My first trip down this road four years earlier was in a car on a beautiful fall day when green and gold foliage obscured what lay beyond. Now, as I walked by, the denuded winter landscape exposed the telltale topography of ravines—deep gashes in the Earth's flesh. They were so much steeper and deeper than I had recalled. Dr. Karandash's voice suddenly intruded.

"I remember it was very bleak, very quiet, and we did not at all like this feeling. . . . We had not gone more than a hundred meters when we saw . . . a human leg, a bare leg, bootless, projecting out of the snow, just as if its owner had dived off the side of the ravine . . . into the snow and had stuck there in the drift, his leg pointing upward."

Finally, the rollercoaster road rises to a wide plateau and the memorial—a soaring white stone arch tapering to a flame shape, which shelters two tablets like those Moses delivered, inscribed with "Thou Shall Not Kill" in myriad languages. Underground is a candle-lit space where the names of 4,300 of the 16,000 victims are etched on marble walls and the ceiling is the black winter sky brilliant with stars—supposedly the last thing the condemned Jews saw, though the designer's anodyne vision surely belies the truth. For most Jews who died here, the final image fixed in their minds likely was the bottom of a ravine filled with corpses.

"All the skeletons embrace one another in the ground," wrote poet Yevgeny Yevtushenko in *The Apple Trees of Drobitsky*, written in 1989, twenty-eight years after publication of his celebrated *Babi Yar*, about the slaughter of 34,000 in the ravines near Kiev. Few outside Ukraine know of the killings at Drobitsky or of Yevtushenko's poem about the earth there "endowed by the dead." The apple trees of Drobitsky, adjacent to the memorial, still bear fruit. I nearly lost a camera to thieves there on my 2006 visit—a material loss so embarrassingly negligible on that sacred-profane ground that I hesitate to mention it.

My mother escaped the march to Drobitsky before reaching the ravine, but her sister, Frina, most likely did not—yet she survived. Like I've said above, Frina has never said how she escaped, but survivor testimony from other yars in Ukraine lends credence to Yevtushenko's poetic vision in *Apple Trees* when he asks a teenager named Ruvin to "tell us how, naked as the day you were born, all smeared with blood, your face drained bloodless, you crawled out from under, shoving bodies aside."

Behind the arch on a lower plateau is a block of reddish Zhitomyr granite, a monument to the victims of the entire Holocaust, with six notches on the side for the six million. It was erected in 1998 to correct—or supplement—the monument next to it put up in 1955 by Soviet authorities, whose official state denial of a Jewish Holocaust is reflected in the cryptic inscription on a small weathered obelisk: "The victims of the fascist terror 1941–1942 lie here."

Just beyond this second plateau, the ground starts to slope sharply toward the bottom of the ravine. I didn't go there on my first visit. I had begun walking down the slope, gravity and momentum quickening my pace, pulling me headlong toward the pit. But something made me stop after thirty yards. I turned and walked along the edge of the abyss. Looking down, I could see discarded tires in the tall grass and brambles, and I could walk no farther. The tour guide at the memorial, a young woman named Irina, said that sometimes on a summer day when she looks at the ravine, "I see strawberries and cranberries growing. It reminds me of blood." She has a recurring nightmare: "Guns firing, children falling, lying in blood. I am inside a huge building. When I want to leave I can't find a door. Someone tells me, 'Use a rope.' Then I wake up."

In 2006, Irina was in her fifth year as a guide at Drobitsky Yar. I wondered why she chose to return every day to a place that will give her visions of bloody strawberry fields forever. "I somehow feel related to all those visiting here," she said.

So it was both homecoming and "family" reunion when, four years later, in 2010, I knocked on the office door at the memorial and Irina answered. She wondered something similar about me—why had *I* come back? To complete my journey, I told her. To walk from the ghetto to the memorial, and then to the bottom of the ravine. We laughed over memories of the first visit when I chased two boys through the apple trees in pursuit of my stolen camera, only to corner them empty-handed—and how Irina had gone into the orchard and returned forty-five minutes later with my camera and a craven apology from the boys. After your walk in the ravine, she said, we shall have hot tea.

There are steps going down one side of the ravine to a path on the bottom leading to steps going back up the other side in a rough U-shape. I started down the left side, treading gingerly as it was hard to make out the steps in the fresh snow. I descended deeper and deeper and began to experience—in the words of Dr. Karandash—"the feeling of being closed in between the walls of the ravine." I was now far below the precipice from which I had stared down into the pit. I was looking up the steep slope at treetops and sky. I was in the crevasse with Dr. Karandash as he heard "a terrible sound . . . a high scream between the ice walls. I imagined at that moment the sound was made by all those people there, those souls in anguish crying in the night, crying at one moment all around us so the sound would seem to shatter the ice and then, diminishing as it rushed upwards, skywards, a long-drawn spirit wail ascending into the black frozen heaven."

The report from Soviet authorities who unearthed bodies from killing fields across Kharkov eerily echoes Blunden's fiction:

"In most graves they lay in extreme disorder, fantastically intertwined, forming tangles of human bodies defying description. The corpses lay in such a manner that they can be said to have been dumped or heaped but not buried in common graves. The fact that before being murdered, Soviet citizens were stripped of their clothes and footwear is fully confirmed by the medico-legal examinations. During exhumations the experts in most cases discovered naked or half-naked bodies."

I reached the bottom of the ravine and stopped. Suddenly, I was angry at how peaceful it was, how beautiful, under the new snow. It seemed a negation of what happened here, a grotesque travesty of truth that this beauty and serenity could muffle the high screams of my grandparents and great-grandparents whose bones lay here, fantastically intertwined.

"That is the one thing I cannot stop thinking about—how they died," my mother has said to me many times. "I don't know how they died."

I have known for some years, with reasonable certainty, how her family died. But I have never responded to her lament by offering the information, because I do not believe that she really wants to know—or rather, she dreads being told what she already must know but has relegated to a black box deep in her subconscious.

In September 1943, with the Nazis in full retreat from Ukraine, the District Commission for Determination and Investigation of the Crimes of the German-Fascist Invaders and their Collaborators issued its report, "On the Mass Shooting of Jews by the German Murderers in the Drobitzki Valley." The eleven-member commission included military, political, academic, and religious representatives from the Kharkov region.

"'The Commission opened up two pits near the village of Rogan in the valley of Drobitzki, one of them 100 meters long and 18 to 20 meters wide, and second 60 meters long and 20 meters wide. According to the finding of the Expert Medical Commission, upward of 15,000 bodies were buried in these pits. Five hundred were removed from the pits, of which 215 were submitted to medico-legal examination. They included the bodies of 83 men, 117 women, and 60 children and infants. It was established that the cause of death of almost all these persons was a wound and hole in the back of the skull caused by the passage of a bullet. This indicated that the shooting was carried out from behind the person to be killed and from a short distance away."

There is little reason to believe that Dmitri Arshansky, his wife, Sara, and his parents eluded this fate. My mother and her sister are the only known survivors of the march from the tractor factory to Drobitsky Yar. After a few minutes, I began my slow ascent, climbing out of the grave step by step. My cell phone rang—it was Candy. "Are you okay?" Never had her voice sounded sweeter.

Irina was waiting for me in the office with hot tea and cookies. I had arranged for the same taxi that dropped me at the ghetto site to pick me up at noon at Drobitsky Yar and take me back to Kharkov for my next appointment. Something must have been lost in translation—he never showed up or called. Around one o'clock, Irina got on the phone and had an animated conversation with someone she obviously knew well. She hung up and said, in English, "We walk . . . to road."

Emotionally spent, I was in no position to argue. We put on our coats and headed out the door. The snow had stopped and a worker was shoveling the broad walkway in front of the memorial arch. Irina, in spiky heels worn by all Ukrainian women in all weather and all terrains, led me back to the winding road. We were marching out of Drobitsky Yar. I looked back at the ravines, vanishing into the landscape like fugitives.

We reached the highway, and Irina motioned me over to one side. "We wait," she said. Behind us was the nine-foot menorah marking the entrance to Drobitsky Yar. I went over for a last look and read the inscription again. "This is the place where the dead teach the living ones." I placed four stones at the base of the menorah in memory of my grandparents and great-grandparents whose bones lie beneath these strawberry fields.

After a few minutes, a little car turned off the highway and pulled up in front of us. A smiling man, Irina's friend, opened the door and we climbed in. On the way back to Kharkov, I thought about my trip to the bottom of the ravine, and wondered what the dead ones had been trying to teach me.

CHAPTER EIGHTEEN

S ince the British packed their wigs and red coats and went home more than two hundred years ago, no foreign army has occupied American soil. Before 9/11, no foreign enemy had struck a city on the U.S. mainland and left thousands dead—though residents of Atlanta during the Civil War would beg to differ. The markers of that conflict are generally found in the countryside at places like Shiloh and Gettysburg and Chickamauga.

In Kharkov, as in other cities in Ukraine, the evidence of foreign occupation and destruction in our lifetime is around every corner in the commercial district—places of torture, imprisonment, and the banal bureaucracy of terror. Some are memorialized with plaques, others are unmarked. High-fashion mannequins in a store window on Sumskaya Street belie the building's past as Gestapo headquarters during the occupation.

Yuri Radchenko knows them all. Born in Kharkov in 1986, he grew up in Severnaya Saltkova, a vast housing development north of the city. Sprouting to 6-6, Yuri's first passion was basketball. He found his next calling at the age of fifteen at a park where the Nazis slaughtered 4,000 residents of Kharkov, many of them Jews. His interest in this period of Kharkov's history grew into a lifelong fascination. He wrote a thesis on Soviet prisoners of war in Nazi Germany and occupied Europe while at V.N. Karazin Kharkov National University. In 2010, he was a post-graduate student completing a dissertation on the Holocaust in Kharkov and eastern Ukraine when he first responded to my e-mail to the history department requesting information for this book about the Holocaust in Ukraine, specifically Kharkov, and the Kharkov trial.

"Of course I want to help in your project," Yuri wrote. "It is our common duty to remember tragic past of the Holocaust. If you will visit Kharkov, I can be your guide— I have some experience. You must know that Jews were killed not just in Drobitsky Yar, synagogue and ghetto. Many Jewish were exterminated in Sokolniky Park and two prisons of SD (SS security and intelligence service)."

We met on a snowy Friday morning in mid-December outside School 13 where earlier I had addressed—with massive help from the school's English teacher—students the same age as my mother when she'd attended the school seventy years before. Yuri had engaged a cabbie he knew,

Sergy, and his sardine-can compact. I climbed in the front, Yuri folded himself into the back, and we were off through the partly plowed streets of Kharkov. Lean and rangy, Yuri has the metabolism of a greyhound and a hyperkinetic intellect. He speaks Ukrainian, Russian, English, German, and Yiddish—sometimes all at once—and soon will add Hebrew to his crowded tower of Babel.

"Now we are going to visit ex-stalag, prisoner of war camp for Soviet prisoners, which was functioning from 1941 to 1943," Yuri said. "It is on Holodnaya Gora—meaning cold hill. Sources say 10,000 Soviet prisoners died here. We don't know exactly the reason why they died. Starvation, disease—another, another, another. Commanders of SD in Kharkov didn't know how to bury these bodies, so they decide to bury them in Drobitsky Yar. It has very big graves, you know. They decided to do it after the mass shootings there. The prisoners were buried with some patients from mental hospital No. 15. There is no information at Drobitsky Yar about these other murders."

We stood in swirling snow outside the long, faceless building, painted a bilious yellow, with old-school barbed-wire—not razor wire—strung along the tops of walls. It had always been a prison, Yuri said, from the time of the Russian empire to Soviet Ukraine, during the Nazi occupation, and now again. "They have museum inside," he said. "But is very hard to come inside. You must prepare many

documents, many papers. And there is nothing, no signifi-
cation, that here died Soviet prisoners of war."

We clambered back into the welcome warmth of
Sergy's cab. "Now, Greg, we are going to visit ex-S.D.
prison, the first Jewish camp in Kharkov," Yuri said, and
a wildly inappropriate memory suddenly intruded. I had
done something like this before. On one of my trips to
Hollywood as a television critic, I took the legendary
"Grave Line Tour" of celebrity death sites, riding upright
in the back of a silver hearse. Unlike the Jews of Kharkov,
most of these celebrities—Marilyn Monroe, John Belushi,
George Reeves (Superman), among others—died by their
own hand. An exception was Sharon Tate, pregnant wife
of movie director Roman Polanski, who was slaughtered
with three friends in her Hollywood Hills home by Charles
Manson and his enthralled acolytes who later argued they
were only following orders. It was almost as if Hitler had
loosed a million Manson families on Ukraine.

The cab turned down a narrow side street and pulled
up at the curb. I glanced up and down Rybnaya Street at
a mélange of storefronts and saw nothing of obvious historical import. Yuri pointed to a brown retractable door like
those on a garage. This is the first place the Nazis imprisoned Jews, Yuri said.

"It was created in November '41 and existed till
December 1941. Maybe 300 or 500 Jews were held here. In
this camp Germans exploited Jews, there was forced labor

here. They killed one Jew, an old man. They hanged him in the garage. In this garage were the so-called *Gaswagens* used to kill Jews." The mobile units were the precursors to the gas chambers at Auschwitz, Bergen-Belsen, Treblinka, and other death camps.

In his research Yuri discovered the names of six Russian and Ukrainian collaborators who drove these *gaswagens* and worked out of this garage, cleaning and maintaining the death vans between assignments. Only one, Michael Bulanov, was captured, and later stood trial with three Nazi officers. The garage was used as a prison for a month, until the Nazis created a larger ghetto at the tractor factory southeast of the city—on the road to Drobitsky Yar.

One place I had discovered while researching my first book and told Yuri that I needed to see was the synagogue on Grajdanskaya Street (then Meshanskaya), once the hub of the Jewish district. Yuri pointed to several brick, two-story apartment buildings nearby, classics of Jewish architecture and housing at the time, he said. What made them "Jewish?" I asked. Dodging slush and piles of dirty snow, we crossed the street and Yuri opened the door to one of the dilapidated buildings, now seemingly vacant. He pointed to a hollowed-out space in the frame, about waist-high, used to place a Mezuzah.

In December 1941, when the Nazis were gathering the remaining Jews of Kharkov for the march to Drobitsky Yar, there were some too old, too young, or too sick to walk.

The Germans locked them in the synagogue, without heat or water, where they froze to death. The one-story building is now a shuttered magazine publishing plant. Two bronze tablets with gold lettering, one in Russian, the other in Hebrew, tell what happened here. No Germans were ever held accountable for this crime, Yuri said, but a collaborator was arrested and executed for killing a young girl in the synagogue. We stood staring at the tablets, and Yuri told a story about the casualties and accidental heroes of war.

"When the Germans were gone, some Ukrainian boys broke into the synagogue and found two Torahs. They saw a lot of Jewish bodies and took the Torahs home. They didn't know what to do with them. Then they have the idea of using the paper for making cigarettes, but this paper didn't want to burn. They then wanted to sell them but nobody wanted to buy. After the war when the synagogue opened, they took these Torahs to show them. The rabbi tells them, 'You did a very good thing because you saved the Torahs.'"

"Now we will visit very important place, so-called Park of Glory," Yuri said. It was a visit to this park as a teenager that first opened Yuri's eyes to the Holocaust. "It was place of mass shooting by Gestapo. Here were exterminated by bullets 3,500 or 4,000 people during Nazi occupation. Jews, Communists—so-called Communists—so-called Partisans, prisoners of war."

One of the leading executioners and traitors was Alexander Posevin, a former officer in the Red Army. "It is well-known that he shooted Jews in this place" Yuri said. "Posevin had very interesting destiny. He could have died in his bed. He had very good pension, but always had the idea of more, more, more. He was so stupid. He was sergeant in battalion of 28th Red Army of southwestern front. On July 4, 1942 he was captured by Germans in Belgorod region. Next he was Soviet prisoner of war in Stalag on Holodnaya Gora. Germans gave him possibility of freedom, but he must serve them in battalion of local collaborators. He became commander of 200 policemen in the S.D. battalion in Kharkov. He and his policemen took part in mass shootings in Sokolniky Park and in S.D. prison. In August 1943 he escaped and was conscripted in Red Army, hiding his past like other collaborators.

"After war he came home and was living like normal Soviet citizen. He became member of Communist Party and was deputy on local government. But in 1985—anniversary of the end of the war—he asked for higher pension, and the KGB found that there is no information about his activity from August 1942 until August 1943. Many witnesses to his crime were found. He was arrested. There was trial and he was executed in 1988."

The Park of Glory is in Sokolniky Park which sits at the edge of a vast national forest northwest of Kharkov. When we arrived, Sokolniky was covered in fresh snow, still pristine, and light snow was falling. It was noon on a weekday, but tranquil as Sunday morning. Near the entrance was a long, straight path between tall firs draped in snow. The path was so long, it narrowed in the distance. At the end I could make out a grey statue, a human shape whose gender was ambiguous at that distance. As we drew closer and the statue loomed up and then towered over us, I could see that it was a woman, a stern, powerful figure in a peasant dress, hair pulled back revealing an expression of eternal vigilance and infinite sadness. "Motherland."

"Listen," Yuri said. "Do you hear thumping sound? It is the sound of heart beating."

Behind Motherland and her electronically beating heart is a memorial wall, perhaps ten feet high and fifty yards long, with a frieze depicting the tragedies and ultimate triumphs of soldiers and Kharkov citizens in their struggle against the occupying Nazis. It is said that 186,000 soldiers alone died in the four battles of Kharkov. Yuri translated the gold lettering for me.

"It says it is for people who fought for freedom and died for freedom. But really it is a place for people who were innocent, people who were killed without weapons. It is classic Soviet-Brezhnev monument—*classic*. Information about partisans, about the underground movement, about people who fought—it is heroization, just heroization. Here were killed many Jews, but there is no information about Jews."

After the war, Soviet authorities exhumed thousands of bodies from pits across Kharkov including Sokolniky Park. "In two pits in the Sokolniky forest park, bodies were found lying in straight rows, face downward, arms bent at the elbow and hands pressed to faces or necks," the report states. "Such a position of the bodies was not accidental. It proves that victims were forced to lie face downward and were shot in that position."

Motherland would have wept at testimony of Alexander Bespalov, a resident of the nearby Sokolniky settlement, about what he saw on a late June day in 1942.

"I saw how some three hundred girls and women were brought to the forest park in ten or twelve lorries. The unhappy people threw themselves from side to side in their terror, screamed and tore their hair and clothes. Many fainted, but German fascists took no heed of this. With kicks and blows with rifle butts and clubs they forced them to rise to their feet. Those who would not rise were stripped by the executioners and thrown into the pit. Several girls who had children with them tried to flee but were killed.

"I saw how, after a tommy-gun burst, some women staggered toward the Germans with heartrending shrieks, staggering and helplessly waving their hands. The Germans fired on them from their pistols. Demented by fear and grief, women tightly clutched their babies and ran around the clearing trying to save them. Gestapo men snatched the children from them by the leg or arm and threw them alive in the ditch, and when the mothers ran after them toward the ditch they were shot."

The Nazis kept coming back to Sokolniky for more killing. Another local resident, Darya Danilenko, told of hearing gunshots and "incredible shrieks of people" coming from the woods one day in January 1943.

"In the spring of 1943 when the snow melted and the earth filling the ditches had settled, I went with other residents to cover up the ditches. When I came to the place where our Soviet citizens had been shot, I saw that both pits were packed with bodies. Naked human arms and legs could be seen sticking out of the thin layer of earth."

Under the steady sightless gaze of Motherland we made the long walk back to the road where Sergy was waiting in the taxi. Our next stop would be the philharmonic hall on Rymarska Street, site of the old opera house where Bulanov and the Germans stood trial. And finally, the public square where Kharkovites witnessed rough justice for the killers with rope and makeshift gallows. Yuri said he wasn't certain of the location. He directed Sergy to a broad square near the intersection of several streets. It was jammed with a sca of vendor tables and booths and vehicles parked seemingly at random.

I recalled the black-and-white photographs I'd seen at the Kharkov Holocaust Museum of the hangings, and tried to imagine this place sixty-seven years ago without the big

JUDGMENT BEFORE NUREMBERG

commercial buildings and the McDonald's on the corner. Yes, I thought, this could be the place.

Sergy parked in what looked to be an actual, if unmarked, space next to other cars, then went off to speak to a man in a uniform twenty feet away who had gestured to him. When he did not return after fifteen minutes, Yuri went to investigate and found Sergy in the front seat of a police car shuffling through papers. He returned holding a $25 ticket for some invisible violation.

"Classic Ukrainian justice," Yuri said, smiling ruefully. He had little doubt in whose pocket the $25 would end up. I laughed. "Classic *Chicago* justice."

The violations of Bulanov and the three Nazis were impossible *not* to see, and the Ukrainian justice they received—perhaps in this square—was a small down payment for incalculable crimes.

Daylight was fading quickly—it would be dark by four o'clock. The first neon signs were flickering on as Sergy guided the cab out of the marketplace through the wintry gloom.

No matter how many memorials were built and plaques posted in Kharkov, I thought, staring out the window, it would never be enough, the numbers were too great. There would always be an army of unrequited ghosts, in the forests and alleys and shadows of old garages—ghosts in search of sanctuary and a single fleeting moment of recognition by the living that they, too, had once been here.

225

CHAPTER NINETEEN

Before 2009, when I began appearing before strangers to promote *Hiding in the Spotlight,* my mother's Holocaust biography, I was never self-conscious about the fact that I knew almost nothing of her amazing story until I was thirty years old, and that I was a teenager when it first dawned on me that I was actually Jewish.

I remember the looks of shock and disbelief from the audience the first few times these facts slipped out during question-and-answer periods. You would think I had told them I was thirty before I discovered my left hand, or that I was a teenager before learning the truth about Santa Claus.

"Wait!" they would say. "You were THIRTY?"—making it sound like ONE HUNDRED THIRTY.

"Well," I would explain sheepishly, "I was never told. And frankly I never thought to ask. My only religion growing up was Hoosier basketball. I'm sorry! Please feel free to leave right now."

People are kind—so far no one has walked out—but I remain very self-conscious about being possibly the most clueless second-generation Holocaust survivor in the world, or so it feels every time the facts come out and jaws drop across the room. This is why it was such a moment of relief and validation for me when Rabbi Moshe Moskovitz let slip the information that he—chief rabbi of Kharkov—knew almost nothing of his father's Holocaust experience until *he* was thirty and had been chief rabbi for five years.

"I always knew he was in Auschwitz and a survivor, but nothing more," the rabbi told me in his office in the beautifully restored synagogue on Pushkinskaya Street. "He didn't talk about the details until the Spielberg interview with him."

Like my mother, the Rabbi Moskovitz's father, Nissan, broke his virtual silence to be interviewed for The Shoah Project, filmmaker Steven Spielberg's effort—launched after the phenomenal success of *Schindler's List*—to seek out and preserve survivor stories before the fast-approaching day when all the subjects will be gone. Born in 1965 in Venezuela, Rabbi Moskovitz represents a reverse Diaspora of Ukrainian Jews, *returning* to the land his father left in Nazi chains.

Nissan Moskovitz was thirteen when the Germans arrived in his hometown of Chumayev near Khust in far western Ukraine. "We don't know the date," the rabbi told me, but it likely was 1942 or later because the Jews of Chumayev were shipped to Auschwitz instead of being shot and buried on the edge of town—the Nazi method early in Operation Barbarossa, before Auschwitz was in operation. At Auschwitz, the Moskovitz family endured the waking nightmare of instantaneous dissolution—an agony unique to the Holocaust.

"His mother and younger siblings were sent straight to the left to the gas chambers and he was taken to the right line to work," the rabbi said of his father. "Until the end of the war, he went from camp to camp until they were freed by the Russians. After the war he met up with his father, who also survived, in Budapest. From there he went to London and then to Colombia. My mother was in Venezuela, also a survivor. We knew my father was a survivor, but he never spoke of it. At home we always discussed the Holocaust, and he was always quiet with his red eyes. He's very religious, a big believer, even though when you hear his story, what he went through—how do you keep your faith? How do you even believe in people? It doesn't work rationally."

After short-term stints at synagogues in South America, Mexico, and the Caribbean, Moskovitz, then twenty-five, was named chief rabbi in Kharkov in the summer of 1990—an historic moment for Kharkov Jews. Only weeks before, Soviet President Gorbachev had officially returned

GREG DAWSON

the great domed synagogue, built in 1913 and closed by the
Communists in the late 1920s, to the Jewish community of
Kharkov. It was the first shuttered synagogue in the Soviet
Union to resume its original purpose after being used as a
secular playground for decades. Moscow authorities had
even turned it into a sports complex at one point.

"The sports complex was in the actual synagogue
building," the rabbi said. "They added a floor in the main
sanctuary so that football and basketball could be played
at the same time. When we received the synagogue back
in August 1990, the Olympic symbols from 1980 were
still on the windows and the walls, and the additional
floor was still there. All the other synagogues in Kharkov
were no longer functioning. Meshansky synagogue was
burned many years ago and in its place is a factory. The
Chebotarsky 17 synagogue was returned to us in 1998—it
had been used as a traffic police station—now we use it as
a dormitory and yeshiva. Another synagogue is now used as
a planetarium."

Kharkov's Jewish population, about 30,000, is a fraction
of what it was before the war, but a much larger fraction
than for cities in western Ukraine where the population had less warning—in most cases *none*—of the Nazi
advance and its attendant atrocities. Kharkov's pre-war
Jewish population was around 135,000, and most fled east
to the Urals before the Nazis arrived in October 1941, in
contrast to many towns and cities to the west where nearly

230

all the Jews were murdered in the first months of Operation Barbarossa. Writing after the Soviets had pushed the Nazis out in 1944, Vasily Grossman, a Jewish journalist working for the Red Army, lamented that "there are no Jews left in Ukraine"—only a slight exaggeration.

If people at my book events were dumbfounded by what I did not know about myself, I was dumbstruck at what they collectively did not know about the Holocaust in the East, which served as the backdrop for my mother's story. And keep in mind, except for classrooms of captive students, these were self-selected audiences with, presumably, an above-average knowledge of the subject. Who could imagine that I would find the same dearth of knowledge at ground zero of the story itself—Ukraine.

"You would be surprised to know how little people know, even here," Rabbi Moskovitz told me. "When we came in 1990, on the small monument at Drobitsky Yar the word 'Jewish' was not mentioned at all. Even people here who wrote history about what happened never wrote about the Jewish Holocaust in Ukraine. And the sad part is, even today in Ukraine the children, our youth, don't know about the Jewish Holocaust. They know about the war between the Red Army and the Germans, the ones who are scholars. But if you go out on the street to ask about the Holocaust, not many people know about it."

This ignorance is the toxic residue of Soviet anti-Semitism coupled with Kremlin policies that pretended there were no ethnic minorities—*especially* Jews—in the dizzyingly multi-ethnic Soviet Union, just "citizens" and "patriots"—a familiar refrain at the Kharkov trial where the primary victims, Jews, were never mentioned by name. Like nuclear waste at Chernobyl, Soviet attitudes about Jews are proving to have a long afterlife. Writing in 2008, Anatoly Podolsky, director of the Ukrainian Center for Holocaust Studies in Kiev, observed that "Ukrainian society seems incapable or unwilling to perceive its national history as a history of various cultures. This is leading to a situation in which Ukrainian society, especially the younger generation, does not know the background to the Holocaust in Ukraine. A notion has even taken hold that the Holocaust took place exclusively in Western Europe and is not of any importance to Ukraine. The fact that the Jews were the Nazis' chief victims is being obscured."[1]

Podolsky's anecdotal impressions were confirmed by Elena Ivanova, professor of psychology at Kharkov National University, who conducted a study in 2002 among 107 students, ages fifteen to seventeen, from private, public, and Jewish schools in Kharkov. They had forty-five minutes to write essays in response to this prompt: "Please write about the Holocaust (the mass extermination of Jews during the Second World War)." She put the definition of Holocaust in parentheses, Ivanova noted, because "the word was still not in widespread use in Ukraine" in 2002.

"The youngsters were clearly surprised, if not taken aback, when they read the essay assignment," Ivanova reported. "They began to exchange glances, laugh, and whisper back and forth. It was obvious that they had never written about anything like this and perhaps had never spoken about it. As the essays would show, many had not really heard about the Holocaust and, according to several students at one of the schools, it had not even been mentioned in their history lessons. It was obvious how difficult it was for the students to write anything on the subject."[2]

This was hardly surprising. Soviet textbooks studiously ignored the Holocaust. It was officially included in secondary school curriculums in Ukraine in the 1990s after the collapse of the Soviet Union, but in the U.S. we would call it an unfunded mandate. Dr. Phil would call it passive-aggressive behavior. The ministry of education did not stop teaching of the Holocaust, but also did nothing to promote it, Podolsky said. There were no training programs for teachers, and not enough class time was allotted to the subject. "So we have a situation where the State and Ministry create no formal hurdles for Holocaust teaching, but real possibilities are also non-existent," Podolsky wrote.

In short, thanks for nothing. And then there were the textbooks, some of which provided "very scant, fragmentary, and even distorted information," Ivanova observed. One eleventh-grade textbook described the massacre at Babi Yar—the most iconic of killing fields in Ukraine—without ever mentioning that Jews were killed there. It's little wonder Ivanova found that "Most students were informed about the Holocaust, but their knowledge was superficial. Most had a murky idea about anti-Semitism as a phenomenon, and did not link it directly to the Holocaust."[3]

This is how you "teach" the Holocaust without really teaching it—by leaving important lessons unlearned. "The number of students manifesting anti-Semitic and racist views was quite large, as was the number more generally under the sway of stereotypes and prejudices," Ivanova concluded. "All of this speaks to the fact that a serious labor of enlightenment is essential in order to overcome negative views and prejudices," especially ones that have been latent in society for centuries.[4]

This is happening in Kharkov through the labors of Rabbi Moskovitz and numerous Jewish organizations— day schools, cultural centers, and the like—which operate freely though with tight security, as I experienced. The Jewish Agency for Israel on Pushinskaya Street, where I passed through an entrance with armed guards, is among the organizations offering Holocaust literature, teaching guides, programs, and other material free of the state's soft-focus filtering. The Kharkov Holocaust Museum, opened in 1996 and unequivocal in presenting the Holocaust as a Jewish catastrophe, is now a popular destination for school groups.

I asked the rabbi about the level of anti-Semitism in Kharkov today.

"Government anti-Semitism is non-existent," he said. "People-to-people anti-Semitism? I think it exists everywhere. Here it is not worse than other countries."

The task of teaching the Holocaust in Ukraine and healing its wounds is complicated by the fact that not everyone was on the same side. Collaboration with the Nazis by Ukrainians—*some* Ukrainians—remains a very big pink elephant in the room as the Ukraine attempts to reconcile with its past. Rabbi Moskovitz said of his father, "He always knew that Ukraine is a place where they (Germans) killed the Jews. And he said the Ukrainians were even worse." Ukraine is still recovering from the civil war within the war against Germany. And unlike the American civil war, in which North and South occupied separate domains, Ukrainian collaborators and patriots shared the same space and passed each other on the street every day. Their sons and daughters still do. To appreciate the magnitude of the pink elephant in Ukraine, take the testy semantic squabble in the U.S. over "civil war" versus "war between the states" and multiply by a thousand.

Two days before I visited Rabbi Moskovitz at the synagogue, we met at an annual ceremony at Drobitsky Yar, where my mother and her sister were destined to die with 16,000 Jews, including their parents and grandparents, had random good fortune not intervened—as it did for the rabbi's father, who was chosen to work instead of die at Auschwitz. We stood at the base of the majestic monument, shivering in the cold, knowing the 16,000 marched in far worse, clothed in much less that December day in 1941. It would be seventy years before their identity as Jews finally was acknowledged, and honored, in this same place. For Rabbi Moskovitz, it was progress, a milestone of sorts.

"One unbelievable thing that happened in Kharkov was that (Leonid) Kuchma, the president of Ukraine, came to open the monument at Drobitsky Yar in 1992. He walked together with me and the ambassador of Israel from the road all the way down to the monument. This was a big event."

After returning to Orlando, I transcribed my interview with Rabbi Moskovitz and e-mailed him some follow-up questions. He replied with rabbinical thoroughness and added a postscript.

"As a note from a rabbi, I would like to point out that since we are both children of survivors who miraculously survived the Holocaust, we have an additional mission to spread good in the world—being that we are also part of their miracle. So, whenever we do a mitzvah we are continuing the life of those who perished in the Holocaust."

CHAPTER TWENTY

You'll know that man-on-the-street knowledge of the Holocaust in America has taken a giant leap forward when "Righteous Gentiles" are household words equal to "Oskar Schindler." I can't say if that will happen in my lifetime, but I'm working it—starting with my mother.

Of course, *she* knows—for very personal reasons—about Righteous Gentiles. What she doesn't know—and has a hard time accepting—is that most other people don't know. We sometimes appear together at schools or bookstores to talk about *Hiding in the Spotlight*, and in telling her story of escape and survival she invariably refers to "my Righteous." I can tell from the sea of glazed eyes that her shorthand reference did not register with the audience.

"You know, mom," I say afterward as gently as possible, "when you say 'my righteous,' they don't know what you're talking about. You need to spell it out."

A small percentage will blink in recognition at "Righteous Gentiles," but I always offer the room a nutshell definition: the mantle of Righteous Gentile is the highest honor the state of Israel can bestow on a non-Jew, given to those who risked their lives to shelter Jews during the Holocaust. The formal name of the honor awarded by the Yad Vashem Holocaust memorial in Israel is "The Righteous Among Nations." Some 23,000 individuals from 44 countries have been so honored. In the U.S., the best-known Righteous is Schindler, the German industrialist who saved 1,200 Jews, but his name was impossible trivia, too, for most Americans before the Steven Spielberg movie.

I suspect that *Schindler's List* did more to make Liam Neeson a star than it did to raise the average Academy Awards show viewer's awareness of Righteous Gentiles as a group, which is understandably dim. We are separated by an ocean—geographically and emotionally—from the Holocaust. Among 23,000+ Righteous, only three are Americans. Individual Americans were, literally, in no position to shelter Jews fleeing death marches, though we did have the opportunity to act righteously, at little risk, as a country—and ignominiously slammed the door. In May 1939, the U.S. government turned away the S.S. *St. Louis*, carrying nearly a thousand Jews from Europe in search of refuge from Hitler. The ship was forced to return to Germany, where many of its passengers died in the Holocaust. Because America lost its nerve or its conscience—or because there was anti-Semitism in high places in Washington—the journey of the *St. Louis* became known as The Voyage of the Damned.

Unlike the U.S., which observed from a safe distance, Ukraine was ground zero of the Holocaust. The mass extermination of Jews began there, creating the first need and opportunities for rescuers. Yad Vashem has named 2,272 Righteous in Ukraine, placing it fourth behind France, Netherlands, and Poland, which is first on the list with 6,195. No country has a greater need for the world to know of its Righteous Gentiles than does Ukraine, whose identity still bears the stigma of anti-Semitism and pogroms and collaboration with occupying Nazis by a significant subset of its population. It needs a homegrown Oskar Schindler to supplant the persistent image of *Schutzmannschaften*— Ukrainian police working for the Germans—dragging Jews through the streets and patrolling death marches.

Twenty-three thousand may sound like a lot, but it's not—about one Righteous for every 260 exterminated Jews, based on six million dead. (The ratio of *Schutzmannschaften* to Righteous Gentiles in Ukraine is roughly 46 to 1.) The vetting process for admission to this august club is rigorous and protracted, as we learned in securing the honor for my mother's Righteous—Evdokiya Bogancha and her husband Prokofiev—neighbors in Kharkov who hid her from the Nazis after she escaped the death march to Drobitsky Yar. Not just anyone can hold up their hand and

claim they sheltered Jews. Verifiable documents and testimony are required. In May 2007, my mother submitted her
testimony to an authorized representative of Yad Vashem in
Atlanta, where she has lived for the past twenty-five years.

"I want to write about the wondrous family, Bogancha.
Everyone knew of the German order to kill on the spot all
rescuers of Jews. Yet, they put their own lives second when
I knocked on their gate's door early that morning of January
2, 1942. I had jumped out of the death march where I was
but one of many walking in a long column of rows and rows
of Jews who were without weapons and weakened by the
cruelest treatment. We were surrounded by German guards
with whips and Ukrainian guards with rifles.

"When my father started speaking Ukrainian to the
Ukrainian guard, he said: 'Look at me, I am not a Jew. I am
going because of my wife.' My father continued: 'Please let
my little daughter go'—at the same time showing him his
gold pocket watch, his lifetime possession. He was taking
off his overcoat and placing it on my shoulders, leaving
himself exposed to one of the coldest winters in the history
of the country.

"I knew I had to dive out of the death procession. I
turned my head looking past my mother and saw a large
roll of barbed wire on the ground and two women standing
there just watching the column. I then jumped out of the
column and the two of them became three of us. I stood
there tied to the disappearing vision of the column . . .

not really knowing where to go. My feet did the thinking for me. They turned me in the opposite direction, toward Kharkov, my city that I loved, 20 kilometers ahead.

"On my way back, I was allowed once again to spend a night in a house of total strangers. They had put me up several days before when I had sneaked out of the ghetto to go back to my street—Katsarskaya—to try to find food for the family. They could guess my origin because they saw thousands of people passing their home in the last two weeks. But they didn't ask questions. They let me spend the night in their little house so I would not freeze to death.

"I got up early and reached Katsarskaya Street. First, I went to see my classmate, Leeda, and her mother. They let me in and explained that they couldn't hide or keep me. They couldn't have been any nicer. I truly understood their position. Next I went to the home of my closest school mate and her mother. This was Svetlana Paganovich. I knocked on their door. They opened it and were horrified to see me, saying, 'Go away, you musn't come here' and slammed the door.

"My last chance was the home of my very favorite boy classmate, Nicolai. I liked him so much that I was afraid to speak to him. We lived on the same side of the same block, but in all the years I never saw inside his gate. When I finally dared to knock on the gate . . . it was opened right away. I saw the most kindly woman imaginable, Nicolai's mother, Evdokiya Nicolaevna Bogancha. I introduced myself because her family and mine had never met. She took my arm and pulled me in, locking the gate. Nicolai's father, Prokofiev Philipovich, was just as welcoming. This welcome would have been pleasing to a queen, but for a persecuted Jewish child who had just lost her family it was heavenly.

"The miracle continued. Two days later a man came to tell the Boganchas that Frina had escaped too and was in another home. Without hesitation, the Boganchas told him to let Frina join me. His appearance meant that people on the street knew that we had escaped, that we were hiding and who was hiding us. No one informed on us and we remained there for one week.

"After a few days Mr. and Mrs. Bogancha started talking to us about the necessity of leaving Kharkov . . . and introduced the thought that we would be two different people than we were before the war. They told us to look for an orphanage where we could hide until the war was over. We changed our names and those of our parents, and the story of how we became orphans.

"The Boganchas arranged with some farmer friends to take us in a cart to the closest train stop. We would then follow the railroad tracks for 25 kilometers to Lubotin where we found someone who let us spend the night. The next morning we walked to the train station where we found an empty boxcar which had some straw on the floor. After a few hours the train started moving to Poltava where we spent the night in the station. Then began our perilous 4-year journey until the end of the war. But that is a very long story for another time."

My mother's story is more than testimony to the courage and selflessness of the Bogancha family. In it we see encapsulated the warring instincts of cowardice, heroism, shame, nobility, bigotry, and enlightenment competing for Ukraine's soul in that terrible time. In her case, the better angels prevailed. She was turned away from two homes, but they were outnumbered by those who sheltered and embraced her: the house on the road to Kharkov, the people on Katsarskaya who brought Frina to her, the farmers who secreted them out of town, the family on the way to Lubotin that opened its door to two fugitive Jews. Even those who turned her away on Katsarskaya did not betray Zhanna, a fact worth noting because there were some who would have—like those who informed on the Arshansky family when the Germans first arrived in Kharkov and were systematically hunting Jews.

The heroism of the Boganchas and the legion of anonymous guardians is heightened by the price they would have paid if discovered. "In Eastern Europe, the Germans executed not only the people who sheltered Jews, but their entire family as well," says the official Web site for Yad Vashem. "Notices warning the population against helping the Jews were posted everywhere. Generally speaking, punishment was less severe in Western Europe, although there too some of the Righteous Among the Nations were incarcerated in camps and killed."

Yitzhak Arad in *The Holocaust in the Soviet Union* says the exact number of would-be Righteous executed by the Nazis is unknown, "but it is feasible to assume that there were many hundreds of them." He provides numerous examples of the Nazis' relentless pursuit and murder of rescuers. They were equal-opportunity killers, showing no mercy to non-combatants. "In the Uvarovo district of the Moscow region, the Germans bayoneted a Jewish woman and her small son and shot the mother and daughter who sheltered them," he writes. A journalist in Kharkov was murdered for sheltering an eleven-year-old girl. The litany goes on and on.

Antonina Bogancha, Nicolai's widow, still lives in the same house on Katsarskaya Street where Nicolai's family sheltered Zhanna and Frina. When I visited in December 2010, Antonina showed me the hiding place under the floor—a hole approximately six by six with dirt walls and shelves that now hold preserved vegetables and fruit. This is where the girls would hide if the Nazis came to the door, she said. When I returned home, I asked my mother about the hiding place. She had never seen it. The Germans never came to the door, she said—further testimony to the unshakable allegiance of her Gentile countrymen—"my Righteous."

Most of those who helped my mother—"my Righteous"—are gone and forgotten. Their names—unknown even to those they saved—will never be added to the list of Righteous Among the Nations. My mother's thoughts moments after escaping the death march to Drobitsky Yar stand as their requiem.

I could feel the eyes and good wishes of many souls on their last march. It was like they were holding me up in the air above the danger, so I would not be harmed. I felt their passion and knew it would never die. Our hearts were connected.

CHAPTER TWENTY-ONE

In 2006, when I visited Ukraine for the first time to do research for *Hiding in the Spotlight*, the most startling double-take moment was finding my still-vibrant mother's name etched on a wall memorializing the 16,000 Jews executed at Drobitsky Yar. Seeing her and her sister listed among the dead was a surreal jolt—a vision of a near-miss epitaph for me, my brother, and our four children, as well as our Aunt Frina's children and grandchildren.

And yet, five years later it's a different moment from that visit, less dramatic at first glance, that I find myself replaying over and over: I turn a street corner, look up, and see on the side of a building in Russian, "48 Katsarskaya"—my mother's address. At Drobitsky Yar, where her parents and grandparents are buried but she never set foot, I could see my mother's name but could not feel her presence.

On the tree-lined sidewalk outside 48 Katsarskaya, it felt like time had collapsed and she was standing there with me, thirteen and carefree again, returning home after a lesson with Professor Luntz, her beloved teacher at the Kharkov Music Conservatory. It had been sixty-five years since the Arshanskys—a candy maker, his wife, and their two girls—were routed from their apartment by Nazis. But something of them lived on, still seemed to possess this space. I recalled what my mother said about her father's violin, taken by a German who looted their home.

He took the violin, which was like "a member of the family," she said. "But he could not take its vibrations that came from our existence. The vibrations would remain, without the body."

And so it was with the apartment at 48 Katsarskaya. I sensed emanations from within, and felt a need to see inside my ancestral Ukrainian home. I wondered if the piano my mother learned on—a Bechstein with a mirrored music stand her father ordered from Germany—was still there. The tall windows facing the street were covered by sheer curtains which beckoned . . . and repelled. I didn't knock on the door that day or on a return visit four years later. It was not just reluctance to invade a stranger's privacy that stopped me. I feared the apartment door could open a Pandora's Box of historical wounds and recrimination. The vibrations remained.

Rumbling west to east across Ukraine in 1941, the *Wehrmacht* was a threshing machine separating Jews from their homes and possessions, discarding the useless human husks in giant graves and distributing the harvest to non-Jewish Ukrainians and ethnic Germans. Some of the booty ended up in the hands of local authorities. Gold and silver objects, and currency (rubles), generally were seized and sent to Berlin. Here is a typical *Einsatzgruppe* report on the harvest from one area in central Ukraine:

"Kiev . . . Gold and valuables, linen, and clothing were secured. Part of it was given to the NSV (Nazi Welfare) for the ethnic Germans, and part to the city administration for distribution among the needy population. Zhitomir . . . About 25–30 tons of linen, clothing, shoes, dishes, etc., that had been confiscated in action were handed over to the officials of the NSV for distribution."

The Nazi "philanthropy" was not always so systematic and controlled. Looting often occurred in the frenzy of Jews being led to slaughter, as described in this scene at Berdichev where 12,000 Jews were murdered on September 14–15, 1941.

"Policemen, members of their families, and the mistresses of German soldiers rushed to loot the vacant apartments. Before the eyes of the living dead, the looters carried off scarves, pillows, feather mattresses. Some walked past the guards and took scarves and knitted woolen sweaters from women and girls who were awaiting their death."

I am thinking of my grandfather's gold watch, furtively slipped to a young Ukrainian collaborator in barter for my mother's life on the road to Drobitsky Yar: does it tell time today in the pocket of the collaborator's grandson? Did the old man tell the boy how time stood still in the moment he took the watch from my grandfather? I am thinking of the Bechstein piano with the mirrored music stand on which my mother learned to play, and my grandfather's beloved violin. Were they plundered and put on trains to Germany for use in beer gardens and the private homes of Nazi leaders—or did they pass into the hands of other Ukrainian prodigies?

The most prized of all the plunder were apartments left behind by Jews. "Thousands of apartments and their contents remained vacant after the deportation and murder of their Jewish owners," wrote Yitzhak Arad. "Some apartments were used to accommodate German administration staff and military personnel; some were requisitioned by the police and local administration and their associates, and some were invaded by local inhabitants."[1]

Nova Ukraina, a newspaper published in Kharkov during the German occupation, reported that 1,700 families moved into new apartments in December 1941—the month my mother's family was ordered to abandon their apartment at 48 Katsarskaya. Probably several families have occupied the apartment since then, but given the decimation of Kharkov's Jewish population, it's highly unlikely that Jews live there now. Collaboration with the Nazis by a minority of Ukrainians remains an exposed nerve in the body politic. I decided that whoever lives there now would not welcome my touching that nerve.

From a strictly military perspective, no city was fought over more often or fiercely during the war than Kharkov. As a major industrial center and producer of tanks, situated on the road to Stalingrad to the east, Kharkov was a strategic plum. "Kharkov, Russia's 'Pittsburgh,' Captured by Nazis" said a front-page headline in *The Bismarck* (North Dakota) *Tribune* on Oct. 25, 1941. It changed hands four times during the war and was the largest Soviet city occupied by Germans (its pre-war population of about 900,000 was actually larger than that of Kiev). Seventy percent of Kharkov was destroyed during the Nazis' on-again-off-again 22-month occupation of the city from October 1941 to August 1943, when it was liberated for good by the Red Army.

The Germans destroyed fifty industrial plants, the railway junction, power stations, telephone and telegraph connections, medical and educational institutions, and most of the city's bridges. The 70% figure would have been much higher if the Soviets had not dismantled many factories—among them the tractor works near Kharkov used by Nazis as a ghetto—and shipped the parts east to the Urals before the Germans arrived. Much of the industrial infrastructure left behind was destroyed by the Soviets under Stalin's "scorched earth" edict.

"Along the battle-scarred Ukrainian countryside, a thin mantle of snow falls to hide or soften the hideous panorama

of destruction that unfolds mile after mile," Edmund Stevens, a correspondent for *The Christian Science Monitor*,
wrote in December 1943 from Kharkov. "Twisted rails,
burnt-out railway cars, wrecked tanks and armored cars
and guns are strewn helter-skelter alongside the track. The
train halts where cities and towns once stood, but little now
remains save shell-pitted walls. Even trees planted along
the right of way are blasted and broken from shellfire."

In the hierarchy of Nazi crimes committed in Kharkov,
the destruction of commercial, industrial, and military
infrastructure—commonplace targets in war—must rank
beneath their larger attempt to disembowel the cultural life
of the community and to usher in a new Dark Age. A week
after taking Kharkov in October 1941, the Nazis ordered
the closing of all institutions of higher learning—more than
forty—in the city. All valuable resources, including apparatus for splitting the atom, files, and books, were either
shipped to Germany or destroyed.

"Under the Germans, Kharkov's cultural life was completely interrupted," Stevens wrote. "They did not so much
as open one library or bookstore for the distribution of
books and magazines, even Nazi propaganda."

The war on literacy was consistent with Himmler's
vision of transforming Ukraine into a German colony—a
"Garden of Eden" in the East—in which the servant/slave
natives would receive only enough education to recognize
and sign their names. As if to drive home the point while

adding insult to injury, the Germans put in charge of eviscerating the great universities of Kharkov "mostly semi-literate noncommissioned officers," Stevens wrote. "Professors and researchers were denied any food ration and either starved or eked out a miserable existence by making boot polish, soap, candles or other small commodities."

The Germans occupied Kharkov, on and off, longer than any other Soviet city, and took the opportunity to commit—even for them—some of their most macabre atrocities there. No person or place was immune to Nazi terror, even wounded soldiers in a hospital. In trial testimony, a hospital worker—one of many witnesses to this particular horror—described the scene at the First Evacuation Hospital of the 69th Army, where Red Army soldiers were being treated.

"In the 8th block of the hospital there were 400 seriously wounded men who needed immediate surgical attention. They were either in the operating theater or being prepared for operating when a dull explosion occurred. The nurses ran toward me shrieking. SS men had driven up to the hospital, nailed up all the entrances and hurled two incendiary bombs into the premises. The first floor was at once enveloped in flames. The fire reached the beds of the wounded. With their clothes burning, they crept toward the windows. Many were so weak they fell dead after crawling a few steps. Those who reached windows and climbed onto sills were shot with tommy-guns by SS troops who had surrounded the building. Similar scenes took place on the second floor, which the fire soon reached."[2]

The Nazis were nothing if not thorough exterminators. They returned to the hospital the next day, the deputy superintendent of the hospital testified.

"The Germans made a round of the other blocks— ward after ward, basement after basement. Coming to a ward, they would first toss several grenades into it, fire a burst from a tommy-gun, then enter the ward and finish off those who were still alive. Wounded men, who, by some miracle, escaped with their lives, later told me that the Germans were accompanied by an officer who flashed a torch into all the corners. On approaching each bed and ascertaining that the patient was dead, he would say: 'Kaput,' and walk on."[3]

But all work and no play makes Hans a dull boy. After transforming the hospital into an abattoir, the Nazis amused themselves with a *coup de grâce*.

"They found a man still alive in one of the basements," said a hospital worker. "They dragged him into the yard and were about to shoot him. One German was already aiming his tommy-gun when another said something to him, and both burst out laughing. The first German ran off and soon returned with a hammer and nails. The Germans seized the half-dead man, stripped him naked, and nailed him to a wall for the amusement of themselves and other German monsters."[4]

On the flip side, one element of Ukrainian society that flourished during the Nazi occupation was the Christian religion, which was anathema to Stalin's secular communist state. Church leaders, especially in western Ukraine in the early stages of German rule, greeted the invaders as liberators from Stalin's godless tyranny. Also liberated and given fresh voice was the anti-Semitism endemic in Ukrainian churches. Pastoral leaders did not use the word "Jews," but it was easy to read between the lines when the leader of the Ukrainian Autocephalous Church praised Hitler for "conducting a tireless and uncompromising struggle against the anti-religious communist regime," code language for the boogieman of "Judeo-Bolshevism."

The non-action of church leaders in the face of violence against Jews spoke louder than their words. Early in Operation Barbarossa, the Nazis had seeded Soviet territory with anti-Semitic propaganda in the hope of inciting "spontaneous" pogroms. "Thousands of Jews were murdered by incited mobs, even before the *Einsatzgruppen* began their murderous operations," Arad wrote. "The heads of the churches were silent when their followers carried out these atrocities."[5]

In Kharkov, newspapers announced that churches would give a prayer of thanks on the first anniversary of the German occupation of the city. Another leader of the Autocephalous Church sent Hitler a telegram on April 5, 1942, wishing him happy birthday and rapid success in the war. The telegram was sent three months after the Nazis marched 16,000 Jews through the streets of Kharkov, under the horrified gaze and occasional anti-Semitic taunts of onlookers, to the tractor factory and then to slaughter at Drobitsky Yar. Even the monkeys who hear, see, and speak no evil would have had difficulty pleading ignorance of these events, which did not take place in barbed-wire–enclosed death camps on the edge of town, but rather on city streets and in open fields.

Averting their gaze from Nazi atrocities was a full-time job for church leaders in Kharkov. In the first two weeks of the occupation, their "liberators" hung 116 people from lamp posts, balconies, and trees on Sum-skaya Street in the center of the city. A magnificent statue of Shevchenko, the Ukrainian national poet, was festooned with corpses. Starvation was another favored weapon of the Nazis against both civilians and prisoners of war. General Field Marshal Walter von Reichenau, in his directive "The Conduct of the Army in the East," minced no words. "Supplying the civilian population and prisoners of war with food is an unnecessary human-itarian act. It is like giving away cigarettes and bread—an example of misdirected compassion."

The bulk of local harvests and food was confiscated to feed the occupying army or shipped to Germany. The daily bread ration for residents of Kharkov was 5.25 ounces. For Jews, it was 2 ounces. The German command expected at least ten to twenty million people in the East to starve to death during the winter of 1941–42. Soldiers were given a mantra to repeat if they felt they were losing their nerve and about to commit an unnecessary humanitarian act: "Each gram of bread or other food that I give to the population in the occupied territories out of good-heartedness, I am withdrawing from the German people and thus my family. The German soldier must stay hard in the face of hungry women and children. If he does not, he endangers the nourishment of our people."

Apparently it worked, at least in Kharkov. "As early as December 1941, starvation was quite frequent, even among the non-Jewish population, and by March 1942, almost half as many people were starving to death in Kharkov each month as in the Warsaw ghetto," wrote historian Dieter Pohl. My mother remembers going through German garbage for potato skins her mother could use for making soup, and later, while hiding in an orphanage, scrounging for much less savory things than potato skins. Upwards of 100,000 residents of Kharkov are thought to have died of hunger during the German occupation.

N.F. Belonozhko was the wife of a soldier. She kept a diary of daily life in Kharkov during the occupation. Her fate is unknown, but Belonozhko's notes were retrieved and published in *The Unknown Black Book*, the Dante-esque testimony of those consigned by fate to Himmler's

"Garden of Eden." What follows are excerpts from Belono-zhko's diary.

"Winter began fiercely this year. No one had a stove. There was no fire wood either. I am working in a caf-eteria. Today it's borscht from frozen beets without bread, then *kozein*, a glue-like, repulsive white substance (made from bones); it tasted like rubber. They say it was used in building airplanes. . . . The first to get sick in our room is Shura and Sonya's mother. Sonya would go to a village to the south to get her milk. Her mother dies slowly. And now in our apartment is the first coffin, made from a chest of drawers.

"In the kitchen in the evenings, everyone looks ner-vously at their legs, squeezing them. Are they swollen? Sonya's and Nyura's are very swollen, and the Mordukhaev girls are just wasting away. They look like they are made of wax. They don't comb their hair, they don't wash, they make something out of potato peelings and snow and eat it. People live by selling things but they've got nothing left to sell.

"Lice are crawling around the apartment. . . . Another one of us has died. Sonya died in the hospital. Her feet became infected and she died of blood poisoning. They buried her in a common grave. There's no one left to recall the past, our life before the Germans. There's no one to dream about. Margarita has gotten sick, too. When will this end? When?"⁶

JUDGMENT BEFORE NUREMBERG

August 23, 1943. That is when it ended, on a Thursday morning.

"By dawn on August 23, the 89th Guards and 183rd Divisions had reached Dzerzhinsky Square, the 89th hoisting its red banner over the Gosprom building," wrote historian Karel Margry. "However, the Russians bagged few of the enemy. The German units had completed their withdrawal from the city, occupying defensive positions south of the Uda River. At noon, the Russians declared the city clear of German troops."

Not completely. Three lower-level German officers had drawn the shortest of short straws fate could deliver to a Nazi invader, leaving them behind in the hands of the Soviets who would use them to show the world the price to be paid by those who blindly saluted Hitler and perpetrated atrocities in his name.

CHAPTER TWENTY-TWO

Since the Holocaust as we know it—the mass extermination of European Jews—began in my mother's back yard in Ukraine, it should come as no surprise that the legal road to Nuremberg also began there. It *should* come as no surprise, but still does nearly seventy years after a military tribunal in Kharkov began the wheels of justice grinding slowly toward the grand denouement in Nuremberg, thence to Jerusalem and the trial of Adolf Eichmann in 1961.

It was in a makeshift courtroom in Kharkov in December 1943 that Nazis were first tried and convicted for wartime crimes, 705 days before chief U.S. counsel Robert Jackson made his opening statement before the International Military Tribunal (IMT) at the Palace of Justice in Nuremberg. In all my travels since publication of *Hiding in the Spotlight* in 2009, I have encountered no one who knew of the Kharkov trial—even amongst university professors and museum curators—and not many who were aware that the mass slaughter of Jews began in Ukraine.

Judge Jackson knew where the road to Nuremberg began, and why. The Nazi drive to exterminate the Jews "achieved its zenith of savagery in the East. The Eastern Jew has suffered as no people ever suffered," Jackson told the International Military Tribunal. "It was against the Soviet people and Soviet prisoners that Teutonic fury knew no bounds." And it was in the East, before the Soviet people in Kharkov, that Nazis first faced legal fury for their crimes in a trial whose testimony and precedents would echo in the chambers at Nuremberg.

The Kharkov trial, and an earlier one at Krasnodar involving only Soviet collaborators, were "the first judicial record of cases on the crimes and criminal responsibility of the Hitlerites . . . paving the way for the application and effectuation of many norms and principles which later constituted the basis of Nuremberg law,"[1] wrote I.A. Lediakh.

Soviet Foreign Minister Molotov was confident that there would be a day of legal reckoning, even in the dark early days of the war as the *Wehrmacht* rolled inexorably east, raping the Motherland in ways unseen in modern warfare. He could not have guessed that it would be on the stage of an opera house in Kharkov. Molotov began building a public record of Nazi crimes and atrocities within months of the German invasion in June 1941. In November, he issued an official note accusing the Nazis of violating the Hague Conventions of 1907 by shooting prisoners of war, starving others, including civilians, to death, looting their personal belongings, and conscripting them for military work.

"Even at this early date, the Soviet government plainly sought to stake out a claim imputing 'all the responsibility for these inhuman actions of the German military and civil authorities on the criminal Hitlerite government,'" wrote George Ginsburgs. "The all-enmeshing web of criminal conspiracy which eventually stretched to embrace the entire Nazi system, directly implicating men at the summit of official hierarchy as accomplices in the misdeeds committed by the lower echelons, figured prominently in the Soviet government's public pronouncements well-nigh from the start."[2]

On January 6, 1942, as Nazis were throwing dirt on the bodies at Drobitsky Yar, Molotov issued a laundry list of "monstrous atrocities" committed by the occupiers, and once again carefully connected the dots from killers on the ground to their masters in Berlin. "Irrefutable facts prove that the regime of plunder and bloody terror against the non-combatant population of towns and villages constitutes not merely excesses of individual *German* officers and soldiers, but a definite system planned and encouraged by the German government and the German High Command, which deliberately foster the most brutal instincts among soldiers and officers," he stated.

GREG DAWSON

Molotov's notion of shared, prosecutable guilt—"from the lance-corporal in the army to the lance-corporal on the throne," as Soviet legal expert Aaron Trainin put it—was endorsed just a week later by representatives of nine occupied countries meeting in London at the Palace of Saint James. The governments in exile vowed "the punishment, through channels of organized justice, of those guilty or responsible for these crimes, whether they have ordered them, perpetrated them, or in any way participated in them."

With the declaration at Saint James, the idea of collective culpability "took root . . . in the diplomatic canon of an important segment of the international community," Ginsburgs wrote. "The concept that a general blueprint drawn up by the state and party hierarchy of the Third Reich accounted for the epidemic proportion of depravities perpetrated by the middle and lower echelons of the Nazi apparatus was destined eventually to emerge as a key theme in the Nuremberg script."[3]

Molotov was as assiduous in documenting the Nazis' crimes as they were in committing them, Ginsburgs wrote. In April 1942, Molotov "returned to the fray with further evidence that the German army was engaged in methodical looting, plunder, and criminal excesses against the civilian population, wanton destruction of towns and villages, enslavement and deportation of civilians, their mass arrest and confinement in P.O.W. camps, destruction

264

of national cultures and all manner of bestialities encouraged on direct orders of superior officers."

The instinctive reaction of the contemporary reader, bombarded and often burned by hoax and hyperbole, is to cast a skeptical eye at such apocalyptic language and divide by two to get the truth. In this case, however, you need to multiply. Not only were Molotov's accusations true, his words failed to convey the full dimension of the horror unfolding across the Soviet Union. It can be seen in the records of the Extraordinary State Commission for Ascertaining and Investigating Crimes Perpetrated by the German Fascist Invaders and their Accomplices (ESC), created in November 1942 to "keep complete records of the vile crimes perpetrated by the Germans and their accomplices." The commission inspected graves and corpses, took witness accounts, studied forensic reports, and interviewed captured Germans. It acquired Nazi maps, books, private correspondence, diaries, memoirs, and transcripts of speeches at Reichstag sessions.

"These records proved indispensable at the IMT," wrote Michael Bazyler, a law professor and expert on international law. And well before the IMT, they would prove indispensable in the Ukraine as the Soviets paved the way to Nuremberg. The first use of the material was in July 1943, when eleven Soviet citizens were charged with treason for collaborating with German forces in the murder of six thousand people in Krasnodar in southeastern

Ukraine in 1942. But there was something curious about these litanies of Nazi atrocities: the primary victims, Jews, were not identified as such. Although they were in large measure the very reason the Germans were there, and were the main quarry of the *Einsatzgruppe* squads that did the killing, Jews appeared only as "Soviet citizens" or "peace-loving citizens" in ESC reports on massacres in Krasnodar, Kharkov, and myriad sites across Ukraine.

"In testimonies gathered by the local committees in each town . . . local inhabitants recalled events they had witnessed," Arad wrote. "They described the persecution and murder of the Jews, as they saw and heard them. The testimonies were written down verbatim, and clearly included the word *Jews* as the main victims. In reports provided by the local commissions, however, the word Jews disappeared gradually, to be replaced by the term *Soviet citizens.*"[4]

Though no Germans were in the dock at Krasnodar, the proceeding clearly was a trial *in absentia* of the Nazis. Prosecutors assigned responsibility to the commander of the German 17th Army, the chief of the Krasnador Gestapo, and thirteen other Gestapo officials. Eight of the defendants were sentenced to death by hanging, the others to hard labor or deportation.

In October 1943, Roosevelt, Stalin, and Churchill met in Moscow to discuss a variety of issues. With the German army in full retreat from Soviet territory, Stalin's attention turned to vengeance in the courtroom—and it turned with a keen vengeance that bespoke the Soviets' exponentially greater degree of suffering to that point in war. By October 1943—eight months before D-Day and the other major conflicts of the European theater to follow—rivers of blood already were running through the Soviet Union. Hundreds of thousands of Russian soldiers had died defending Moscow and Stalingrad and in the epic tank battle at Kursk. In the siege of Stalingrad alone, the Soviets lost nearly 480,000 men—more than all American losses for the war. It's estimated that for every American soldier killed fighting the Germans, eighty Soviet soldiers died. Millions of Russian civilians had died, including close to 1.5 million Jews systematically murdered in Ukraine.

"Americans have little conception of the Soviet Union's experience in World War II," wrote J.T. Dykman in a paper for The Eisenhower Institute. "About the only way we can begin to understand is through imagination. The distance between Moscow and Berlin is about the same as that separating New York City and Atlanta. Imagine twenty million people being violently killed between those two American cities in four years." In his memoir, Eisenhower attempted to describe the unfathomable destruction. "When we flew into Russia, in 1945, I did not see a house standing between the western borders of the country and the area around Moscow."[5]

The documented horror explains Stalin's focus on harsh legal remedy when he met with Churchill and Roosevelt in October 1943. Edmund Stevens wrote in the *Christian Science Monitor*: "The Russians insisted on a declaration concerning the punishment of individuals responsible for German atrocities in the occupied areas. The Russians contended that the category of such war criminals embraced everyone from the Nazi higher-ups who issued the directive for extermination . . . down to the meanest *Wehrmacht* private who mowed down unarmed civilians with a machine gun, or used his bayonet in gruesome fulfillment of the directives."

The Russians got their wish. The leaders signed a statement on atrocities which sent a chilling message to Germans who had committed, and perhaps were *still* committing, atrocities—as well as a blunt warning to those without blood on their hands to not even think about it, lest the Allied powers "pursue them to the ends of Earth." For the Soviets, the key sentence of the Moscow Declaration addressed legal jurisdiction over suspected German war criminals.

"Those German officers and men and members of the Nazi Party who have been responsible for, or have taken a consenting part in, atrocities, massacres and executions will be sent back to the countries in which their abominable deeds were done in order that they may be judged and punished according to the laws of these liberated countries and of the free governments which will be erected therein. Thus, Germans . . . who have shared in slaughters inflicted on the people in areas of the Soviet Union which are now being swept clear of the enemy will be brought back to the scene of their crimes and judged on the spot by the people whom they have outraged."

The Soviets wasted no time in exercising their jurisdiction. Less than two months after the Moscow conference, three Nazi officers and a Russian collaborator were brought before the Military Tribunal of the 4th Ukrainian Front in Kharkov, charged with having "taken a direct part in mass and brutal extermination of peaceful Soviet people." The Western Allies had not expected such trials to occur until *after* the war, and were deeply concerned the Germans would retaliate with trials of captured U.S. and British airmen. But despite intense gnashing of diplomatic teeth in private, the Allies held their tongues as the trial proceeded. "The Kharkov trial thus became the principal test, right up to the war's end, of the ability of the three Allies to stand behind the Moscow Declaration," wrote historian Arieh Kochavi.[6]

The indictment offered by Soviet prosecutors at Kharkov contained themes and principles that would be reprised at Nuremberg, not least a continuum of Nazi guilt in which those who ordered and those who shot were inextricably bound together. "All these crimes and outrages are not isolated facts, but only a link in the long chain of crimes which have been and are being committed by the German invaders on the direct instructions of the German government and the Supreme Command of the German Army," the indictment stated.

Law professor John Quigley has written, "It was the Soviet Union that, during the war, promoted what was to become perhaps the most significant legal innovation in the Nuremberg proceedings, namely the notion that waging of aggressive war is a crime to which individual responsibility attaches. Soviet representatives proposed the idea to the other Allies, and that is how this crime found its way into the London Charter, which defined the crimes to be tried at Nuremberg."[7]

In his indictment at Nuremberg, Jackson said the defendants were guilty of five categories of crimes, including preparation and waging of wars of aggression, and persecution and extermination of Jews and Christians. "The prosecution submits that these five categories of premeditated crimes were not separate and independent phenomena but that all were committed pursuant to a common plan or conspiracy," Jackson stated. "The central crime in this pattern of crimes, the kingpin which holds them all together, is the plot for aggressive wars."

The Soviets had a large hand in "defining the legal theories under which the defendants would ultimately be tried," wrote Bazyler. Their novel idea that governing cliques such as the Nazis could be viewed and prosecuted as criminal organizations was met with resistance by the other powers. "In the end, the Soviet position prevailed, and became an important prosecutorial tool during the trial."[8]

Molotov's extensive homework had paid off. Chief Soviet prosecutor R.A. Rudenko and his team may have been the best prepared of the four Allied prosecution teams. They came armed with reams of information and damning evidence meticulously gathered by the Extraordinary State Commission for the past three years. "The Commission's extraordinary efforts resulted in an impressive list of hundreds of Germans, from generals to humble privates, and a specific and detailed enumeration of the crimes of which they stood accused," Bazyler wrote. "The Soviet presentation of their case through extensive documentary evidence played a critical role in the thorough documentation of Nazi crimes and exposure to the world of brutality of the Nazi regime."

Bazyler concludes that "Soviet contributions to the trials were numerous, from their scrupulous gathering of evidence, to the precedents set by their domestic trials of war criminals, to their presentation of the records of massive Nazi atrocities on Soviet and foreign soil alike. Such contributions cannot be underestimated."[9]

Yet they have been. The record strongly suggests that it was the Soviet scholar Trainin, in his 1944 book *Criminal Responsibility of the Hitlerites*, who first argued that the

Nazis at Nuremberg should be charged with a "crime against peace," which he contended was the gravest international offense. The idea had been batted around in conferences, but "Trainin gave the concept its definitive formulation, which would later serve as a basis for the Nuremberg Charter," wrote historian Francine Hirsch. Ginsburgs called Trainin's thinking "revolutionary." None of that has altered "the common misperception that it was the United States that came up with the formula for 'crimes against peace,'" Hirsch wrote.[10]

What happened? A classic case of history being written by the winners. The IMT was a public-relations proxy battle in the Cold War, and the Soviets lost. As much as we may wish to exalt the trials as an expression of pure and ultimate justice, "Nuremberg was as much about politics as it was about justice—and it could not have been otherwise," Hirsch wrote. "It was the U.S. that seized control of the IMT and made Nuremberg its own."[11] The not-ready-for-prime-time Soviet delegation was mocked for its drab clothing and inept translators. The Western Allies allowed embarrassing information about Soviet actions not related to the Nazis' crimes—e.g., the Soviet-German Non-Aggression Pact of 1939 and the murder of Polish officers in the Katyn Forest—to be raised in court by defense attorneys for the Germans.

"The IMT became a devastating propaganda failure for the Soviet 'propaganda state,'" Hirsch wrote. "It exposed

Soviet inadequacies before the world and ultimately shaped Soviet leaders' attitudes toward the postwar order." As for the Soviets' many important contributions to the IMT process, "These would soon be forgotten in the West—a direct result of the Cold War."[12]

Another early casualty of the Cold War was justice *after* Nuremberg. Eagerly catering to West Germany, their new ally against the Soviets, the U.S. and Britain began granting clemency to Nazis the way Shriners toss candy to kids on a parade route. The High Commissioner of Germany, American John McCloy, paroled sixty convicted German war criminals at the end of 1949. The U.S. and Britain turned a blind eye on West Germany's hear-no-evil-see-no-evil pursuit of suspected war criminals which netted a pathetic 13 death sentences and 163 life prison terms out of 103,823 investigations from the end of the war until 1992.

"In many respects the punishments meted out against German war criminals by Allied and German courts alike bore no relation to the horrible crimes that had been perpetrated," wrote Kochavi. He thought it no coincidence that the U.S. and Britain did not experience firsthand the horrors of Nazi occupation. "The physical distance of government officials from the crime scenes may have led to a certain callousness. Those who dealt with the issue proved simply insensitive to the suffering that people under German domination endured."[13]

In the meantime, the Soviets had to endure criticism from the West that the Kharkov trial and others which followed across the U.S.S.R. were carbon copies of the tainted "show trials" of the 1930s, which railroaded Soviet citizens "guilty" of nothing more than fabricated disloyalty to Stalin. That impression was compounded by Stalin's insistence at Yalta on the forced repatriation of Russian soldiers and civilians whom he bizarrely considered traitors for being stuck in German prisons or displaced persons camps at the end of the war. Many of those dragged back to the Motherland were executed or sent to gulags, the likely fate of my mother, who was in a DP camp near Munich and set to return *voluntarily*, but would not go without her sister Frina, who adamantly—presciently—refused. Between Stalin's outrages and the showcasing of Soviet dirty laundry, the mountains of crucial evidence gathered by Soviets against the Nazis and presented at Nuremberg never received the attention or credit it deserved. My goal is to ensure that that does not happen to the trial at which the evidence was first used to convict Nazis of their crimes.

"The importance of domestic war crimes trials such as the Kharkov trial lies not only in their bringing of Nazi war criminals to justice, but also their effect, as put by Professor Ginsburgs, of pointing the way toward the grand finale at Nuremberg," Bazyler wrote.[14]

Ginsburgs concedes that the Kharkov trial "was a methodically staged *mise en scène*," but adds, "We have no indication that the German defendants had either been rehearsed or coerced. Nor has any solid evidence ever been adduced that the accused were not in fact guilty of the crimes to which they so willingly confessed."

The road to Nuremberg from my mother's back yard, from my grandparents' and great-grandparents' grave at Drobitsky Yar, from the courtroom in Kharkov was paved with vengeance, yes, but also with something resembling true justice. John McCloy should have done half as well.

CHAPTER TWENTY-THREE

O n Wednesday morning, December 15, 1943, hundreds of residents of liberated Kharkov filed into the
Opera House on Rymarska Street, which runs parallel to
Sumskaya Street, where the SS and German military command were headquartered during occupation of the city.
A grand, neo-classical structure, the Opera House had
miraculously emerged unscathed from two years of brutal
Nazi rule, punctuated by four battles for the city, which
left much of Kharkov in ruins. The ornate hall had been
transformed into a courtroom where three German officers and a Russian collaborator were cast as antagonists in
a drama whose denouement was as predictable and eagerly
awaited as the grand operas presented on the stage.

Each person entering the Opera House held a red
ticket good for that session only. Every day the seats would
be filled by a different group of lucky citizens holding the

toughest ticket in town—even more coveted than a ticket to a Deanna Durbin picture showing in one of the reopened movie theaters in Kharkov, which was slowly coming back to life after the suspended animation of the Nazi occupation. The tickets "were distributed to factory workers and office employees through their trade union organizations, so that the audience kept rotating," Edmund Stevens wrote in the *Christian Science Monitor.*

The Soviets prepared for and gained international coverage of the trial—and not just from correspondents for major newspapers such as the *New York Times* and *Christian Science Monitor.* Stories from Reuters, Associated Press, United Press, and other agencies ran on the front pages of small-town newspapers across America. "First War Guilt Trial Held On Kharkov Deaths" was the headline in *The Oelwein* (Iowa) *Daily Register.* "Nazi Soldiers Describe Brutal Execution Methods During Trial at Kharkov," said *The Rhinelander* (Wisconsin) *Daily News.* Page 1 of *The Charleston* (West Virginia) *Gazette:* "Traitor Bares Nazi Horrors."

Foreign reporters were admitted only to the final day of the four-day trial (and were free to witness the subsequent public executions). Their earlier stories were based on published accounts by Soviet writers—the crème de la crème of Soviet journalism—whose reports were funneled through Moscow. This led to confusion at some U.S. newspapers such as *The Port Arthur* (Texas) *News,* which ran a bold-type headline: "Murder Of Children Described At Moscow Trials."

Klieg lights were set up in the makeshift courtroom to film the trial for a feature-length documentary. In format and presentation it certainly was an elaborate *mise en scène* like the infamous show trials of the 1930s. And what better place for a staged production than an opera hall? The Soviets were hungry for payback and eager for the world to learn about Nazi crimes against the Motherland. A good "show" would further that goal. But there was a show, a masquerade, *within* the show—like two matryoshka dolls, the larger one missing a crucial detail, a single paint stroke. Hidden inside was the true face, the momentous truth Soviet authorities were denying: this was the first trial of Germans for crimes that would become known as the Holocaust. The murdered Jews of Kharkov were among the first of the six million to die. Yet, they were invisible at the Kharkov trial.

"Both the Krasnodar and Kharkov trials omitted mention of the Nazi murder of Jews," wrote Alexander Prusin. "Although by 1943 the Holocaust had become common knowledge and the ESC (Extraordinary State Commission) possessed massive evidence of the scope of the genocide, the tribunals referred to the executions of Jews as 'massacres of Soviet citizens.' The indictment in Kharkov referred to the ghettoization of Jews as 'forceful resettlement of Soviet citizens' to the outskirts of the city."[1] The

Soviet government knew for certain in January 1942 "that the Jews were being annihilated, and up to the end of the war, neither Stalin nor his counterparts in Soviet leadership made any public reference to the matter," Arad wrote.

The charade was dutifully maintained by Molotov in notes he sent to diplomats of friendly nations. In an April 1942 note, Molotov "detailed the murder of 3,000 civilians in Taganrog on October 27, 1941, of 7,000 inhabitants of the Crimean town of Kerch, of 6,000 people in Vitebsk, of 10,000 in Pinsk, of 12,000 in Minsk, and of 14,000 in Kharkov. Nowhere in the note does Molotov mention that the murdered victims were Jews."[2]

The determined air-brushing of Jews from the picture reached Alice in Wonderland heights of absurdity in subsequent Soviet trials held in 1945–46 "where defendants and eyewitnesses revealed the horrors of ghettos, concentration camps, and mass executions, and where the charge of perpetrating the Holocaust—without its explicit mention— would frequently constitute the only basis for indictment," Prusin wrote.[3]

Stalin had complex reasons, personal and practical, for maintaining the fiction of a non-Jewish Holocaust in the Soviet Union. Stalin was fervently anti-Semitic, but it was bloodless pragmatism that led him to sell out the Jews after signing of the Ribbentrop–Molotov treaty in August 1939. All reports of Nazi persecution of Jews in German-occupied territories suddenly vanished from the Soviet press,

TOP: Bus shelter with red-and-blue floral design. Sign in Russian reads: Drobitsky Yar. BOTTOM: Menorah at the end of the entrance road to Drobitsky Yar.

ABOVE: Dueling monuments at Drobitsky Yar killing field south of Kharkov. Obelisk to left, erected by Soviets in 1955, makes no mention of Jews. Monument to right, built in 1998, corrects the historical record. OPPOSITE TOP: Heroic statuary in Kharkov center. OPPOSITE BOTTOM: Monument in Sokolniky Park where thousands of Jews and Russian soldiers were murdered.

OPPOSITE: Motherland statue, with beating electronic heart, at Sokolniky Park near Kharkov. ABOVE TOP: Babushka in balcony at Kharkov music conservatory, December 2010. ABOVE BOTTOM: Site of the Kharkov synagogue where 400 elderly, crippled Jews and children were locked in by the Nazis and perished in December 1941.

OPPOSITE: Author at the Kharkov Holocaust Museum (2010) with founder Larisa Volovik (left) and daughter Yulana Volshonok, curator. ABOVE TOP: Plaque at the site of the old Opera House where the 1943 trial was held before an audience of local residents. ABOVE BOTTOM: Students at School 13 where Zhanna attended at same age.

TOP: First and third generation survivors—Zhanna Dawson and granddaughter Aimee—at Timber Creek High School in Orlando, FL, January 2011. *Photo by Wendy Doromal.* BOTTOM: The Arshansky extended family, circa 1935 in Kharkov. Zhanna is second from left between father Dmitri and mother Sara. Both perished at Drobitsky Yar.

which began strewing rose petals in the Führer's path. Consequently, Jews never knew what hit them two years later when Hitler tore up the treaty, invaded, and sent the *Einsatzgruppen* after them. Hitler's betrayal had the effect of distancing Stalin even further from the discrete plight of the Jews. The consistent theme of his wartime speeches was that Nazi Germany aimed to exterminate the Slavic and Russian people—a narrative that would be watered down by reference to Jews, the only group of Soviets in *actual* danger of extermination. Stalin also meant to blunt German propaganda that it was making war not against the Russian people but rather "Judeo-Bolshevism"—a notion that might appeal to anti-Semitism among Ukrainian soldiers and lessen their hatred for the invaders. Stalin's erasure of the Jews was not simply a wartime expedience, as demonstrated by his post-war banning of *The Black Book*, a collection of eyewitness testimonies to Nazi crimes against Jews in Ukraine and other territories. Soviet censors stopped publication of *The Black Book* in 1947, and it did not see full light of day until 1980 when Yad Vashem published it in Russian.

Thus, it is hardly surprising—indeed, it is entirely consistent with the delusion fostered by Stalin—that in the first state-run trial of Germans there would be no mention of "Jews," the primary victims whose slaughter was the very reason for the trial. Here is a key passage from the indictment read in court:

"In Kharkov, on Gestapo orders, many peaceful Soviet citizens were moved from their flats in the city to specially designated barracks on the territory of a workers' settlement of the Kharkov tractor plant. The Soviet citizens on their way to the workers' settlement were repeatedly plundered and subjected to humiliations. Having put the people in barracks, the Germans divided them into groups of two or three hundred people, including adolescents, children, and old folks, and then drove them to a gully four to five kilometers away from the tractor works where they were shot near large pits that had been prepared beforehand."

This is a sanitized, *Judenfrei* version of the story my mother told me and which I recounted in *Hiding in the Spotlight*. In December 1941, her family and 16,000 other Jews were marched by Germans and Ukrainian collaborators from Kharkov to the tractor factory, where they were held for two weeks without food and water before being taken to Drobitsky Yar for execution. The singularly Jewish quality of this slaughter—contrary to the Soviet whitewashing at the trial—is found in numerous accounts by civilians and soldiers, both Russian and German. The small obelisk erected in 1955 at Drobitsky Yar with the inscription, "The victims of Fascist Terror 1941–1942 Lie here," now stands as a monument to the madman's denial of the Holocaust. Stalin lied here.

In September 1943, an eleven-member commission of Kharkov city officials, academics, an army general, a priest, and two representatives of the ESC issued a report titled "On the Mass Shooting of Jews by the German Murderers in the Drobitzki Valley." During German occupation of Kharkov, "The Jewish population was totally destroyed one by one," the report stated. "Upwards of 15,000 Jewish residents of the city were shot during the months of December 1941 and January 1942 alone near the so-called valley of Drobitzki. The barbarity inflicted on innocent victims was confirmed by evidence obtained from witnesses, from protocols by medical experts, and from other reliable documents." By the time the report reached the courtroom in Kharkov, all references to "Jews" had been removed and replaced with various euphemisms such as "peace-loving citizens."

The two-stage death march of Kharkov Jews—first to the tractor factory for temporary warehousing, then to Drobitsky Yar—is chronicled in *Einsatzgruppe* field reports sent back to Berlin, and by testimony of German soldiers in later inquiries by the West German government. In one deposition, a former member of a German police battalion said he was sent to a secluded area outside Kharkov sometime after Christmas 1941. "We were taken to hilly terrain where we had to form a huge seclusion ring that the civilian population was not allowed to enter. Into this the Jews from the ghetto were taken with trucks. The Jews had to undress and to lie down nearby or right inside crevices in the earth. The crevices were natural ones and not tank ditches or other dugouts. In these pits the Jews were shot by the S.D."

Despite similar stagecraft, the Kharkov "show" was no rerun from the thirties. There was no need for fabricated evidence in the opera hall, wrote Prusin, because "traces of German crimes in the Soviet Union were visible, widely known, and undeniable."

And they *continued*—even as the Kharkov trial proceeded. Kiev and Kharkov were now liberated cities, but in areas to the west the retreating Nazis were still burning villages and slaughtering civilians. At the same time, the most gruesome cover-up in history was underway across Ukraine—the exhuming and incinerating of more than a million bodies, most of them Jewish, under the supervision of tormented Col. Blobel. It seemed an odd task for a man who quaked at the sight of fifty bodies in a gangswagen, much less tens of thousands of corpses festering in their own blood and vomit.

By December 1943, the tide was turning dramatically against Germany—Berlin and other cities had been under heavy Allied bombardment since mid-November—but the end of the war was still eighteen months away. The Kharkov trial came as a surprise to Churchill and Roosevelt, co-signers with Stalin of the Moscow Declaration just six weeks earlier. The Declaration stipulated that any accused Germans be returned to the scene of their crimes for trial and punishment, and in language unusually vivid for official statements it noted that "in their desperation the recoiling Hitlerites and Huns are redoubling their ruthless cruelties. This is now evidenced with particular clearness by monstrous crimes on the territory of the Soviet Union which is being liberated from Hitlerites, and on French and Italian territory." Still, no one expected the Soviets to act on the Declaration before the ink was dry.

"After the Moscow meeting many persons regarded the decision about war criminals as something for the future, something to be attended to after the fighting was over," Edwin James wrote in the *New York Times* on the third day of the Kharkov trial. "Many recalled the now famous 1919 cry of 'Hang the Kaiser' and recalled that it came to nothing, and classified the Moscow ruling as something for later on. Not so Stalin."

Stalin's reasons for jump-starting the judicial process are not known but could have included: boosting the morale of the battered Soviet people for the battles ahead; putting the rest of the German military on notice about what to expect if it committed similar atrocities; and establishing in the public mind a straight line between the criminal acts of German soldiers in the field and Hitler and the Nazi High Command. And perhaps, in addition, to throw a veil over his own crimes against humanity, including those from the past decade and those he was still planning to commit.

John Balfour, the British minister in Moscow, believed
that Stalin was conducting the Kharkov trial in order to
throw "a cloak of legality" over random hangings of German
prisoners which had been reported in Kiev—where bodies
were left twisting in the wind from balconies—and in a village west of Kremenchug after a hasty field court-martial.
"The gallows was a tree where a village woman had been
executed for killing poultry without permission of the
German agricultural authorities" a few months prior, the
New York Times reported.

If the Kharkov trial was designed as a cloak of legality,
it was exceedingly threadbare by Western standards. There
was no presentation of documentary (physical) evidence;
defense attorneys (state lawyers) were not permitted to
cross-examine witnesses; the judge often acted as a prosecutor in questioning defendants and witnesses; and the
guilt of individual defendants was established through con-
fessions, and by linking them to similar crimes committed
by *other* German military in the region—guilt by non-
association. Two of the defense attorneys had "represented"
defendants in the show trials. As Stevens noted, "This, too,
was a military tribunal: judges, prosecutor, and attendants
were all in uniform."

In short, the Kharkov trial—along with those held
later at the time of the Nuremberg trials—was typical
Soviet justice. "While the war crimes trials followed the
format of the prewar show trials, they were administered

in full accordance with contemporary Soviet laws and definitions of legality," wrote Prusin. In its own way, Soviet justice was blind. The principles and procedures of the Kharkov courtroom were identical to those used to convict eleven collaborators at Krasnodar just months earlier.

The Soviets held thousands of German prisoners in December 1943. Their reasons for choosing these three— Reinhard Retzlaff, Wilhelm Langheld, and Hans Ritz—to prosecute are as uncertain as Stalin's motivation for having the trial. Prusin has speculated, "The German defendants were selected to represent an assortment of military ranks and branches of the German armed forces: an NCO (non-commissioned officer) of the Secret Field Police, a captain of military counterintelligence, and an SS second lieutenant. They appeared in court in full military regalia—a rare practice in Soviet trials. The prosecution pointed out that the decorations were rewards received for atrocities committed against Soviet people."[4]

With the seats filled and all the actors in place, the Military Tribunal of the 4th Ukrainian Front came to order. Before the packed hall, under bright lights and the hum of motion picture cameras, the Secretary of the Court, Justiciary Captain Kandibin, read the indictment, "In the case of the atrocities committed by the German fascist invaders in the town of Kharkov during the period of their temporary occupation."

"Under the direction of their superiors, the German fascist troops asphyxiated in specially equipped 'murder vans,' hanged, shot or tortured to death many tens of thousands of Soviet people; plundered the property of state, economic, cultural, and public organizations; burned down and destroyed entire towns and thousands of inhabited places; and drove to slavery in Germany hundreds of thousands of the peaceful population. All these crimes and outrages are not isolated facts, but only a link in the long chain of crimes which have been and are being committed by the German invaders on the direct instructions of the German government and the Supreme Command of the German Army."

The opening salvo was supported by a lengthy rehearsal of Nazi atrocities described by civilian and military witnesses including several Germans. In this nightmare litany, murder by gas wagon seemed the gentlest of methods—a mercy killing compared to the fate of starving prisoners in one camp waiting for food. "During the distribution of scanty rations, soldiers used to set dogs on the exhausted and hungry people," the indictment stated. "The dogs jumped into the crowd, tore to shreds the clothes and bodies of the war prisoners, knocked them down, dragged and mauled them on the ground. Some of the badly mauled prisoners and civilians were then shot by soldiers and thrown over the fence so as to avoid bothering about their treatment."

The indictment asserted that the "whole weight of responsibility" for atrocities committed by Nazis in Kharkov "is borne by the leaders of the predatory fascist government of Germany and by the Supreme Command of the German Army"—but that the instruments of their terror were equally guilty. One by one, the indictment detailed the crimes of Retzlaff, Ritz, Langheld, and Mikhail Bulanov, the Russian collaborator.

"As a result of the foregoing exposition," the indictment concluded, "the persons enumerated are committed for trial before the Court of the Military Tribunal."

Symbolically at least, this was the trial of the men who murdered my grandparents and great-grandparents at Drobitsky Yar. Yes, it could have been worse. They could have been torn to pieces by dogs. If this was a "show trial," it was because the victims were showing the perpetrators far more justice than they deserved.

CHAPTER TWENTY-FOUR

A fter the painfully deliberate reading of the indictment in German, all the accused pleaded guilty, and questioning of the defendants finally began in the trial which "opens the period of great, awful judgment on Germans who have been transgressing the law of humanity," wrote journalist Alexei Tolstoy in *Pravda*.

In dramatic illustration of the Soviet theory of equal guilt for the whole Nazi machine, from the Führer in Berlin to the gaswagon driver in Ukraine, the first German to bear the weight of that "awful judgment" for the greatest crime of the century was a man whose name and face were otherwise destined for anonymity.

William Langheld, 52, was the oldest defendant, born in 1891 at Frankfurt-on-Main. He joined the Nationalist Socialist Party in 1933. Before the war, he was an official of the Town Council in his hometown. A captain in the

Counter-Espionage Service, Langheld was charged with taking part in shootings and atrocities against both prisoners of war and civilians, Jews and Gentiles alike. He allegedly used torture to extract false information from prisoners and, when that failed, fabricated evidence that led to the murder of innocents. A *Time* report described Langheld as "a horse-faced, clean-shaven, lipless veteran of World War I who told his story coldly." "A red-faced and unemotional Nazi," said the *New York Times*.

The most chilling portrait was painted by Edmund Stevens, who noted that Langheld and the other defendants "almost seemed to revel in their wickedness, gratuitously filling in all the lurid details." In a story under the headline "Nazi Captain in War Trial Boasts of Slaying and Cruelty," Stevens wrote: "With his carriage and heel clicking, Langheld is the epitome of a German soldier of the old school. He rocks back and forth on his heels while calmly confessing the most horrible crimes, evincing an apparent zeal to omit no detail, however damaging to his case."

Standing before the tribunal in his uniform "spangled with decorations," Langheld clearly and with no trace of remorse recounted why it was necessary for him to invent evidence against innocent civilians. "My immediate superior, a major, reproached me because there were not enough executions under my command," he testified. "I apologized and said that I had only been at the camp a short time and had not yet had an opportunity to show my diligence."

"Did you not try to prove to the major that the prisoners of war had not committed any crimes?" the prosecutor asked.

"Yes, I knew there had been no crimes, and no cases," Langheld said. "But I understood the major's remark as an order to create cases—to invent them if they did not exist. I ordered one of the most exhausted prisoners to be brought to me, assuming it would be easier to obtain the necessary evidence. I asked whether he knew who was preparing to escape from the camp and at the same time promised to improve his food. The prisoner refused to mention any names, saying he knew nothing of such rumors. But as I had to carry out the major's orders, I ordered the prisoner thrown to the ground and beat him with sticks until he lost consciousness. Then I drew up a statement, kicked the prisoner till he sat up, and tried to force him to sign it. He again refused."

"Who signed the statement after all?" asked the prosecutor.

"The interpreter," Langheld said.

The fabricated testimony with the forged signature stated that twenty prisoners were plotting to escape the camp. Langheld then chose the names of twenty prisoners at random from the camp list and presented them to the major who had criticized the low body count under his command. The prisoners were shot the following day. In another instance, Langheld demonstrated that he was not only diligent but resourceful in padding his body count.

Six women from nearby villages came to the camp
seeking information about missing relatives. Langheld
arrested the women and accused them of attempting to
establish communication between prisoners and gue-
rillas outside the camp. According to the official trial
narrative, "They were undressed, flung on a bench and
beaten with sticks and rods. But no tortures could force
these Soviet women to give false evidence. They fell
unconscious, but did not say a word."

One of the women had brought with her a five-year-
old child. The prosecutor asked how the child reacted
to the beating.

"The child at first clung to its mother crying, and
then crept away to a corner and crouched there in
terror," Langheld testified.

The next day, Langheld presented trumped-up
charges against five of the women, and they were sum-
marily shot. The sixth woman, the mother of the child,
died that night from the beating. And what became of
the child?

"He clung to his dead mother, crying aloud," Langheld
testified. "The lance-corporal who came to take away the
woman's body got tired of this, so he shot the child."

Civilians as well as Red Army soldiers were herded
into so-called prisoner of war camps in Ukraine, which
in practice were holding cells for the walking dead,
and arenas for sadistic sport. In one camp, Langheld

testified, prisoners were forced to live in the open. Camp authorities allowed them to light fires at night for warmth—then stood by as soldiers opened fire on the huddled figures as if they were plastic ducks at a carnival midway firing range. The fun did not end there for the captors.

> **Prosecution:** Tell us why, when German officers and soldiers came to the camp, as you testified at the preliminary examination, they tore off the caps of war prisoners and threw them into a forbidden zone?

> **Langheld:** The soldiers practiced this as a sport in order to show their contempt of the Russians.

> **Prosecution:** And what happened afterwards?

> **Langheld:** When the prisoners tried to pick up their caps, the guard fired at them. Naturally there were occasions when they were killed.

> **Prosecution:** Were there other occasions when prisoners were fired at?

> **Langheld:** Yes. I myself witnessed similar incidents in the camp at Poltava.

Prosecution: So it means that war prisoners were chosen as shooting targets?

Langheld: Yes, it may be said that at the given moment they were regarded as game to be shot at.

Prosecution: Did German officers and soldiers take the prisoners' clothes from them?

Langheld: Yes. All the good things they had were taken from them.

Prosecution: That is to say, they were robbed.

Langheld: Yes, that is so.

Prosecution: And did you take part in this robbery?

Langheld: Yes, I did.

The prosecutor asked Langheld how many Soviet citizens he had personally exterminated. Langheld hesitated, rolling his eyes upward in calculation. "I cannot give the exact figure," he said, "but I imagine there were at least one hundred." The prosecutor wanted to know if soldiers or officers were ever punished for brutalizing or killing civilians.

Stevens wrote that Langheld "pondered a moment . . . and then answered in the same quiet, measured voice in which his entire testimony had been delivered, that on the contrary such treatment was deliberately encouraged and rewarded. At the conclusion of his testimony, Langheld turned on his heels and strode back to the prisoners' box."

Next up was Hans Ritz, at 24 the youngest of the defendants, and also the most talkative and eager to heap blame on higher-ups. Born in 1919 in Marienwerder in eastern Germany, Ritz was the son of a professor and attended Königsberg University, where he studied law and music. He was a member of the Hitler Youth from age fourteen and served as President of the Court of Honor of Hitler Youth in Poznan while working there as a lawyer. In 1943, Ritz was drafted for service on the Eastern Front, and rose to the rank of *Untersturmbannfuhrer* (lieutenant) in the SS.

Ritz was "a small man with a caved-in chest, a gnome-like bald head and an infantile expression," said a *Time* magazine story. Ritz's appearance belied a curious mind and excellent memory for detail. He had been intrigued by stories of mobile gas chambers, Ritz testified, but not until he was posted to Kharkov in May 1943 was his curiosity satisfied.

"Lt. Jacobi told me they had much work to do in connection with arrested persons detained in the Kharkov prison but that, thank God, they had a special method of clearing the prisons," Ritz told the court. "When I asked him what this method was, Lt. Jacobi told me it was the 'gas van.' I remembered that I had heard about this vehicle in Germany. I asked Lt. Jacobi to let me have a look at the vehicle. He said there would be a good opportunity to do so at six o'clock the next morning, as the machine would be loaded and if I came to the prison yard I would see it."

At dawn the next day, Ritz watched as some sixty prisoners were packed into the truck. He noted "they were emaciated, their hair was matted, and there were traces of blood on their faces." Some balked at the sight of the truck and were driven inside by kicks and blows from the butt ends of SS rifles. The inquisitive Ritz wondered how the resisters knew what awaited them. "Lt. Jacobi replied that . . . the gas van had been so extensively used in Kharkov, many people appeared to have learned what the van portended," Ritz testified.

Having witnessed the loading of the gas wagon, Ritz naturally was curious to observe what happened when it reached its destination. Learning that three thousand civilians were to be shot for having welcomed Soviet authorities when Red Army troops briefly recaptured Kharkov, Ritz asked to watch and Major Kranebitter, S.D. commander in Kharkov, was happy to oblige.

Prosecution: Tell us in detail about it.

Ritz: Major Kranebitter took me and several officers and drove out to a village near the town of Kharkov where the shooting was to take place. On the way we overtook three lorries loaded with prisoners accompanied by SS going to the same place. The car in which I rode arrived at a forest clearing where pits had been dug. This clearing was surrounded by SS men. Soon the lorries arrived with the prisoners. The prisoners were divided into small groups and were shot by SS men with automatic rifles. Major Kranebitter said to me: "Show us what you are made of." As a military man and an officer I did not refuse. I took the automatic rifle from one of the SS men and fired at the prisoners.

Prosecution: Were there women and children among the people shot?

Ritz: Yes. I remember a woman with a child. The woman, trying to save the child, covered it with her body. But this did not help her because the bullet went through her and the child.

Prosecution: How many people were shot on that occasion in your presence?

Ritz: Major Kranebitter told me about three hundred people were to be shot on that day.

Prosecution: In the pits in which people were buried, did you see any who had been asphyxiated in the gas vans?

Ritz: Yes. Lt. Jacobi showed a pit covered with a thin layer of earth through which showed the outlines of human bodies. Lt. Jacobi said these were the passengers of yesterday's ride in the gas van.

Later in his testimony, Ritz told of moving from observer of massacres to supervisor and trigger man.

Prosecution: Did you personally take part in the shootings in the pits in the vicinity of Taganrog?

Ritz: I was ordered by the Chief of the *Sonderkommando*, Ecker, to detail a firing squad. After giving my orders, I went to the site to check up whether my instructions had been accurately carried out.

Prosecution: What did you see on the spot?

Ritz: I saw a pit approximately 50 by 50 meters and 4 meters deep. Inside it were a group of persons to be shot, approximately fifty. Sergeant-major Turkel reported that every-thing was ready for the shooting. The prisoners were poorly clad and had been beaten up. I said "Begin" and fire was opened. A mass of bloodstained bodies piled up in the pit, but some were not dead. I ordered two privates to go down into the pit and finish off those who were still alive. Soon after that, two SS men and I got into the pit. Two persons who were still alive but wounded, I finished off with my pistol.

Ritz's eagerness to learn new things and techniques was evident throughout his testimony:

Prosecution: Tell us how you questioned Soviet citizens.

Ritz: At first, I questioned the prisoners according to my knowledge of jurisprudence. However, soon the Chief of the *Sonderkommando* came to me and declared that I could not continue in

this way, that these people were thick-skinned
and other methods ought to be applied. Then I
started beating them.

Prosecution: Was beating part of the system of
interrogation of Soviet citizens?

Ritz: Yes. In Kharkov, I had the opportunity of
being present at interrogations, and everyone
from the commander to the lowest ranks of the
Sonderkommando beat up people and beat them
hard.

Prosecution: You, Ritz, are a person of higher
legal education and apparently consider yourself a man of culture. How could you not only
watch people being beaten but even take an
active part in it, and shoot perfectly innocent
people—not only under compulsion but of
your own free will?

Ritz: I had to obey orders, otherwise I would have
been court-martialed and certainly sentenced to
death.

Prosecution: This is not quite so, because you
yourself expressed a desire to be present when

people were loaded on to the gas vans and nobody specially invited you to be there.

Ritz: Yes, that is true. But I beg you to take into consideration that I was then still a newcomer on the Eastern Front and wanted to convince myself as to whether it was true these lorries of which I had heard were used on the Eastern Front

Prosecution: Now, Ritz, you are a man with some knowledge of the law. Tell us, were the standards of international law observed to any extent by the German Army on the Eastern Front?

Ritz: I must say that on the Eastern Front there was no question of international law or any other law.

Prosecution: Who is actually to blame for all of this?

Ritz: I consider the primary and chief culprit to be Hitler, who calls first of all for a system of cruelty and, secondly, speaks of the superiority of the Germano-Aryan race whose mission it is to establish order in Europe. Further, I would like to point out that Himmler stated repeatedly that . . . the death sentence must be imposed according to one's Aryan instinct. This Germano-Aryan instinct had to be covered up to a certain extent in Germany, but on the Eastern Front the German troops acted openly. Further, I want to speak about Rosenberg, the propagandist of the superiority of the German race. This propaganda of Russians as barbarians caused the German soldiers to behave as they do.

In freely admitting crimes he committed by his own hand, then easily shifting blame to others, Ritz was in many ways the poster boy of the homicidal psychopathy which made the Holocaust possible. Wrote journalist Alexei Tolstoy: "So much for university, music lessons, and a professor's family—all bounced off Hans Ritz's conscience like peas off a wall. I declare I have never yet seen such moral degradation."

Of the three German defendants, Reinhard Retzlaff came closest to personifying the "banality of evil" which Hannah Arendt memorably attached to Adolf Eichmann. Unlike the heel-clicking soldier Langheld and the eager Hitler Youth Ritz, Retzlaff seemed to have drifted on a sea of his own inertia and ineffectuality as a radio operator and prison guard until washing up on the shore of the Eastern front, where he found himself supervising massacres as a Senior Corporal in the German Secret Field Police.

Retzlaff, 36, was born in 1907 in Berlin and had a secondary education. His father worked in a health insurance bureau, and before the war Retzlaff himself was an assistant department head in a Frankfurt newspaper. He joined the German army in 1940 and served as a radio operator with an artillery unit in France. After the French campaign he was assigned to a reservist battalion whose main responsibility was guarding French and Belgian prisoners in Pomerania. Deemed no longer fit for active military duty, Retzlaff then was transferred to the "Altenburg" Battalion, which trained officials for the German Secret Field Police.

A *Time* story described Retzlaff as "weak-chinned and pompadoured," his demeanor during trial "bored, contemptuous."

Prosecution: What subjects were studied in the Altenburg Battalion?

Retzlaff: Chiefly, criminal law, methods of examination, arrests, searches, espionage activities among the civilian population. In addition, special lectures were given us.

Prosecution: What kind of lectures?

Retzlaff: Leading Gestapo officials gave us special reports explaining the mission of the German people as a representative of a superior race and its tasks in the establishment of a "New Order" in Europe and measures related to it.

Prosecution: What are these measures?

Retzlaff: We were told that the Soviet people as one of the inferior races must be exterminated.

Prosecution: Thus, in the battalion you were taught methods of extermination of the Soviet people?

Retzlaff: Yes.

Prosecution: Was this policy ordered by the German government?

Retzlaff: Yes. In the course of a number of years the German government impressed this policy upon German minds through press, cinema, and radio.

Prosecution: Thus you were trained in this battalion not as officials but as hangmen?

Retzlaff: Yes, one may say so, as I later saw in practice.

Prosecution: How many Soviet citizens were exterminated by means of the gas van with your direct participation?

Retzlaff: I personally took part twice in loading people into the gas van. I put there about twenty persons each time.

Prosecution: How were the people murdered in the gas van buried?

Retzlaff: The bodies of the murdered people were buried in a gully to the south of Kharkov or burned.

Prosecution: They were burned?

Retzlaff: I was ordered to accompany a gas van to the area of the barracks of the Kharkov Tractor Plant. The gas van drew up in front of a gray-painted barrack. The S.D. men jumped out of their car and began to unload the bodies of the murdered people from the gas van and carried them into this barrack. When

I entered, I saw the rooms on the right and left of the corridor were already packed with bodies which had apparently been brought there earlier.

Prosecution: Approximately how many bodies were there in the barrack together with those you had brought?

Retzlaff: There were approximately 300 to 350.

Prosecution: Continue your testimony.

Retzlaff: When the bodies had been stacked in the corridor, the S.D. men entered the barrack and poured petrol over them. They also poured petrol over the outside wall of the barrack. Then the S.D. men flung blazing torches inside and set fire to it. I saw six other barracks burnt down in the same manner.

Prosecution: What was the purpose of burning the bodies of people finished off in the gas van?

Retzlaff: So that the use of the gas van should be kept secret, and therefore traces of its work—dead bodies—were to be burnt.

Retzlaff told the court how he was schooled in a special brand of torture by a commissar of the 560th Group of the Secret Field Police at Kharkov. It happened during interrogation of two arrested workers.

> **Retzlaff:** Karchan warned me that it was necessary to convict them of guerilla activities and obtain from them information about their accomplices. During the interrogation . . . I got the impression that these persons were not guilty and I reported this to Karchan. He asked me whether I resorted to beatings. I replied in the negative. Karchan then ordered me to beat up the prisoners.

> **Prosecution:** Relate in detail how you carried out Karchan's order.

> **Retzlaff:** I borrowed a rubber truncheon from Sergeant-major Tichner which he usually used at interrogations. I failed to achieve anything by this means and reported this to Police Commissar Meliss, who then came to the office in which I examined the prisoners. Meliss told me that in examinations one must display greater resourcefulness. Pointing at the prisoners, he said, "Look, this prisoner has a fine beard. Pluck out the hair from it and prick the other with a

needle." I obeyed this order too, but failed to obtain any result.

Prosecution: Tell us what happened to the workers whom you had examined.

Retzlaff: Police Commissar Karchan ordered me to obtain through the Kharkov Passport Bureau a list of workers of the Tractor Plant and to copy out fifteen names. I carried out this order and the next day handed him a list of fifteen workers. The two prisoners whom I had examined were asphyxiated in the gas van and the fifteen workers on my list were shot.

Prosecution: Do you remember the names of the two workers from the Kharkov Tractor Plant who were finished off in the gas van and those fifteen workers who were shot?

Retzlaff: No, I do not remember. During my work I had to deal with so many prisoners that I could not remember all these Russian names.

Not among them was Mikhail Petrovich Bulanov, a driver—or "chauffeur" as he sometimes said—for the Gestapo in Kharkov from October 1941 to February 1943.

Ironically, less is known about the one Russian defendant than about the three Germans. Bulanov, 26, was born in 1917 in Kazakhstan, and was not a member of any political party. In testimony he alluded to being married. I found no other personal information about him.

In the transcripts and reporting of the trial, Bulanov emerges as a fearful, reticent cipher amid his more formidable, unabashed co-defendants (he "looked like a man in a waking dream," in Stevens' vivid phrase), a pawn of history who invites pity—until his heinous crimes as a paid accomplice are recalled.

> **Bulanov:** Early in December 1941, on the orders of the Gestapo Chief, about nine hundred sick people undergoing treatment in Kharkov hospital were shot.

> **Prosecution:** What was your part in this affair?

> **Bulanov:** I was ordered to bring a three-ton truck to the hospital. When I arrived, nine more three-ton trucks had arrived besides mine.

> **Prosecution:** How many trips did you make?

> **Bulanov:** I made four trips during which I brought to the shooting site approximately 150 persons.

Prosecution: Tell the Court how this was done.

Bulanov: When I arrived at the hospital . . . Gestapo men began to lead out patients dressed only in their underwear and load them into the trucks. I drove the truck to the shooting site approximately four kilometers from the city. When we arrived, screams and sobs of patients who were already being shot filled the air. Some begged for mercy and fell down naked in the cold mud, but the Germans pushed them into the pits and shot them.

Prosecution: Tell the Court what you know about the shooting of children in the Children's Hospital of Nizhne Chirskaya.

Bulanov: On August 25 and 26, 1942, I—together with chauffeur Blokhin—was ordered to get the trucks ready. We were ordered to drive them to Nizhne Chirskaya Children's Hospital. Upon our arrival, Gestapo men began to lead the children out of the hospital and load them on the trucks. The children were ragged, and swollen from hunger. Many resisted and would not board the trucks. The Gestapo men assured them they were going to their uncles and aunts in Stalingrad. Some children yielded to persuasion and got on the trucks, while others resisted. The Gestapo men forcibly put them in and I was ordered to fasten the canvas at the back of the truck. Three to four kilometers from Nizhne Chirskaya, a pit had been prepared. Having reached the pit, I and other Gestapo men began to take the children toward the pit near which stood a Gestapo man, Alex. Point-blank he shot the children in the head with an automatic rifle and then pushed them into the pit. Seeing this, the children struggled and tried to break away, crying, "Uncle, I am afraid!" and "Uncle, I want to live, don't shoot me!" and so on. But the Germans took no notice of this.

Prosecution: What was the age of these children?

Bulanov: They ranged in age from six to twelve years.

Prosecution: Did you, Bulanov, see the gas van in which people were murdered with carbon monoxide?

Bulanov: In January, 1942, such a van arrived at our garage from Germany.

Prosecution: Did you have occasion to repair it?

Bulanov: I had occasion to repair it and clean it. When cleaning it and sweeping the inside I saw children's caps and tiny shoes which had evidently fallen off the murdered children.

Prosecution: What remuneration did you receive from the Germans for your traitorous activities?

Bulanov: I received 90 reichmarks, or 900 rubles, as wages. I also received a soldier's ration. Furthermore, the belongings of executed Soviet citizens—what remained after the Germans had selected the best for themselves—were given to us.

Prosecution: What things did you receive?

Bulanov: I received overcoats for my wife and myself, also two suits of clothes and footwear.

Prosecution: Accused Bulanov, it follows from your testimony that you betrayed your motherland, that you sold yourself to the Germans for ninety marks, took an active part in the systematic shootings and extermination of innocent Soviet people. Do you plead guilty to this?

Bulanov: Yes, I do.

CHAPTER TWENTY-FIVE

The Tribunal heard from a series of witnesses, German and Russian, who added to the tapestry of horror woven by the testimony of the four defendants. In an ordinary murder trial, the loved ones of the victim fill a few seats in the courtroom but most are occupied by curious strangers with no personal stake in the outcome. This was not the case in the Opera House where, to some degree, all the onlookers were victims of the German occupation. And although the word "Jew" was never uttered in the courtroom, there could be little doubt among onlookers about the identity of their fellow citizens singled out as the primary targets of Nazi terror in Kharkov. Despite the Soviet charade, the Kharkov trial and others "exposed the overwhelming tragedy of the Soviet Jews," wrote Alexander Prusin. "In the localities where the largest Jewish communities had lived before the war—the Baltic states, Belorussia, and the Ukraine—the population was well aware of the horrors of ghettos, camps, and execution sites."[1]

The audience was mostly female and old because the men of fighting age had gone off to war, or been imprisoned and killed. "The faces of these Kharkov civilians who had lived through two years of Nazi occupation were charged with a breathless tenseness that never once relaxed through the long hours of interrogation," Edmund Stevens wrote. Fluent in Russian, Stevens spoke with people in the crowd during recesses in the trial.

"I discovered that many of the people in the audience had personal knowledge or experience of the events and atrocities described and had seen or known the defendants during the German occupation," he wrote. "Several times during more gruesome bits of evidence, there were stifled sobs from some woman—not out of pity for the defendants. For the most part, the proceedings took place against a background of concentrated silence."

It is difficult to isolate the *less* gruesome bits of evidence in the catalogue of atrocities provided by the witnesses. How to compare, on the gruesomeness scale, the sport-shooting of starving prisoners scrambling for food packets tossed into a huge crowd, to the killing of prisoners with shovels and spades when guards ran out bullets? Can either compare to the sight of arms and legs poking through knee-deep mud in a prison/death camp? Or the screams of children before being shot point-blank?

The testimony on one topic, *gaswagens*, produced an element of dark humor—a mordant running commentary on Nazi arrogance, self-delusion, and guilt. Karl Kosch, an architect by training and a field engineer for the German army, testified about the wagons, as did many witnesses.

"Waiting on the road for a truck to take me back to my battalion, I saw a big van coming in my direction. It stopped near me. An *Unterscharfuhrer* (sergeant) came out of the driver's cabin and asked if I had seen a big truck with SS troops in it. Then he came closer and lit a cigarette and I noticed that he was slightly drunk. I asked if he could give me a lift in the direction of Mariupol. He laughed and, taking me to the back door of the van, said: 'Well, climb in. There is plenty of room in here.'

"When he opened the door a wave of terrible stench came out. The truck was completely empty. It occurred to me that this was the gas van of which I had heard. I said, 'So you want to give me a ride to heaven in this truck?' The *Unterscharfuhrer* stopped talking, looked grave, and asked me: 'What do you know about this machine?' I answered that I had heard a great deal about the gas van. He said that this was a gas van, but I must not say a word about it to anyone because the machine was strictly secret."

The gas wagon was the worst-kept secret in Ukraine, possibly in the entire Nazi-occupied East.

Prosecutor: From whom did you first hear about this gas van?

Kosch: I first heard of it from N.C.O. Hass. Previously Hass had been in the central sector of the Eastern Front and said he had seen the gas van on the outskirts of Smolensk and in Vitebsk and Byelgorod. I also heard about it from Winn and Bernhold, who served in the 179th Battalion, 79th German Infantry Division. These men also said they had seen and heard about the gas vans in the central sector.

The second-worst kept Nazi secret was the unearthing and cremating of bodies at the many killing fields across Ukraine and the occupied territories in a futile attempt to destroy the evidence of the genocide. The obsession with hiding these public crimes which could not be hidden bespoke awareness on the part of the Nazi leadership, starting with Hitler, that it was engaged in unprecedented acts of criminality which violated every written and unwritten rule of warfare.

Hitler, Himmler, and the rest feared for themselves the judgment day which had now arrived for three of their tools, murderous minions named Langheld, Ritz, and Retzlaff. Over the course of three days in the Opera House the Soviet prosecutors had laid out the panoply of Nazi crimes and atrocities visited on Ukraine and Kharkov in particular. On the morning of December 18, it was the task of chief state prosecutor Col. N.K. Dunayev in his closing statement to summarize a litany of violence and sadism which beggared the imagination.

"Citizen judges, since the treacherous attack of Hitlerite Germany on our motherland, the peoples of the Soviet Union learn of new crimes each day, new monstrous villainies committed by the German fascist invaders of our land," Dunayev began. "Mountains of bestially murdered, peaceful Soviet citizens have been piled up by the Hitlerites wherever they have set their foot. Thousands of murdered children, of women and aged people killed, of sick war prisoners burned to death—such are the ghastly traces left by German occupation. Turning over the gory pages of this case, one might think that one is dealing with the darkest period of medieval barbarism which, however, has been far outstripped by the German hangmen of our times."

In a clear signal that the trial of the four defendants was also—perhaps even primarily—a trial of Hitler and the Third Reich *in absentia*, Dunayev named the international laws which Germany had signed—the Hague Convention of 1907, the Geneva Convention of 1929—then tossed aside when it suited Hitler's purposes. "Having solemnly endorsed these Conventions of her own free will, Germany then cynically and basely violated them, just as she violated the treaties of peace she has concluded," said Dunayev, no doubt referring to the 1939 non-aggression treaty with Stalin which Hitler casually crumpled the day he sent three million men and three thousand tanks across the Soviet border in June 1941.

Hitler's paternity of the aggressive war and its atrocities did not absolve the implementers of his criminal vision, Dunayev said. He cited the Washington Treaty of 1922 on piracy and its principle that a service member is not immune from trial and punishment if he commits a crime, even if he was following orders from a superior.

"Numerous orders of the Hitlerite government and military prescribe actions which are, manifestly and beyond doubt, major crimes and flagrant violations of international law," Dunayev told the court. "The German servicemen who set fire to peaceful towns and villages, who shoot civilians, who force women, the aged, and children into burning houses cannot but know that such actions constitute a travesty of international law and the laws of all civilized countries.

"The former servicemen of the German Fascist Army who are today in the docks are criminals, and must bear deserved punishment for the criminal offenses they have committed. The evidence of unheard-of crimes committed by the base Hitlerite is not far away, citizen judges. It is in the suburbs of Kharkov, in the forest park, on the territory of the tractor plant, and in many other places converted by the fascist hangmen into the ghastly graves of victims in tens of thousands.

"I appeal to you, citizen judges, to inflict severe punishment on the three base representatives of fascist Berlin, and on their abominable accomplice, to punish them for their bloody crimes, for the sufferings and the blood, for the tears, for the lives of our children, of our wives and mothers, of our sisters and our fathers. Today they are answering to the Soviet Court, to our people, to the whole world, for the felonies they committed on a scale and of a baseness far surpassing the blackest pages of human history. Tomorrow their superiors will have to answer—the chieftains of these bandits.

"In the name of the law and of justice, in the name of tens of thousands of people maimed and tortured to death, in the name of the entire people—I, as state prosecutor, beg you, citizen judges, to sentence all four base criminals to death by hanging."

Dunayev's request for the death penalty unleashed raucous applause from the onlookers. The defendants' state-appointed counsel pleaded for mercy—something they had denied their victims—offering arguments and mitigations which sound lifted from a trial on Court TV. The Germans were products of their environment and a "monstrous" system of education, argued N.V. Kommodov. "These men were made into assassins by killing their souls, and it is this doubt which gives me, comrade judges, the moral right to pose the possibility of a lesser penalty than that demanded by the prosecutor."

Counsel S.K. Kaznacheyev spoke of Retzlaff, 36, as if he were the member of a teenage biker gang in need of rehab, not hanging, asking the court to consider that he "served in an army of bandits where human feelings were considered a weakness, and ruthlessness and fanaticism a virtue." He asked the court to spare the confessed killer's life because he was "conscious of what he has done and has undergone a psychological transformation."

Finally, the accused were given the opportunity to address the court. Langheld asked to be spared because he was old, Ritz because he was young, Retzlaff so he could return to Germany to "open the eyes of the German people to Hitlerite propaganda." Bulanov simply begged for mercy. All the defendants admitted their crimes but said ultimate responsibility belonged to those who ordered them to kill. Langheld played the victim card, eloquently.

"I flogged Russian prisoners of war," he said. "I issued orders for them to be shot. On my orders, civilians were arrested and subsequently shot. But . . . I am not the only one. The whole German Army is the same. I was not the only one to perpetrate atrocities. I do not want to minimize my guilt in any way but . . . the underlying reasons for all the atrocities and crimes of the Germans in Russia are to be found in the German government.

"The Hitlerite regime has succeeded in stifling the finest feelings of the German people by implanting base instincts in them. One might quote the words of a German poet: 'Accursed evil in its turn engendering evil.' This evil found expression in the orders and directives of the higher German military authorities. To fail to carry them out would have meant to sentence oneself to death. I was also the victim of these orders and directives."

Ritz, in a rambling mea-not-culpa, told the court he did not want to minimize his crimes—"an atrocity remains an atrocity"—then attempted to minimize them by telling the judges that he derived no "satisfaction" or "gratification" from the murders he committed. ("I was acting on orders.") He pleaded that he was "a child of only thirteen" when Hitler came to power and had been subjected to relentless Nazi propaganda. Like Retzlaff, Ritz claimed a death-bed conversion from his ardent embrace of Hitler's mission to exterminate the "uncultured and inferior" Russian people. He had lived and learned.

"When I reached the Eastern Front I was convinced that there was not a word of truth in these fables of Hitler, Rosenberg, and the others," Ritz said. "I realize that destruction of this system would be an act of justice. I request you spare my life so that I may devote myself to the struggle against that system."

Stevens, who was in the Opera House for the final day, wrote that Ritz's plea "thawed none of the ice in the court. Every face in that room outside the prisoner's box wore the same expression of hatred and contempt that signified too clearly 'thumbs down!' There was no room for mercy in that surcharged courtroom. It was crowded out by the unseen audience of uncounted thousands of tortured and massacred Ukrainian men, women, and children whose blood the defendants and others like them had shed."

After hearing the final pleas, the judges retired to deliberate, but there was little suspense. Everyone in the courtroom knew what was coming, Stevens wrote. "Most of them had seen the gallows being erected in the center of the marketplace." Around midnight, the judges returned. The presiding judge, Major-General A. Myasnikov, read the verdicts—detailing the crimes of each man—and the sentences.

"During the temporary occupation of the city and region of Kharkov, the German fascist invaders shot, hanged, and burned alive, or asphyxiated by means of carbon monoxide, more than thirty thousand completely innocent Soviet civilians including women, old folk and children . . . deported into German slavery hundreds of thousands of Soviet citizens . . . pillaged, burned and destroyed the material and cultural treasures of the Soviet people," Myasnikov summarized.

"On the basis of Article 296 of the code of criminal procedure of the Ukrainian Soviet Socialist Republic and the decree of the Presidium of the Supreme Soviet of the U.S.S.R., the Military Tribunal of the Front sentences William Langheld, Hans Ritz, Reinhard Retzlaff, and Mikhail

Petrovich Bulanov to death by hanging. The verdict is final and not subject to appeal."

The Opera House erupted in applause. "Bulanov and Langheld seemed on the verge of collapse," the *New York Times* reported. "Both were led from the hall by guards. Ritz started to cry when the demand for death sentences was being translated into German." This was puzzling. The court had simply granted Ritz's wish not to minimize his crimes.

At the conclusion of *Eichmann in Jerusalem*, her brilliant meditation on the trial of Final Solution facilitator Adolf Eichmann, Hannah Arendt offers her own sentencing statement to the convicted Nazi. It was almost as if she were addressing the Kharkov defendants. In her peroration, Arendt addresses Eichmann:

"Let us assume, for the sake of argument, that it was nothing more than misinformation that made you a willing instrument in the organization of mass murder; there still remains the fact that you have carried out, and therefore actively supported, a policy of mass murder. For politics is not like the nursery; in politics, obedience and support are the same.

"And just as you supported and carried out a policy of not wanting to share the Earth with the Jewish people and the people of a number of other nations—as though you and your superiors had any right to determine who should and who should not inhabit the world—we find that no one, that is, no member of the human race, can be expected to want to share the Earth with you. This is the reason, and the only reason, you must hang."[2]

CHAPTER TWENTY-SIX

Observing the insouciant Germans in the dock on the final day, Stevens was not convinced that they had fully grasped the reality—the utter finality of their situation. Not so the traitor Bulanov. "From the very start, the quaking fear that convulsed his frame and the wild horror in his eyes showed he knew full well the shadow of the gallows was upon him," Stevens wrote.

In the back of the Germans' minds, he said, may have been stories of an old Russian ruse—walking men into the shadow of the gallows before revealing at the very last moment that it was a grand bluff. "Apparently the illusion still persisted," Stevens wrote, observing the Germans' stolid demeanor (excepting Ritz's tears at hearing the death sentence). The sentence was read about midnight; less than twelve hours later, it was carried out.

"Not until the following morning when they were hustled out of a Black Maria (police van) and saw the four erected gallows against the grey December sky, saw the close-packed crowd that thronged the marketplace, surging against the cordon of soldiers struggling to keep the space around the gallows clear—not till that moment did they realize the jig was up indeed," Stevens wrote.

The market itself had been burned down by the Germans, leaving a wide expanse of rutted ground for a quartet of gallows made from freshly hewn wooden posts. Each gallows tree had a "trunk" some fifteen feet high with a cross beam on one side, forming a 7 shape, for suspending the rope. From each beam hung a noose and beneath it a one-ton military truck. On the bed of each truck were three stools made of white birchwood.

Clustered in an area near the gallows were members of the Military Tribunal, representatives of the Extraordinary State Commission which gathered evidence for the trial, Kharkov city officials, and a gaggle of Russian, British, and American correspondents. Guarding the VIP section were fur-capped Red Army soldiers with machine guns slung over their shoulders. Surrounding the island of elites was a sea of ordinary people—forty to fifty thousand, reporters estimated—in heavy coats, head scarves, and caps. Young people gathered on rooftops; others watched from windows. Soviet fighter planes patrolled the sky above the square. Newsreel cameras hummed.

At 11:15 A.M. a Black Maria entered the square and rolled to a stop near the gallows, lined up like telephone poles. The doors of the van opened and the four convicted war criminals, hands tied behind their backs, were led by soldiers toward the nooses. They were hoisted up onto the trucks and placed on the stools beneath the rope. They were not given blindfolds. Soldiers stood on the stools beside them to carry out the sentence.

"The Germans were in full uniform with epaulettes and ribbons and they wore forage caps," wrote the correspondent for Reuters news service. "Capt. Wilhelm Langheld wore good-quality military trousers with high boots." From his perspective, Stevens noted, "Three of the four prisoners had to be propped up. Bulanov had fainted. Ritz and Retzlaff turned pasty white; they drooled at the mouth, and their knees gave way. Only Langheld, the old soldier, remained stiff as a ramrod throughout, never once flinching."

The Red Army attendants slipped nooses around the necks of the condemned men. Major-General Myasnikov, presiding judge at the Tribunal, stood on a platform to one side of the gallows. As the drivers of the trucks started the rumbling engines, Myasnikov read the sentences into a microphone, then ordered, "Carry out the sentence!" The trucks moved forward. The stools fell away and the ropes jerked taut. The killers hung in the air like resting mari-onettes, arms slack, heads lolling to the side. Cheers swept through the sea of onlookers.

"Langheld, Retzlaff, and Bulanov died within three minutes," the Associated Press reported, "while Ritz twitched on the gallows for almost five minutes."

I studied a close-up photo of the crowd. It's impossible to know at which moment the photo was taken, but several people in front are looking up, perhaps at something dangling before their eyes. Here and there in the multitude is a haunted stare which seems to be focused inward, revisiting a private horror. But mostly I saw wide smiles, hands clapping, opened-mouth awe, joy, and, yes, unmistakable expressions of vengeance fulfilled—just a small down payment on imperfect justice, really, since these were only four among thousands of murderers who had perpetrated the mass slaughter and largely achieved Hitler's goal of a *Judenfrei* Ukraine. There is a deep and melancholy irony to this snapshot: it is highly unlikely that any of the faces are Jewish. Most of the Jews of Kharkov fled before the Nazis arrived in 1941. Those who did not, like my mother's family, were now in the ground at Drobitsky Yar. It was left to their non-Jewish countrymen, who had seen their city devastated by the Nazis, to celebrate this moment.

On December 19, 1943, my mother and her sister were in Berlin, where they had been taken a month before under heavy guard by the retreating Germans, who did not know that their prized Russian pianists were Jews. I'm confident that had she been in the marketplace in Kharkov with her liberated countrymen that day, my mother would have been among the celebrants. As I studied the frozen images of this judgment day, her bitter words about her mother and grandmother being forced to squat in the open ditches of the tractor factory came rushing back.

I wanted to put those who created this hell in the same place. That's where I wanted Hitler and Himmler and Goebbels.

She would have settled for these gallows, I thought, and for these men—Langheld, Retzlaff, Ritz, Bulanov. If not these exact men, it was others like them, an army of faceless assassins dispatched by Hitler, who had pulled the triggers and buried her family with the sixteen thousand in the yawning pits at Drobitsky Yar.

I want to take all the leftover butchers, put them on the verge of a high and steep hill, put them on the edge of it, and then start the automatic guns. Not a tear would be lost by me.

Nor, I suspect, by the babushka in the headscarf I saw that December day sitting alone in the balcony of the conservatory, enveloped in sadness, as the student orchestra rehearsed Prokofiev, and later downstairs drifting ghost-like through the hallways in search, it seemed to me, of something precious taken from her long ago. I can't give a name to it, the thing taken from her, but I believe I saw it in the smiling eyes of the young Ukrainian girl in terminal A at the Kiev airport, pirouetting across the floor, beaming, floating free—"Mama! Papa!"—at that moment in time, the happiest child I think I had ever seen.

EPILOGUE

I n 2008 when I listened with amazement as NBC anchorman Brian Williams employed the lofty tone of *expose* for a report on "an invisible part of the Holocaust" in Ukraine— sixty-seven years after the well-documented and previously reported fact—he was following in the tradition of an icon of his profession, CBS broadcaster Edward R. Murrow.

Early in the war, Murrow had held Americans spellbound with his rooftop broadcasts from London during the blitz. In the ensuing years before the end of the war, the existence of Nazi death camps and Hitler's attempt to exterminate all European Jews had been reported in thousands of newspaper stories in the U.S. Yet, almost like clockwork, as the war was ending, the myth of American innocence was born.

"The myth that we have nurtured in the intervening half-century—and that was fostered at the time—is that

Americans, the ordinary man and woman on the street, first learned of the Final Solution in April and May 1945, when Fox-Movietone newsreels showed the walking skeletons and the bodies stacked like cordwood," wrote Ron Hollander, a professor at Montclair State University, in his book *We Knew: America's Newspapers Report the Holocaust.*

After studying newspaper stories from 1941 to 1945, Hollander concluded that "we knew. Not just in 1945 when we stumbled unpreparedly upon Dachau and Buchenwald while chasing the retreating Germans. But for at least the last three years of the war, while 3.5 million Jews were being murdered, *we knew.*"

Murrow must have known—how could he not?—but if so, by the end of the war he was either unconsciously repressing the information or conveniently "forgetting" it for dramatic purposes. Hollander wrote:

"Broadcasting for CBS from Buchenwald on April 15, 1945, Edward R. Murrow spoke as if he were breaking the news for the first time. 'I pray you to believe what I have said about Buchenwald,' Murrow begged his presumably skeptical audience. 'Murder has been done at Buchenwald.'"

Emory University historian Deborah Lipstadt, who haunts Holocaust deniers the way Simon Wiesenthal hunted old Nazis, reinforced the point in *Beyond Belief,* her withering autopsy of American newspaper coverage of the Holocaust from dawn to dust, 1933 to 1945.

"Each time a report confirming some aspect of the Final Solution was released, the press treated it as if it were the *first* official confirmation. Previous reports and news stories were ignored," Lipstadt wrote. "In December 1944, *Newsweek* claimed that the War Refugee Board's description of Auschwitz constituted the 'first time' an American governmental agency had 'officially backed up' charges made by Europeans of mass murder. But the United States government had backed up the charges two years earlier in December 1942."

To illustrate this curious and disturbing amnesia—a less polite but more honest term would be willful ignorance—Lipstadt quoted from a May 1945 editorial in the *Chicago Herald American:* "Last week Americans could no longer doubt stories of Nazi cruelty. For the first time there was irrefutable evidence as the advancing Allied armies captured camps filled with political prisoners and slave laborers, living and dead."

Conspicuously missing from that passage is the word Jewish. To demonstrate the absurdity of omitting Jewish in this instance, imagine the omission of "slave" or "Negro" in a different historical context—the Civil War: "Last week Americans in the North could no longer doubt stories of Southern cruelty. For the first time there was irrefutable evidence as advancing Union armies entered plantations filled with political prisoners and forced laborers."

Anyone can have an off day and simply forget, but it's very likely that the editorial writer's omitting "Jewish" was not just an oversight. The reluctance to identify the victims as Jews—especially on front pages—was one aspect of American newspapers' dysfunctional coverage of the Holocaust and a major reason the coverage did not plant itself in the minds and consciences of readers.

Lipstadt cited the headline above an eight-line story on page one of the *New York Journal American* in June 1942 reporting a World Jewish Congress statement that "the Nazis have established a vast slaughterhouse for Jews" in Eastern Europe and a million Jews already had died as part of Hitler's "proclaimed policy of exterminating the Jewish people."

"JEWS LIST THEIR DEAD AT MILLION."

"This was a *Jewish* story,' Lipstadt dryly observed, "worthy of reporting, but not worthy of complete trust because Jews were 'interested parties'."

And not the most beloved minority in the land at the time. Newspapers historically have been more eager to pander than to lead, keeping a nervous finger on the pulse of the reading public, and in 1942 anti-Semitism in America was "slightly below the boiling point," wrote sociologist David Riesman. In June 1944, with the U.S. fighting a two-front war in the Pacific and Europe, and the Final Solution no secret, a poll asked who represented the gravest threat to America. Six percent said Germans, 9%

named the Japanese, and 24% unaccountably identified the Jews.

Studying those results, I was reminded of my favorite scene in the 1965 movie *Ship of Fools*, set on a German cruise ship in 1933, the year Hitler seized power. Jose Ferrer plays a character named Rieber who issues a constant stream of anti-Semitic remarks. After he concludes a diatribe blaming Jews for all of Germany's woes, a Jewish traveler, Lowenthal, replies, "Well, yes. The Jews and the bicycle riders." A puzzled Rieber replies, "Why the bicycle riders?" Lowenthal: "Why the Jews?"

The other major reason that stories about the Jews became a drop of blood in the ocean of war coverage was the hide-and-seek manner in which they were "played," or presented, by editors. For readers, it was like receiving one piece every few days of a million-piece jigsaw puzzle of a picture they had never seen. Eli Wiesel has made the crucial distinction between "information"—sheer data—and "knowledge," grasping the meaning and significance of data.

The most trenchant, slam-dunk riff I've seen on the failure of the press to transform information into knowledge came from Laurel Leff, a professor at the Northeastern School of Journalism, who did an exhaustive study of Holocaust coverage in the *New York Times*—more than a thousand stories between Germany's invasion of Poland on Sept. 1, 1939 and May 31, 1945, three weeks after the war ended. In that period, the Holocaust—from early persecution to Final Solution—was *never* the lead story of the day, and made the front page only twenty-four times.

"You could have read the front page of the *New York Times* in 1939 and 1940 without knowing that millions of Jews were being sent to Poland, imprisoned in ghettos, and dying of disease and starvation by the tens of thousands," Leff wrote. "You could have read the front page in 1941 without knowing that the Nazis were machine-gunning hundred of thousands of Jews in the Soviet Union.

"You could have read the front page in 1942 and not have known, until the last month, that the Germans were carrying out a plan to annihilate European Jewry. In 1943, you would have been told once that Jews from France, Belgium, and the Netherlands were being sent to slaughterhouses in Poland, and that more than half the Jews of Europe were dead, but only in the context of a single story on a rally by a Jewish group that devoted more space to who had spoken than to who had died.

"In 1944, you would have learned from the front page of the existence of horrible places such as Maidanek and Auschwitz, but only inside the paper could you find that the victims were Jews. In 1945, (liberated) Dachau and Buchenwald were on the front page, but the Jews were buried inside."[1]

In a Gallup poll taken in the immediate aftermath of the war when reports and images of the death camps were still fresh in the public mind, on average the respondents said only one million Jews had been murdered. The failure of American press coverage to leave readers with a coherent picture of the Holocaust was not one of quantity. The *Times'* output was multiplied manyfold by newspapers big and small which ran stories by their own correspondents or picked up reports from wire services such as Associated Press, United Press, and Reuters. Nor was it a problem of quality. Read a random selection of stories and you find a high level of writing and reporting. Consider United Press correspondent Joseph Grigg's report, filed in spring 1942, on the fate of Jews in western areas of the Soviet Union:

"Thousands lie in unmarked graves, many in mass graves they were forced to dig before the firing squads of SS troops cut them down. One of the biggest known mass slaughters occurred in Latvia in the summer of 1941 when, responsible Nazi sources admitted, 56,000 men, women and children were killed by SS troops and Latvian irregulars. This slaughter went on for days. One German rifleman boasted to correspondents that he had killed thirty-seven in one night, picking them off as a hunter does rabbits."

Still, much of the coverage by America's most influential newspapers remained muted by a persistent, almost pathological skepticism, some of it rooted in the memory of fabricated tales of German atrocities in World War I—raping of nuns, bayoneting of babies—which the press swallowed whole. The only problem was, now it was true.

But even *seeing* was not believing for the *Times'* Lawrence. In October 1943, with other American reporters, he visited Babi Yar, the ravine outside Kiev where the Nazis killed 34,000 Jews in two days. This was nearly a year *after* the Allies had issued a formal statement acknowledging the Nazi plan to exterminate all European Jews.

"On the basis of what we saw, it is impossible for this correspondent to judge the truth or falsity of the story told to us," Lawrence wrote after the tour conducted by Soviet officials. "It is the contention of the authorities in Kiev that Germans not only burned the bodies and clothing, but also crumbled the bones, then shot and burned the bodies of all prisoners of war participating in the burning, except for a handful that escaped."

Not everyone on the tour that day was so skeptical. United Press correspondent Henry Shapiro told of seeing remnants of human bones, hair, shoes, and dental bridgework in the dirt at Babi Yar. The *New York Journal American* put his story on the front page under the banner headline, "100,000 KIEV CIVILIANS KILLED BY NAZIS. Wholesale Massacre Revealed." Predictably, the *Times* ran Lawrence's story on page 3.

It's hard to argue with the assessment of Max Frankel, former managing editor of the *New York Times*, who—in a November 2001 article in the *Times* under the headline "Turning Away From the Holocaust"—called his paper's Holocaust coverage "surely the century's bitterest journalistic failure." Yet on a personal level, thinking of my Ukrainian grandfather and imagining walking a mile in Lawrence's shoes at Babi Yar, it is possible to feel their existential pain and doubt—and to understand how both could have made such terrible misjudgments.

Indeed, Lawrence's eyes-wide-shut reporting for what was regarded as the most sophisticated newspaper in the U.S. reflected the view of Americans from Main Street to Washington, D.C., where Supreme Court Justice Felix Frankfurter famously said he knew that the reports were true, he just didn't "believe" them. And neither did my grandfather, Dmitri Arshansky. As a boy during World War I, Dmitri befriended the German soldiers who passively occupied his hometown, Poltava. In the fall of 1941 when rumors of Nazi atrocities in western Ukraine reached Kharkov, Dmitri refused to believe them, and resisted his brother's pleading to join his family in fleeing east to the Urals before the Nazis arrived. "I know the Germans," Dmitri told his brother, "they are not capable of such things." *People* surely could not be capable of such things. Yet such things soon came to pass.

The virtual disappearance of the Kharkov trial from contemporary memory cannot be blamed on lack of coverage at the time. It received ample, ongoing front-page coverage in newspapers big and small across America, as well as *Time* and *Life* magazines. The *Life* spread had sixteen photos, including mug shots of the accused and stark images of the hangings in the marketplace. "In Kharkov on Dec. 13, 1943, a beginning was made toward Germany's expiation of the immeasurable guilt that hangs over Europe today," the story began. The caption under one photo of the executions noted that "The bodies hung for three days and nights."

Days after the hangings, *The Berkshire County Eagle* in Pittsfield, Mass., was among many, many newspapers that devoted page-one space to a story by Glen Perry, a correspondent for the North American Newspaper Alliance.

"WASHINGTON—Nothing happening on the war front attracted as much attention in official circles here today as did the announcement that three Germans and a Russian traitor had been hanged in the public square of Kharkov after being tried and confessing their guilt in the mass killing of Russian civilians of the city before the Nazi army was driven out. The importance of the news, as Washington sees it, is out of all proportion to the mere fact that four men have been killed in a land which has seen millions of soldiers slain in battle. It is taken as notice to the world from Moscow that the Soviet Union was not fooling when it agreed that war criminals should face trial and punishment in the very towns their crimes took place. These four are the first of thousands who will pay the penalty for their misdeeds."

Ironically—prophetically—*Life's Picture History of World War II*, published in 1950, included no mention or photo of the Kharkov trial, or the extermination of Jews anywhere in Europe. The photos in *Life's* 1944 feature were taken from a Russian film of the trial, *We Accuse,* shown in London and The Little Carnegie Playhouse in New York in June 1945, a month after the war ended.

The reviewer in *Time* said the film "documents the Kharkov war-criminal trials with the force of a pile driver. It shows hideous photographs and testimonials of the kinds of atrocities to which the accused plead guilty. Even more overwhelming are shots of bereaved women as they touch and caress the wounds and the frozen feet of their dead; or the restrained but colossal grief and passion for retribution in the faces of men and women in the audience as they react to the German secret field policeman's admission that he is responsible for the deaths of 'no more than forty' Russian civilians."

"As the first pictorial document of the swift bringing to justice of Nazi war criminals, *We Accuse* is a valuable casebook," wrote the critic for the *New York Times.* "When the convicted four are led to the public square and hanged before surging mobs, the spectacle presented is more shocking than the surfeit of shots in the picture showing dead Russian women and children."

We Accuse might have contributed more than it did to the American public's awareness of events not yet known as the Holocaust. But distribution of the film was limited because it failed to gain the seal of approval of the

Hays Office, which from 1930 to 1968 was charged with protecting public sensibilities and morality from what it deemed to be malign thoughts and images such as homosexuality, miscegenation, and certain dirty words. Thumbs down from Hays meant the film would not be shown in any theaters that honored the code.

The high priests of morality in the Hays Office objected to We Accuse, reported Time, because "some of the atrocity shots are shown more than once, and the word 'damned' is used—attributed to the Germans in the line, 'Let them (Russians) bury their dead and be damned'."

The Hays Office gave Hitler a posthumous victory. In stifling We Accuse, it shoveled more dirt on the graves of the Russian dead, burying them and their stories even deeper, so that one day no one would remember or give a damn.

"Could it be we are all beneath great ruins and we'll never crawl out?" Yevtushenko wrote in The Apple Trees of Drobitsky. "We are working our way out. An ignominious task, though enormous! Only don't let the demolition shovel succeed again in finishing off those who are trying to crawl out."

It's left to us—the children and grandchildren of the survivors—to deny Hitler's ghost, and to ensure that the greatest coverup in history does not succeed.

NOTES

Chapter Two

1. Alan Berger, *Second Generation Voices: Reflections by Children of Holocaust Survivors & Perpetrators* (Syracuse University Press, 2001), 3.

Chapter Four

1. Yitzhak Arad, *The Holocaust in the Soviet Union* (University of Nebraska Press, Lincoln; Yad Vashem, Jerusalem, 2009), 51–52.

Chapter Five

1. George Friedman, "Does Ukraine Really Want to be Sovereign Nation?", *Kyiv Post* (December 3, 2010), 5.
2. Arad, *The Holocaust in the Soviet Union*, 109–110.
3. Anatoly Podolsky, "A Reluctant Look Back: Jews and the Holocaust in Ukraine," *Osteuropa* (2008).

Chapter Six

1. Raul Hilberg, *The Destruction of the European Jews* (Quadrangle Books/Chicago, 1961), 3–4.

2. Hilberg, *The Destruction of the European Jews*, 17.
3. Emily Paras, "The Darker Side of Martin Luther," Digital-Commons@IWU (2008), 1.

Chapter Seven

1. Richard Rhodes, *Masters of Death: The SS Einsatzgruppen and the Invention of the Holocaust* (Vintage Books, New York, 2002), xii.
2. Interview, "An Insidious Evil," *The Atlantic Monthly* (February 11, 2004).
3. Hilary Earl, *The Nuremberg SS-Einsatzgruppen Trial, 1945–1958* (Cambridge University Press, 2009), 134.
4. Hilberg, *The Destruction of the European Jews*, 187, 192.

Chapter Eight

1. Hilberg, *The Destruction of the European Jews*, 257.
2. Ilya Ehrenburg and Vasily Grossman, eds., *The Black Book* (Yad Vashem, 1980).
3. Ernst Klee, Willi Dressen, and Volker Riess, *The Good Old Days: The Holocaust as Seen by its Perpetrators and Bystanders* (The Free Press/Macmillan, 1991).
4. Klee, Dressen, Riess, *The Good Old Days*, 154.
5. Klee, Dressen, Riess, *The Good Old Days*, 28.

Chapter Nine

1. Karel Berkhoff, "Hitler's Clean Slate: Everyday Life in the Reichcommissariat Ukraine, 1941–1944" (PhD diss., University of Toronto, 1998).
2. Arad, *The Holocaust in the Soviet Union*, 413.

Chapter Ten

1. Nora Levin, *The Holocaust: The Destruction of European Jewry 1933–1945* (Thomas Y. Crowell Company, New York, 1986), 261.
2. Levin, *The Holocaust*, 261.
3. Rhodes, *Masters of Death*, 282.
4. Levin, *The Holocaust*, 261.

Chapter Eleven

1. Hannah Arendt, *Eichmann in Jerusalem: A Report on the Banality of Evil* (Viking Press, New York, 1963), 76–77.
2. Arendt, *Eichmann in Jerusalem*, 77.
3. Wendy Lower, "The Holocaust and Colonialism in Ukraine: A Case Study of the General Bezirk Zhytomyr, 1941–1944" (paper presented at a symposium on the Holocaust in the Soviet Union at the United States Holocaust Memorial Museum, Washington, D.C., September 2005).

Chapter Thirteen

1. Earl, *The Nuremberg SS-Einsatzgruppen Trial, 1945–1958*, 164.
2. Arad, *The Holocaust in the Soviet Union*, 349.
3. Earl, *The Nuremberg SS-Einsatzgruppen Trial, 1945–1958*, 290.

Chapter Fourteen

1. Christopher Browning, *Ordinary Men: Reserve Police Battalion 101 and the Final Solution in Poland* (HarperCollins Publishers, New York, 1992), 2.
2. Meredith Meehan, "Auxiliary Police Units in the Occupied Soviet Union, 1941–43: A Case Study of the Holocaust

in Gomel, Belarus" (Honors thesis, United States Naval Academy, 2010).

3. Klee, et al., *The Good Old Days*, xiii.

4. Konrad Kwiet, "Rehearsing for Murder: The Beginning of the Final Solution in Lithuania in June 1941," *Holocaust and Genocide Studies* (Spring 1998), 11.

5. Jürgen Matthäus, "Controlled Escalation: Himmler's Men in the Summer of 1941 and the Holocaust in the Occupied Soviet Territories," *Holocaust and Genocide Studies* (Fall 2007), 229–230.

Chapter Nineteen

1. Anatoly Podolsky, "A Reluctant Look Back: Jews and the Holocaust in Ukraine," *Osteuropa* (2008), 4–5.

2. Elena Ivanova, "Ukrainian High School Students' Understanding of the Holocaust," *Holocaust and Genocide Studies* (Winter 2004), 406–407.

3. Ivanova, *Holocaust and Genocide Studies* (Winter 2004), 417.

4. Ivanova, *Holocaust and Genocide Studies* (Winter 2004), 418.

Chapter Twenty-One

1. Arad, *The Holocaust in the Soviet Union*, 407.

2. Ignatik Federovich Kladov, *The People's Verdict: A Full Report of the Proceedings of the Krasnodar and Khakov German Atrocity Trials* (Hutchinson & Co., London 1944).

3. *The People's Verdict.*

4. *The People's Verdict.*

5. Arad, *The Holocaust in the Soviet Union*, 443.

6. *The Unknown Black Book* (Indiana University Press, Bloomington, 2008), 104–105.

Chapter Twenty-Two

1. I.A. Lediakh, "The Application of the Nuremberg Principles by Other Military Tribunals and National Courts," in *The Nuremberg Trial and International Law*, ed. George Ginsburgs and V.N. Kudriavtsev (Martinus Nijhoff Publishers, 1990), 263–264.

2. George Ginsburgs, *Moscow's Road to Nuremberg: The Soviet Background to the Trial* (Kluwer Law International, The Netherlands, 1996), 31–32.

3. Ginsburgs, *Moscow's Road to Nuremberg*, 34.

4. Arad, *The Holocaust in the Soviet Union*, 540.

5. JT Dykman, "The Soviet Experience in World War Two" (paper presented at The Eisenhower Institute, 2002).

6. Arieh Kochavi, "The Moscow Declaration, the Kharkov Trial, and the Question of a Policy on Major War Criminals in the Second World War," *History* (October 1991).

7. John Quigley, "Soviet Influences on International Criminal Law in the Nuremberg Era," review of *Moscow's Road to Nuremberg* by George Ginsburgs, *Criminal Law Forum* (1996), 447–448.

8. Michael Bazyler, "The Role of the Soviet Union in the International Military Tribunal at Nuremberg and Impact on Its Legacy," *Titel des Artikels*, 2.

9. Bazyler, "The Role of the Soviet Union in the International Military Tribunal at Nuremberg and Impact on Its Legacy," *Titel des Artikels*, 7–8.

10. Francine Hirsch, "The Soviets at Nuremberg: International Law, Propaganda, and the Making of the Postwar Order," *American Historical Review* (June 2008), 707.

11. Hirsch, "The Soviets at Nuremberg," 703.

12. Hirsch, "The Soviets at Nuremberg," 710.
13. Arieh Kochavi, *Prelude to Nuremberg: Allied War Crimes Policy and the Question of Punishment* (University of North Carolina Press, 1998), 231, 247.
14. Bazyler, "The Role of the Soviet Union in the International Military Tribunal," *Titel des Artikels*, 4.

Chapter Twenty-Three

1. Alexander Prusin, "Fascist Criminals to the Gallows!: The Holocaust and Soviet War Crimes Trials, December 1945–February 1946," *Holocaust and Genocide Studies* (Spring 2003), 6.
2. Arad, *The Holocaust in the Soviet Union*, 537.
3. Prusin, "Fascist Criminals to the Gallows!", *Holocaust and Genocide Studies* (2003), 21.
4. Prusin, "Fascist Criminals to the Gallows!", *Holocaust and Genocide Studies* (2003), 6.

Chapter Twenty-Five

1. Prusin, "Fascists Criminals to the Gallows!", *Holocaust and Genocide Studies* (2003), 21.
2. Hannah Arendt, *Eichmann in Jerusalem: A Report on the Banality of Evil* (Viking Press, New York, 1963), 279.

Epilogue

1. Laurel Leff, "When the Facts Didn't Speak for Themselves: The Holocaust in the New York Times, 1939–1945," in *Why Didn't the Press Shout?*, ed. Robert Moses Shapiro (KTAV Publishing House, 2003), 70.

BIBLIOGRAPHY

Arad, Yitzhak, *The Holocaust in the Soviet Union* (University of Nebraska Press, Yad Vashem, 2009).

Arendt, Hannah, *Eichmann in Jerusalem: A Report on the Banality of Evil* (Viking Press, 1963).

Bazyler, Michael, "The Role of the Soviet Union in the International Military Tribunal at Nuremberg and Impact on Its Legacy," *Titel des Artikels.*

Berger, Alan and Naomi Berger, *Second Generation Voices: Reflections by Holocaust Survivors & Perpetrators* (Syracuse University Press, 2001).

Berkhoff, Karel, *Harvest of Despair: Life and Death in Ukraine Under Nazi Rule* (Belknap Press of Harvard University Press, 2004).

Berkhoff, Karel, "Hitler's Clean Slate: Everyday Life in the Reichskommissariat Ukraine, 1941–1944," PhD diss., University of Toronto, 1998.

Blunden, Godfrey, *The Time of the Assassins* (J.B. Lippincott Company, 1952).

Brandon, Ray and Wendy Lower, eds., *The Shoah in Ukraine: History, Testimony, Memorialization*. Indiana University Press, 2008.

Brown, Paul, "The Senior Leadership Cadre of the Geheime Feldpolizei, 1939–1945," *Holocaust and Genocide Studies* (Fall 2003): 278–304.

Browning, Christopher, *Ordinary Men: Reserve Police Battalion 101 and the Final Solution* (HarperCollins Publishers, 1992).

Browning, Christopher, "Initiating the Final Solution: The Fateful Months of September–October 1941." Paper presented at the Center for Advanced Holocaust Studies of the United States Holocaust Memorial Museum, March 13, 2003.

Dykman, JT, "The Soviet Experience in World War Two." Paper prepared for The Eisenhower Institute, 2002.

Earl, Hilary, *The Nuremberg SS-Einsatzgruppen Trial, 1945–1958* (Cambridge University Press, 2009).

Ginsburgs, George, *Moscow's Road to Nuremberg: The Soviet Background to the Trial* (Kluwer Law International, 1996).

Heckler, Cheryl, *An Accidental Journalist: The Adventures of Edmund Stevens 1934–1945* (University of Missouri Press, 2007).

Hilberg, Raul, *The Destruction of the European Jews* (Quadrangle Books, 1961).

Hirsch, Francine, "The Soviets at Nuremberg: International Law, Propaganda, and the Making of the Postwar Order," *American Historical Review* (June 2008).

Hollander, Ron, "We Knew: America's Newspapers Report the Holocaust." In *Why Didn't the Press Shout?*, edited by Robert Moses Shapiro. KTAV Publishing House, 2003.

Ivanova, Elena, "Ukrainian High School Students' Under-standing of the Holocaust," *Holocaust and Genocide Studies* (Winter 2004): 402–420.

Kalb, Marvin, "Journalism and The Holocaust, 1933–1945." In *Why Didn't the Press Shout?*, edited by Robert Moses Shapiro. KTAV Publishing House, 2003.

Kladov, Ignatik Federovich, *The People's Verdict: A Full Report of the Proceedings at the Krasnodar and Kharkov German Atrocity Trials* (Hutchinson & Co., London, 1944).

Klee, Ernst, Willi Dressen, and Volker Riess, eds., *The Good Old Days: The Holocaust as Seen by its Perpetrators and Bystanders* (The Free Press/Macmillan, 1991).

Kochavi, Arieh, "The Moscow Declaration, the Kharkov Trial, and the Question of a Policy on Major War Criminals in the Second World War." *History* (1991): 401–417.

Kochavi, Arieh, *Prelude to Nuremberg: Allied War Crimes Policy and the Question of Punishment* (University of North Carolina Press, 1998).

Kruglov, Alexander, "Jewish Losses in Ukraine, 1941–1944." In *The Shoah in Ukraine: History, Testimony, Memorialization*, edited by Ray Brandon and Wendy Lower. Indiana University Press, 2008.

Kwiet, Konrad, "Rehearsing for Murder: The Beginning of the Final Solution in Lithuania in June 1941," *Holocaust and Genocide Studies* (Spring 1998): 3–26.

Leff, Laurel, "When the Facts Didn't Speak for Themselves: The Holocaust in the New York Times, 1939–1945." In *Why Didn't the Press Shout?*, edited by Robert Moses Shapiro. KTAV Publishing House, 2003.

Levin, Nora, *The Holocaust: The Destruction of European Jewry 1933–1945* (Thomas Crowell Company, 1986).

Lipstadt, Deborah, *Beyond Belief: The American Press and The Coming of the Holocaust 1933–1945* (The Free Press, 1986).

Lower, Wendy, "The Holocaust and Colonialism in Ukraine: A Case Study of the Generalbezirk Zhytomyr, Ukraine, 1941–1944." Paper presented at the Center for Advanced Holocaust Studies at the United States Holocaust Memorial Museum, September 2005.

Margry, Karel, "The Four Battles for Kharkov," *After the Battle* (2001).

Matthäus, Jürgen, "Controlled Escalation: Himmler's Men in the Summer of 1941 and the Holocaust in the Occupied Soviet Territories," *Holocaust and Genocide Studies* (Fall 2007): 242.

Meehan, Meredith, "Auxiliary Police Units in the Occupied Soviet Union, 1941–43: A Case Study of the Holocaust in Gomel, Belarus." Honors thesis, United States Naval Academy, 2010.

Podolsky, Anatoly, "A Reluctant Look Back: Jews and the Holocaust in Ukraine." *Osteuropa* (2008).

Pohl, Dieter, "The Murder of Ukraine's Jews under German Military Administration and in the Reich Commissariat Ukraine." In *The Shoah in Ukraine: History, Testimony, Memorialization*, edited by Ray Brandon and Wendy Lower. Indiana University, 2008.

Prusin, Alexander, "Fascist Criminals to the Gallows!: The Holocaust and Soviet War Crimes Trials, December 1945–February 1946." *Holocaust and Genocide Studies* (2003).

Quigley, John, "Soviet Influences on International Criminal Law in the Nuremberg Era." Review of Moscow's *Road to*

Nuremberg: The Soviet Background to the Trial, by George Ginsburgs. *Criminal Law Forum,* 1996.

Rhodes, Richard, *Masters of Death: The SS-Einsatzgruppen and the Invention of the Holocaust* (Vintage Books, 2003).

Rubenstein, Joshua and Ilya Altman, eds., *The Unknown Black Book* (Indiana University Press, 2008).

Telushkin, Joseph, *Jewish Literacy: The Most Important Things to Know about the Jewish Religion, its People, and its History* (William Morrow and Company, 1991).

Todd, Albert, ed., *The Collected Poems, Yevgeny Yevtushenko, 1952–1990* (Henry Holt and Company, 1991).

Wortman, Marc, *The Bonfire: The Siege and Burning of Atlanta* (PublicAffairs, 2009).

ACKNOWLEDGEMENTS

A host of people helped in big and small ways to bring this book to fruition, but there are two without whom the first word never would have been written. Larisa Volovik and her daughter Yulana Volshonok operate the Kharkov Holocaust Museum where I learned about the historic 1943 trial that history forgot. Had I not happened across an exhibit on the trial during a visit to the museum in 2006, there's little chance I ever would have known about it.

When I returned to Kharkov in December 2010 to do research for this book, I would have been little more than a sightseer without the help of a small village of friends and strangers. I would have been speechless without my gifted and patient translators—Daria and Victoria Plis, and Anna Kakhnovska. I'm grateful to Mariana Yevsyukova for introducing me to Daria and Victoria, and to her grandmother, Antonina Bogancha, for welcoming me into her home as she did in 2006—the same home where the Bogancha family sheltered my mother and her sister after their escape from the death march to Drobitsky Yar.

Victor Melikhov provided an invaluable seminar on Ukrainian history, telling me things I would not have discovered on my own. Yuri Radchenko took time out from his doctoral studies in Holocaust history to show me the places in and around Kharkov where Jews were jailed, murdered, and buried. Moshe Moskovitz, chief rabbi of Kharkov, shared his own story as a Second Generation survivor and told me what life is like today for Jews in Kharkov.

Irina Ferenzova, the chief guide at the Drobitsky Yar memorial who retrieved my camera from thieves on my visit in 2006, gave me hot tea after my solitary walk through the ravine on a snowy morning—then left her post to get me back to town after my cabbie was a no-show. Gala Dobrovolska, my seatmate on the flight from New York to Ukraine, enlisted her son to drive me to the train station in a snowstorm the night I left Kharkov.

I was welcomed like family at Jewish organizations in Kharkov, and by the students and teachers of School 13, the last school my mother attended before the Nazis arrived in October 1941. An administrator at Kharkov Conservatory dropped everything late in the day to give us a tour. There was no end to the cheerful assistance provided by the young, bilingual staff at the Chichikov Hotel.

Special thanks to friends Alan and Naomi Berger whose book, *Second Generation Voices: Reflections by Children of Holocaust Survivors & Perpetrators*, helped me better understand the impact of the Holocaust on my own family and the crucial importance of sharing the story with succeeding generations.

I owe a great debt to the readers who came to hear me speak about *Hiding in the Spotlight* (www.hidinginthespotlight.com) at more than 150 events around the country. Their evident fascination with the history of this overlooked chapter of the Holocaust and a hunger to know more was a major factor in my decision to turn an idea into a manuscript. Once again, as with *Hiding in the Spotlight,* Pegasus Books publisher Claiborne Hancock took a brave leap in buying the manuscript, and my editor, Jessica Case, provided the go-for-it enthusiasm and astute editorial guidance that made the manuscript all it could be.

Like its predecessor, *Judgment Before Nuremberg* is animated by the remarkable spirit and words of my mother, Zhanna, who did not hesitate for a moment when I asked her to relive these terrible memories one more time for the benefit of others. And through it all, from inception to fruition, I was sustained and inspired by the love, patience, and creative insights of my wife Candy, who once again helped me push beyond the cold facts of the story to the beating heart.

INDEX

Bailey, Anne, 103
Balfour, John, 286
Banner, John, 22
barbarism, 92, 110, 117, 121–26, 283, 304, 321
Bazyler, Michael, 265, 270–71, 274
Beautiful Mind, A, 143
Becker, August, 129, 132
Belarus, 59, 64
Belonozhko, N. F., 258
Belushi, John, 218
Belzec, 54, 145, 151
Benigni, Roberto, 151
Bergen-Belsen, 59, 219
Berger, Alan, 28, 35
Berger, Naomi, 28
Berkhoff, Karel, 115
Berkshire County Eagle, The, 344
Bespalov, Alexander, 223
Beyond Belief, 336
Biberstein, Ernest, 160, 178–79
Bismarck Tribune (North Dakota), 251
Black Book, The, 104, 281
Blobel, Paul, 107, 133, 159–68, 172–73, 284
Blume, Walter, 86
Blunden, Godrey, 205
Bogancha, Antonina, 244
Bogancha, Evdokiya, 239–43
Bogancha, Nicolai, 241–44
Bogancha, Prokofiev, 239–43
Böhme, Hans Joachim, 177–78

Bolshevism, 70, 85–87, 91, 95–98, 106–8, 119, 171, 255, 281
Bonfire: The Siege and Burning of Atlanta, 109
Brodsky, Alexander, 116
Brokaw, Tom, 169–70
Bronner, Ethan, 59
Browning, Christopher, 3, 85, 140–42, 145, 175–77
Buchenwald, 336, 340
Bulanov, Mikhail Petrovich, 134, 219, 224–25, 289, 310–15, 324–33

C

Carter, Jimmy, 57
Cask of Amontillado, The, 154–55
CBS, 335, 336
Charleston Gazette (West Virginia), 278
Chicago Herald American, 337
Children of the Holocaust, 29
Christian Science Monitor, 11, 252, 268, 278
Churchill, Winston, 266, 268, 284
Civil War, 71, 99, 215, 235, 337
Clay, Lucius, 21
Cold War, 21, 64, 67, 186, 272–73
concentration camps, 29, 99–100, 115, 132, 151, 165, 175, 191, 194, 280. *See also specific camps*